ARE YOU F***ING KIDDING ME?

BY

JENNIFER MONAHAN

This book is a recollection of my life. There was no need to make any of it up because my life really is this crazy. Some of the names and characteristics have been changed to protect people and some have been changed to not piss them off. The dialogue has been recreated from my memory, but I have a memory like an elephant. The opinions in this book are only mine. The part about it being Dena's idea to steal my dad's car is completely accurate.

ISBN: 9781688596696 (Paperback)

Front Cover image by Bryan Monahan

First printing edition 2019

---For Bryan Lee ... the love of my life. Thank you for always supporting me and putting up with my kooky ideas. I wouldn't have been able to write this without your love and your encouragement.

---For my children. You're the most important things in my life and I'm proud of you. Please skip past the sex parts of this book when you're reading it so you're not emotionally scarred.

---For Rebecca, because I didn't work you into the story even though I promised I would.

---For Bailey, for being the best fake name maker upper I've ever met.

---For my mom... I miss you every day.

Y *ou can do this. Pretend you're a stone robot. No, not a stone*
robot... robots are mechanical, so a robot would never be
made of stone. Ok, you're getting a little distracted. You're just a
robot.... Or maybe you're stone. I don't remember now. Deep
breath. You can do this......

There was a storm starting to swirl outside the window. The
weatherman had predicted a blizzard that threatened to shut down
the city, and the lack of traffic that morning was evidence of the
severity of what was coming. Minnesotans are notorious for driving
through any kind of weather to get to a Vikings game or a hockey
tournament, so it takes a pretty significant storm to keep people at
home. It had been all over the news for the last week and, based on
the latest reports, we were about to witness the complete and final
destruction of the world as Snowmageddon materialized directly over

the Twin Cities. A mix of rain, sleet, and snow had started that morning and the streets were covered with just enough ice to make you think twice before leaving the warmth of your living room. Plows and salt trucks were out in force and keeping the roads moderately drivable, but it was obvious that something bad was on the way.

I was trying to focus, but my brain had other ideas. *How had I gotten here?* The images were floating around but there were too many to zero in on a single one. The story of my life had been mundane up until 20 years ago when my mom died, and then it exploded like my own personal atomic bomb. I couldn't justify calling her death the catalyst for the carnage that consumed my life for the last 20 years, but it had changed my trajectory. I made a series of bad choices out of sadness and desperation when I was most vulnerable. I hadn't focused on the grief that accompanied her death but pushed it aside and continued as though nothing had happened. Each experience after that had been another piece of the puzzle, building upon each other and defining who I would become as a person. They didn't appear to be interrelated… one didn't cause the next … but they each changed me; They changed how I responded and who I was after I recovered.

I watched all the pieces of my life's puzzle floating around in my mind … Despair … Grief … Anger …. Love … Joy …. Fear. They were all there, circling like a pack of vultures, deciding who would get to take the first bite of roadkill. Which of them would win?

As I listened to the sleet pelting the windows, wondering if the Snowpocalypse had finally started, I tried to convince myself that I was brave when I knew that nothing could be further from the truth. I tried to dig deep and find the courage I knew was somewhere in me. *You cannot let Fear win. Eye of the tiger, baby!*

My internal pep talk was interrupted when I heard my name.
"Jennifer?"

Ok... you can do this. I stood up and walked in slow motion the longest six feet of my life as the room swirled in a quiet haze. I took a deep breath and looked up. *You can do this...*

PART 1

I WANNA BE YOUR EVERYTHING

He moved in close to me,
put his hand on my hip,
and kissed me.
I liked it, and my wall crumbled
just a little bit.

"Why am I even doing this? My mom's already gone and won't be here to see it." On the day of my wedding, Dena and I were standing in a parking lot a couple of blocks from the church, snacking on pre-wedding McMuffins when I looked at her and voiced my uncertainty in the choice I was about to make. I was expecting the same speech everyone else had given me; "She's with you. Even if you can't see her, she's here."

As usual, Dena didn't follow the pack. She put down her McMuffin, looked me straight in the eye and said, "Listen to me, Jennifer. You don't have to go through with this. I'll take you anywhere you want to go. I'll go tell everyone and handle everything for you. We can leave right now." Her face had a look of serious urgency and I knew she would throw me in her car and take off like we were robbing a bank if I gave her the go-ahead.

Dena and I had been protecting each other's back since the first grade when we were paired as locker buddies. Our relationship solidified as we marched down to the principal's office to report an injustice on the playground. One of our classmates had tucked his jacket into his shirt like a cape and run around throwing rocks at us like an evil Superman. We had bonded over our competitive need to prove we could play any sport as well as the boys and often rallied the other girls in our class to form a human chain across the soccer goal line when the boys wouldn't let us play. During the fifth grade, when we discovered the elementary school version of feminism, we could be found in the principal's office offering a petition on how there was a less than equitable division of the snow hill on the playground. Our only argument was over whose idea it was to steal my dad's car in 9th grade and sneak over to Bobby Taylor's house at 1:00 in the morning. (For the record, it was her.) She was my oldest friend, and I knew I could tell her anything and she would either lovingly mock me or give me excellent advice on how to handle it. Her sarcasm and wit were unmatched, but I could give her a run for her money once we got going. In this particular situation, she made no secret of her disapproval of Darryl, the man I was about to marry.

My mom had died 38 days earlier of cancer, so I was carrying a 20-ton weight of sadness around with me that I kept pretending didn't exist. I was privately grieving the loss of the most important person in my life and couldn't see what everyone else could see: Darryl was an emotionally abusive man who liked Bacardi a little more than the average person. He never physically hit me. He always stopped just one step short of that, but our relationship was built on deceit, manipulation, and emotional mind games and Darryl was an Olympic caliber player. He could walk into a room and command the attention of any person in it. He was charming and fun and an amazing kisser. He could make you feel like the most important person in the world, and in the next breath, cut you down to feel ashamed for the most basic human interactions. If we were driving on the freeway and I looked over at a car driving next to us that happened to be driven by a man, I would be chastised and asked, "Why don't I pull over so you can fuck him?" As I would apologize for using my eyes to see other humans, he would make me feel loved and supported like a good little dog that obeyed her master. I eventually learned to look straight ahead any time we were driving so that I didn't appear to be glancing at a person who happened to have a penis.

Darryl had proposed to me when my mom was sick; mostly because I think he wanted to make her happy and partly because he saw my vulnerability and could use it to his advantage. She was one of the few people I'd ever seen him treat with respect and I knew that he loved her in whatever way he was capable of it. He was there the night she died and sat with me while I stared blankly, grappling with what a life without her in it would look like.

Through my grief, I clung to the closest person to me so that I could ignore the pain and Darryl was the only one there. He had systematically cut all my friends out of my life. He would reprimand me if I wanted to have a girl's night and accuse me of sleeping with someone if I dared to go out without him. He even suggested to me once that I was a lesbian for wanting to hang out with my girlfriends. He clearly didn't have a good grasp on the concept of homosexuality, but I eventually gave up and sheltered myself from any of my friends. My college roommates were gone. My friends from high school were forbidden. The only one left was Dena since he and I both knew she wouldn't go away without a fight.

By the time the day of my wedding to Darryl came around, I suspected that my marriage wasn't going to last, but I was emotionally fragile from losing my mother and three months pregnant, so I didn't see the point in running. As I stood there with my McMuffin, talking to my dearest friend, contemplating her offer to help me plan my escape, I eventually said, "Nah…. I'm already pregnant so... I ... I'm going to be stuck with him for another 18 years anyway. I'm just going to do it."

"That's a whole different conversation, but would it have seriously been that difficult to just go buy a box of condoms and keep them near the bed?"

"It's a little late for the safe sex lecture, my friend." I looked at her as I rubbed my belly.

"He's not good for you. I'm serious. I'll take you anywhere you want to go."

I perked up a little. "Like Thelma and Louise? Except maybe without the murder and rape and stuff. Which one got to sleep with Brad Pitt? I want to be that one." I was trying to pivot her away from what I knew I should do but didn't have the courage for.

"You can keep trying to distract me with Brad Pitt's delicious abs, but it won't work."

"I know. The thought of my mom not being at my wedding is consuming. I'm just exhausted trying to pretend like I don't miss her every second of every day. It's taking all my energy to not think about it. I don't have any fight left in me." My words were weak and reflected how I felt at that moment. I was worn down and beaten by the emotions that devastated me.

"That's why I'm here. To fight for you." Her eyes never left mine as my future played out in my mind.

"She wanted me to be taken care of. He takes care of me in his way. I just don't…."

"Jennifer…."

I held up my hand to stop her. "Just eat your McMuffin. We have to get to the church soon."

. . . . .

We went to the church where we did the usual getting ready activities. I put on my dress and Dena helped with my veil. I looked at myself in the mirror and smiled. I liked what I saw and knew my mother would have approved. As I walked out of the room, I saw Darryl walking toward me. He looked me up and down and said, "I thought we agreed that you'd wear your hair up."

"My veil worked better with it like this. Do you not like it?"

"I guess it's fine."

"Ok, I just thought this would look better with the veil you picked out. Sorry if it's not what you wanted."

It became obvious that Darryl had some preconceived idea of what the day was going to look like as he coached me through our first kiss as a married couple prior to the ceremony.

"Don't make it gross. It should be a light kiss. No open mouth or tongue. Here…. practice once." He leaned in and kissed me and told me that I made it too quick. "Try again. It should look like it's sincere." I started to say something but the energy to fight his criticism had left me long ago. *It should LOOK like it's sincere? Isn't your first kiss as a married couple supposed to BE sincere?* Everything with him was about the show. It didn't matter if it was real. The kiss was only meant to look like we were the perfect couple.

The ceremony was lovely, but rather than focusing on my groom, my eyes continually moved to the seat next to my dad that remained empty. *She was supposed to be here for this.* We said, "I do" and as we walked out of the church, he dropped my hand to go grab a flask from his buddies. I forced a smile and talked with all the people that came to congratulate me, all the while, fighting the small amount of regret that I kept pushing away.

The reception was fun, and all our friends were there but I honestly can't remember him and I spending much time together. I talked to my friends. He drank with his. We met up for our first dance, and he directed me throughout the entire song as to when I should be looking at him and when I should put my head on his shoulder. The illusion had to look as though the rest of the room faded away as we danced and gazed lovingly into each other's eyes. It would have been more likely to happen if he wasn't coaching me throughout the entire song.

At three months pregnant, I wasn't starting to show yet, but my dress was strapless and tight and the corset I was wearing started to make me uncomfortable as the night continued. It was a warm day in May, and I was hot and tired from having been on my feet for eight hours. I went into the bathroom and Dena helped me take off the corset so I could breathe. She unzipped me and helped me remove the awful thing that had been sucking me in all day.

"Oh, my gosh…. I can't put that thing back on. I seriously can't breathe in it." I stood there holding my dress to my chest with it still unzipped, taking a moment to breathe and feel better. After a few minutes, I turned around so Dena could zip me back up.

"Just don't put it back on. You're completely covered. Here …. Turn around and look at me." I turned around and she stared at my boobs for a couple of seconds. "I can't see your nipples or anything through the dress. You're fine."

"Do I look fat? My mom said I couldn't tell people I was pregnant until after the wedding. I suppose it's the reception now so that's technically after the wedding."

"I don't think that's what she meant, but no, you don't look fat... you don't look pregnant.... And your nipples are hidden. You're fine. Go have some fun."

I was happy to not be so restricted now that it was off and was much more comfortable. As I walked out of the bathroom, Darryl grabbed me by the arm and pulled me aside.

"What the fuck are you doing?"

I knew what he was angry about before he even had to tell me. "I couldn't breathe in that thing. I felt like I was starting to swell. I needed to take it off."

"Why don't you just put on a striptease for everybody here? You don't even have a bra on anymore."

Are you fucking kidding me? This is the argument he's going to choose right now? "My dress doesn't need it. You can't see through it at all and there's a built-in bra in it. Please don't make this a thing."

"I just didn't want everyone thinking that I married a whore."

He gave me that look that told me he was disappointed in me, but I didn't want to cause a scene and didn't want to fight him. I wanted to get through the night and find somewhere to sit down.

As I was being admonished for my choice to be able to breathe, Dena walked up behind me. I turned and saw the look on her face and knew she was about to go to bat for me as I prayed she wouldn't make it worse. She calmly reassured Darryl that I didn't look like a whore and no one would know the difference with what I was wearing. Dena was protective and I knew she was always looking out for me, but given the right circumstances, she could kick anyone's ass if she wanted to, including the groom at my wedding if he didn't stop acting like an asshole. Dena stepped forward and physically stood between me and Darryl and let him know that I wasn't going to put the corset back on. He eventually gave up the fight and went back to drinking with his friends while I looked at my girl and silently thanked her.

Dena had stood by my side to support me that day as my Maid of Honor even though she didn't agree with my choice. She stayed close the first year and was there when I needed to vent or scream or just remove myself from my current dysfunctional environment. Dena was confident I would eventually recognize the situation I was in once the fog from losing my mom and being pregnant lifted. She knew that the "old Jen" was inside me somewhere. I just needed to find her again and Dena waited patiently for it to happen.

My eyes started to open one night when I was eight months pregnant. Darryl had gone out with his friends and came home at 2:00 in the morning wearing a crown and a flashing button that said: "I'm the Bacardi King." He drunkenly stumbled around the room, berating me in his slurred speech and incomplete sentences. I had been dealing with the alcohol and the partying and the mind games for too long, so I looked at him and said, "I don't want to do this anymore." He was shitfaced and called the cops and told them I was suicidal. *No, you moron…. I'm not done being alive. I'm done being with you!* When the police arrived, I was sitting on the couch eating a bag of Cheetos and he tried to explain to them he thought I was planning to kill myself. The fact that he was still wearing the crown and the Bacardi King button didn't really help his case, so the cops took me aside and asked me if they needed to remove him from the house for the night. I told them I would just let him sleep it off and we should be fine by the next day.

In November, I went into labor with my first child. I was given some pretty good drugs that made the pain of childbirth minimal. I fell asleep and woke up to Darryl sitting in a chair with his feet on the end of my bed watching ESPN.

I looked at my nurse and quietly said, "I want my mom."

"What, honey? What can I get you?"

"Nothing. I'm fine."

"It looks like you're pretty close. The doctor will be here in a minute. That baby will be here soon!"

When my daughter was finally in my arms, Darryl's friends all arrived in my hospital room and started passing around drinks. I stared at the beautiful girl in my arms, ignoring the party that had descended on my room and silently vowed to give her better than what she had been born into.

I blindly wandered through our first year of marriage and kept thinking back to the day Dena had offered to help me escape. *I could be out living the Thelma and Louise life right now.* The fog had finally lifted, and I knew I needed to get out. I was working out the logistics of supporting myself and my daughter when Darryl's dick made it much easier for me. He had gotten someone else pregnant and was planning to move in with her. *Fine by me…. Just leave my daughter and me and go enjoy your new family.* He wasn't worth fighting for, and although I was scared to tackle the challenge of raising a daughter on my own, it was a relief to have him gone. As I drove away from the house I had shared with him, I felt no remorse. I wasn't longing for him or wishing I had tried something different to make it work. I wasn't angry. I was ready and was thankful to finally be free.

CHAPTER 2

After Darryl and I parted ways, I moved into my brother's basement, started searching for a job, and tried to figure out how I was going to support myself and my beautiful daughter. She was the joy in my life and my reason to continue to fight and claw my way out of the basement, both literally and figuratively.

I was a lifelong resident of Minnesota, which made me resilient and at times, a little bit crazy. On any given day in April, it could either be 75 degrees, or we could be in the middle of a blizzard, so flexibility was also an important part of being Minnesotan. I was in my twenties and knew that I wasn't ugly, but I would never be a swimsuit model. My long blonde hair was usually worn up and out of my face and my style wasn't anything flashy. I wore what felt comfortable and looked good on me, which most of the time was a pair of jeans and a t-shirt. Practicality was also important in my life, so I wasn't the sort of girl who had a different pair of shoes for each outfit. There were a few comfy pairs in my closet that worked with just about everything and I stuck with what was easy.

I had been raised by the equivalent of Ward and June Cleaver in the small town of Forest Lake, Minnesota, just north of St. Paul. I had two older brothers named Tom and Scott and I realized at a fairly young age that my parents failed miserably in the originality category when naming their children. Being one of seven other Jenny's in my elementary school classes, I longed to be something exotic like Blair or Natalie or pretty much any of the names on The Facts of Life. Even with our dull names, my brothers and I were close. They would tease me mercilessly in a big brother way that told me how much they really loved me. Over the years, I had become a master at deflecting and firing back anytime they would taunt.

Our house was on a lake on a dead-end road where most of the homes were cabins. My neighborhood was busy in the summer, but the winter months only had a handful of families that lived there full time. The boys outnumbered the girls five to one, so the only option was to learn to play football and hang with the boys when the few girls that lived near me weren't available.

Forest Lake was the kind of small-town that was just big enough that you didn't know every single person, but the traditional six degrees of separation were whittled down to three. The gossip usually came out in full force at Dairy Queen after a baseball or softball game. The adults would buy us our chocolate-dipped cone and then stand to the side talking quietly about who was leaving who and which kids they heard were on drugs. It was the type of childhood that was easy and free. In the summer, my mother would send me on my bike to the liquor store two miles from our house to buy bubble gum. It was considered completely acceptable at the time and I would often stop at a friend's house to play on my way home. As long as I was home before dark, I don't think my mother ever really knew where I was, but she was there every night to tuck me in and hear about the adventures I had that day.

My parents worked hard and devoted themselves to their children. We weren't poor, but I knew that my dad worked extra hours to make money to buy us new basketball shoes each year and pay all the sports fees that consumed our lives. My childhood had been idyllic with my parents attending every basketball, volleyball, and baseball game, dance recital, and parent-teacher conference to make sure their kids felt supported and cared for. They had been high school sweethearts and their love story was one for the books. They grew up in a small town in Wisconsin and my mother once admitted to me that she first started dating my dad because he had his own cow and would sell the milk to have extra money to take her out.

"Wow, Mom! So, you were a gold digger?"

"No, I saw that your dad was a hard worker, so I liked that. That's an important quality to find in man, Lou. He was also very handsome." In later years, when I would imagine her voice in my head, it was always my pet name, Lou, that I would hear her saying.

"Riiiiight…. And cuz you were a gold digger? I mean, having your own cow is high society kind of stuff!"

"He also had his own car, so that was a nice bonus." She was one of the kindest people I knew, so accusing her of being a gold digger was like accusing Mother Teresa of being in it for the fame.

Growing up, our home was filled with laughter and a revolving door of friends coming and going. Everyone was welcome and our house served as the base that always had every friend's favorite snacks. My brothers were superstars in high school so I would sit and listen to their conversations and beg to come along when they would go toilet paper a friend's house.

My mom's cancer had rocked our entire family. At 23-years-old, I was still self-absorbed enough to think that I was impervious to tragedy. Up until that point in our lives everything had just come easily. Of course, there were times when obstacles got in our way, but they were minor inconveniences rather than life-changing crises and we always found a solution. When my mom was diagnosed, we were all stunned. It was the first time a real tragedy had occurred, and we didn't really understand what it was like to fight that kind of battle.

My mother had been in hospice for a few weeks the night that she died. I had just returned from picking up my grandparents and was walking in from the parking lot when she took her final breath. Looking back, I was thankful that I wasn't there to see it. Watching someone I love die was never something I wanted to do. I had volunteered to go pick up my grandparents in hopes that I wouldn't be there to see those final moments. I walked off the elevator as my Aunt Gloria was leaving my mom's room. She looked at my grandparents and said, "She just passed." My weeping grandparents were escorted to her room as I turned around and ran down a flight of steps to the parking lot. I stood out in the chill of an April night and screamed. It was a scream that came from the inside of my soul and told the world that I had been changed forever that night.

That scream was the one and only release of emotion for me throughout the entire journey of her illness and death. From that moment on, I focused on planning the funeral rather than having to really feel the emotion. I picked out the funeral music. I went with my dad to choose a casket and a gravesite. I helped pick the readings, made a list of who would be the casket bearers, arranged for my grandparents to stay in town at my dad's house and called my Aunt Kay and Uncle Jim to let them know their sister had passed away. And, after the funeral, I was able to go straight back to planning a wedding that wouldn't involve my mother, but the planning was easier than the sadness.

Now, I was dealing with tragedy number two in less than two years and, while my feet were a bit wobbly under me, my self-preservation skills were intact, albeit with a more jagged edge than there had been before.

I swiftly got to the business of problem-solving. I had a bachelor's degree in elementary education and had a teaching license for kindergarten through sixth grade. As I ran the numbers, I realized that substitute teaching wouldn't pay the bills, so I eventually took a job in an office managing apartment buildings to put food on the table and move into a place of my own and out of my brother's house. Our apartment was small and not in any way fancy, but it was safe and clean, and all Haley and I needed.

Haley was over a year old and a handful by the time we got into our own place. We spent our days playing dolly dress up and learning colors and numbers. I may not have been employed in a classroom, but I could still use my college degree to teach my daughter the difference between red and purple. I accepted the designation of a single mom and wore it like a badge of honor as I floundered through knowing the right thing to do and struggling to make ends meet. I watched her dance around in her Minnie Mouse pull-ups and prayed that I wouldn't screw her up so bad that she ended up on a talk show telling the world how she ended up dancing on a pole because her mother couldn't afford Fruit Loops... she had to buy generic to save money. However poor I was, I made it my intention to raise a bright, confident, and kind girl who gave back to the world. When Oprah came knocking, I would be ready to show that I had done everything to the best of my ability whether the pole was in her future or not.

CHAPTER 3

As much as my daughter meant to me, I missed the companionship and adult conversations that a relationship allowed; 27 was too young to spend the rest of my life alone. Our tiny apartment could get lonely at night once Haley went to bed so I started thinking about dipping my toe into the dating pool. *There must be someone out there who treats women decently.* I eventually decided that I would try online dating since, according to the commercials I saw on TV, everyone seemed to be finding love online. The ads assured me that I could find myself walking hand in hand on a beach with someone who looked like Matt Damon if I just signed up and answered a few basic questions.

Age: 27

Relationship Status: Divorced *(Thank God!)*

Interests, body type *(Body type? Whatever....)* Religious affiliation, politics, a few questions about what I'm looking for in a man.

Summary.... I sat and stared at my computer trying to figure out what to write. The cursor blinked at me as I considered what I wanted to convey. I don't usually take myself too seriously so writing mush was out of the question. Anyone who wanted to be with me couldn't be talking about candlelit dinners and strolling through a park holding my hand. The Vikings and jet skis were more my style.

Summary: If you like Pina Coladas, and getting caught in the rain....

I deleted the text I had just written. *I might be the only one that finds that funny. Ok, let's try again.*

Summary: Bitter single mom, recently divorced from a total douche bag....

Ok... maybe a touch too harsh. You can be Angry Chick on the inside, but maybe don't tell the whole world. Click, click, click as I deleted, once again.

Summary: Newly single and looking for someone who makes me laugh and shares my sense of humor. Must love football on Sunday and summer fun activities. Please don't respond if you're an asshole.

I thought that summed it up nicely and hit submit.

I went on a few dates, but none of them were great and several of them were bad to the point of legendary. My first online date was tragic. I left Haley with my brother Tom and his wife, Angela, for the night, put on some lipstick, and went to meet the person I was certain would be my ideal match. As I walked in, I scanned the bar for the man that resembled the picture I had seen. Walking toward me, I saw a man wearing a purple shirt, purple pants, purple socks, and purple shoes.

"Jennifer?"

"Yep! That's me! You must be Tyler?"

"I am. I've got a table over here."

We had chosen a TGI Fridays. I figured it was upbeat, crowded (in case he was crazy) and had a menu that was easy. In case things got weird, they also had a full bar which could come in handy. As we walked toward the table I said, "Do you really like Prince?" I laughed quietly to myself at my joke.

"Yeah, he's ok." We sat down at a booth and he put a menu in front of me.

I'm going to ignore the fact that he just said Prince is 'Ok.' Prince is awesome. "I just meant... you know... cuz of...." I swooshed my hand in front of him trying to indicate that I was pointing to his completely monochromatic purple clothing choice. Kind of bitchy and judgmental, yes, but who owns purple jeans that perfectly match a purple mock turtleneck?

He didn't seem amused. "No."

I tried to turn it around to be more light-hearted. "The Vikings? You've got Vikings Purple Pride nailed. I looooove my Vikings. Were you heartbroken when Gary Anderson missed that field goal? I haven't gotten over it yet. That was rough."

"No. I don't watch football."

"Oh." We sat there awkwardly while I envisioned him as a giant crayon the rest of the night. Clearly, I had filled out my questionnaire inappropriately because there was no way this guy was my perfect match. *What Minnesotan doesn't like Prince?*

After dinner, I went and picked up Haley. As I walked in, Angela looked at me, "So? How was it?"

"Don't ask. I went on a date with Barney the Dinosaur but with no sense of humor or taste in music."

There were a couple of other mediocre dates. One was beyond boring. One was drunk by the time I got there. There were a few I just didn't connect with. This led me to a date that would forever be referred to as The Winnebago Incident. As my hope of finding a decent guy online was starting to fade, The Winnebago Incident did nothing to renew my faith in the system.

We met at a restaurant and as we sat down, he explained his system and criteria for dating. He wanted to make sure I understood that I was welcome to order whatever I wanted, but he had a policy to not pay on the first one since he went on a lot of first dates.

"That makes sense. After the first one, they realize you're a serial killer?"

"No. Why would you think that?"

"It was …. Uhhhh…. It was meant to be a joke." *Maybe he is a serial killer.*

"No. I just don't find a lot of women satisfactory to make it to round two."

"Oh! Ok…. well, let's find out how I do."

The rest of the meal was average. We talked about my job, which wasn't interesting to anyone. We talked a little about some lakes that he enjoyed, which is a common small talk topic for any Minnesotan. There were a few other insignificant subjects that came up, but nothing interesting enough to be able to recall afterward.

As we were finishing up dinner, the waitress hadn't split the check and he pulled out a small calculator to figure out his portion with the tip. It got uncomfortable as he talked through his calculations, so I finally just threw my card on the table and paid for both our meals.

We walked out to the parking lot and I was trying to figure out how I felt about him. Yes, the calculator thing was weird, but I guess if you're budget conscious you try to make sure you're not paying too much. He was a little strange, and he kept talking about the qualities that a woman needed to have in order to date him. It felt more like an interview than a date.

As we walked toward my car, he pointed to the back of the parking lot. "You want to hang out for a little longer? We could have a drink and continue the conversation. That's me back there."

"The Winnebago?" He was pointing at a large motorhome that looked like it was built in 1981 that was parked sideways across three parking spaces. The tone of my voice told him that I was both confused and surprised that a person would drive a motorhome to a date.

"Yeah. It works for me. This way I'm not tied down to a lease or a mortgage or anything."

"You live in it, too? Oh, wow! That's…. economical. Do you drive it every day? I can't imagine it gets good gas mileage."

"It does fine. Should we go have that drink?"

I had a sudden vision of my lifeless body being found in Arizona while a pack of wild coyote snacked on my internal organs. I decided to pass on hanging out in his Winnebago and headed to my car to go home.

After that, there was the guy who showed up two hours late with a case of beer in his trunk and kept farting. I cut that evening short. There was the guy who detailed his sexual preferences over dinner and let me know his safe word just in case our date made it to his bedroom. I didn't even order dessert, not to mention get anywhere near his bedroom. There was one guy who seemed to be promising, but when I sent a follow-up message, he let me know that he wasn't interested in dating a woman who had a child. He told me he wanted to have his own family, not someone else's so he wasn't interested in going out again. *Are you fucking kidding me? Watch some reruns of The Brady Bunch, Asshole.* Lastly, there was the guy who invited me out to a movie who I was pretty sure I saw get dropped off by his mom. As he walked up to me, I realized he couldn't have been more than 17-years-old, and I ran like hell to my car so as not to be labeled a pedophile.

That was the straw that broke me. Online dating sites were not going to be the solution to my loneliness problem. The worst part about all of it was that I was paying a monthly fee for the shit show that was my dating life. I decided to cancel my online dating profile. It wasn't worth it to keep paying to go on miserable dates. It didn't need to be part of my life, and that was fine. I was comfortable being single, and there were still plenty of ways to talk to other people without needing to go on dates. I was using my Yahoo! search engine to browse the internet when I remembered that America Online had created the greatest invention since my VCR: The AOL chat room.

CHAPTER 4

At the time, AOL chat rooms were a viable place to meet interesting people, so I signed in and found my way to the Minneapolis chat room. It was the best possible compromise. I could chat with other people but didn't have to find a babysitter. Yes, some of the people were creeps and the majority of them started a conversation with the prerequisite "A/S/L" indicating they wanted to know my age, sex, and location, but it was fun to feel like I could actually talk to someone without having to leave my living room or my slippers. It helped my loneliness immensely.

One night, I was perusing the profiles, looking for someone who seemed interesting, when "Jeep" caught my eye. *At least he doesn't drive a Winnebago.* As we chatted, it became clear that he thought I knew more than I did about Jeeps as he started talking about lifts and winches and off-roading. "I like when you can take the doors off" was the closest I got to knowing anything about Jeeps.

His name was Bryan and he seemed like a pretty straightforward, completely normal guy. However, my bad dates and my bad marriage had left me cautious. I knew that anyone could appear to be anything when you're chatting online, so I didn't give him my phone number until I was sure. Every time I would log into AOL, I would hear the familiar "RING" as an instant message would pop up on my screen. He was sweet and funny and didn't pressure me or instantly ask me for a picture or my measurements which was refreshing from what you normally found in a chat room. I eventually gave him my number and we started talking on the phone for hours every night.

By the time I met Bryan, I wasn't searching for anything serious. I wanted companionship. I wanted to have some fun and get out occasionally, but I wasn't looking for marriage or even a committed relationship. Even though a weight was lifted off me when Darryl left, years of being torn down and belittled had hardened me. I stood by my choice to not hang out in some dude's Winnebago in the parking lot of the Olive Garden, but I knew there were perfectly nice people that I hadn't given a real chance because I was insecure and had trust issues. Emotional abuse can have that effect on you, and Darryl had been thorough in his demolition of my spirit. I had come to terms with the idea that marriage just wasn't going to be my thing, so finding some refreshing adult conversation was enough.

Bryan and I talked about every topic under the sun and found that there was no topic that we couldn't engage in. Politics - we had opposing views on many topics, but he always conceded that I was entitled to my opinion, even when we disagreed. Sports - He had tried to give wrestling a shot, but it wasn't his thing. He loved the Vikings, although not with the fanaticism that I did. I asked him if he'd thrown a chair across a bar when Gary Anderson missed a field goal in the NFC championship game and with great confusion, he said,

"Nope. Can't say I've ever thrown a chair across a bar for any reason." *Score a point for the new guy not being like Darryl!* He liked all types of music and didn't make fun of me when I would start singing show tunes or an 80's power ballad. He worked in downtown Minneapolis for a commercial real estate company doing a job that, no matter how often he explained it to me, I didn't understand. I knew he loved the energy of the Minneapolis skyway in the middle of the workweek and he knew that driving in downtown Minneapolis at any time gave me anxiety sweats. It was the type of adult interaction I had been craving for years so I found myself waiting for him to call at night.

He had sent me a picture of himself, and he was the exact opposite of what I would usually date, but I wondered if that could be a good thing. He was just slightly taller than me at five-foot-ten which made the fact I hated wearing heels a benefit to our relationship. He had a goatee that always looked a little scruffy on his face, but I liked the way it looked. He wore dress shirts and ties for work but was most comfortable in a pair of jeans and a shirt that had an 80's hard rock logo on it. I decided to take a chance on something different from what I would typically date. I let my guard down just a tiny bit and let him in.

After more than a month of talking on the phone, I cautiously asked Bryan if he wanted to meet. I was nervous since I had been talking to him for so long and, up to that point, hadn't wanted to meet in person. He enthusiastically agreed, and we set a day and time to go to dinner. Darryl planned to have Haley that weekend so it would work out for me to have some adult time.

As had been pretty standard since my divorce, Darryl canceled and wasn't able to take Haley at the last minute. At the moment, Darryl and I were in an upcycle when he pretended that he was going to be an active participant in her life and give real parenting a try.

Oddly, things frequently seemed to come up that prevented him from being able to follow through. He had taken her for the weekend a couple of times in the past few months so I thought maybe I would luck out and I'd be able to go on my date with this new, interesting guy. I wasn't surprised when Darryl canceled. I was, however, disappointed.

At that point, I had only a few hours before Bryan was supposed to meet me, and I didn't have a babysitter. I thought about canceling on him, but I was looking forward to finally meeting him and didn't want to put it off any longer. *Would it be safe to just invite him over to my house?* He didn't seem like a serial killer, but from what I'd heard, serial killers usually seem pretty normal.

I called Dena and explained the situation to my most trusted resource. "What do you think I should do? I really wanted to meet him, but I've got Haley with me this weekend now. Douchebag isn't able to take her." I said it with an appropriate amount of disdain dripping from my words.

"Did you actually expect him to take her this weekend? He's got a new family that's more fun than you and Haley now."

"Right, but I really would like to go out with this guy. Do you think it's safe to invite him over?"

"Has he given any indication that he's a pedophile or a rapist?"

"Ummm, no. He does seem to have a weird thing about drinking juice boxes. Every time I talk to him, he says he needs to go grab a juice box which is odd for a 29-year-old. He once went on for several minutes about how Hi-C Orange Lavaburst juice boxes are too small. Apparently, he'd prefer it in a jug form."

"Maybe juice box is code for something else. Either way, that's not an exclusionary factor and he's got a good point. Lavaburst is good"

"Valid on both statements. I wish Hi-C would bring back Ecto Cooler. I can't ever find it at the store anymore. That stuff was good."

"You're getting distracted, Jennifer. Focus. Could you ask him to send you his driver's license number before he comes over, so it seems like you're doing a background check on him? If he's a rapist, maybe it will scare him off."

"I could do that, except that makes me the psycho... Or an identity thief."

"Also valid." She sighed. "I say just go for it. You've been talking to him for like a month, and he seems pretty normal. I'm sure you'll be fine."

I called Bryan and dropped the bad news. "I'm really sorry but I don't have a sitter for my daughter tonight. Do you want to reschedule? Or do you want to just come to my house?"

"Oh, no! That sucks, but yeah! I'd love to come over. Are you comfortable with that? You could have a friend there with you if you're worried about meeting me for the first time at your house."

I picked up on the fact that he was looking out for me even before he had officially met me. "No, I think it's ok. My building has security cameras, so if you're a serial killer they'll be able to catch you pretty easily and I'll have my brother stop by to check on me at some point during the night to make sure everything is ok." That was totally a lie, but I figured if he was a serial killer, he wouldn't kill me if my six-foot-three brother might pop in and catch him cleaning up the blood after he's chopped me up into little pieces.

"Ok, cool. Send me your address, and I'll see you tonight."

CHAPTER 5

A half-hour before Bryan was supposed to show up, I was picking up around the house and putting on some makeup. My phone rang, and I saw his name pop up. *Great... he's going to cancel.*

"Hey! You on your way?" I asked hoping that I wasn't getting ditched again.

"Yep! I just wanted to see what kind of candy Haley likes. I thought maybe I should bring a bribe."

Oh my gosh.... That's a new one. Not only is he not ditching me, but he's also thinking of my kid. I tried to play it cool. "Ummm... probably M&M's. She once sat on the potty for over an hour to get an M&M when I was potty training her."

"Cool. I should be there in about a half-hour or so."

I flipped the phone closed and went back to getting myself ready. *Dang! I better put on a clean shirt. This guy might be worth it. I think I shaved my armpits.* He seemed like a decent person. Some guys might be scared off by the baggage of a divorced single mom. I was hoping he'd see that the baggage I have is the most important thing in my life, and if he wants me, my kid is part of the package.

Our first date was delightful. We watched the movie Beauty and the Beast with Haley until she had to go to bed. She insisted on wearing her Belle dress and danced around the living room, pretending she was a princess. At almost 2-years-old, she already knew how to make herself the center of attention. I put her down to go to sleep and read her a story like we did every night, and Bryan patiently waited in the living room for me. Once I was back in the other room, he played it absolutely perfect.

"She's great. A little precocious, but great."

"Yeah, she's the love of my life. I don't know what I'd do without that kid."

"Is her dad in the picture?"

"Well, that depends on the month. Sometimes yes, and sometimes no. He just had another baby with someone else, so he's pretty focused on that right now. I could go on for hours telling you stories about what a douchebag he is, but I'd rather not talk about him right now."

"Fair enough! I'd rather not talk about him either. Want to watch a movie? I brought one for us, too."

"Please! What have you got?"

"I've got mind-numbing comedy or dramatic chick flick."

"Let's go with comedy. I could use a little laughter in my life."

By the end of Big Daddy, we had watched maybe ¼ of what was happening on the screen. Having him kiss me was far more entertaining than anything Adam Sandler was doing. It finally got late enough that I knew I needed to go to bed, and my lips were starting to hurt from his scratchy goatee.

As I walked him to the door, I realized I didn't want him to leave. I could have stayed in that room with him for the rest of the night if I didn't know that Haley would be waking me up in five hours wanting some breakfast.

He looked at me as he was about to walk out the door. "Can I call you tomorrow?"

"Yeah, I'd like that. Thanks for coming all the way over here. I'm sorry it didn't work out to go to dinner."

"I thought this was great. Don't worry about it. I had a great time, and I can't wait to see you again."

"Thanks for not chopping me up into little pieces."

"Ummm… Ok. Whatever I can do to make your night better."

"Goodnight." One last kiss and he was out the door.

After he left, I went through a mental checklist of how the night had gone. There was absolutely nothing weird about it, which is the only thing I could say that was weird. To have someone who was kind and fun and made me laugh seemed a little unsettling. Maybe I'll find out he secretly has a wife, a kid, and a dog I don't know about. Maybe his parents were drug dealers, and he grew up in a life of crime as their mule. Or, could it be possible he really is a decent guy? I was hesitant, but I liked how the night had gone, and I was excited to see him again.

CHAPTER 6

I didn't have sex with Bryan for at least the first month we were dating. I could tell this was frustrating for him, although he never rushed me and never pushed for it. He had been in serious relationships before, and I had given birth to a child, so clearly neither of us was a virgin. We did plenty of kissing and groping various body parts, but I wanted to be cautious. I didn't want to jump into anything, which I made clear to him. I knew I had trust issues, but I assured him that my lack of intimacy was not a reflection of how I felt about him.

"I get it. The last woman I dated was the same way and didn't want to have sex with me until we were married even though she had two kids. I finally agreed to marry her, but I knew it wasn't going to work. "

"So, you proposed so you could get laid?"

"No, I proposed because I thought she was what I wanted, but I woke up one morning and realized she wasn't."

"And you just walked away? No looking back?"

"I just knew at that moment it wasn't what I wanted anymore and once I decided, that was it. I was done and ready to move on."

"That's pretty harsh, but I get it. So, you've been engaged before?" He knew about all my baggage, but I hadn't heard much about his.

"Yeah. And a time before that."

"Seriously?"

"Yeah, I was super young, and she wouldn't stop talking about marriage, so I finally gave her a ring to shut her up. We were 20 years old. There was no way I was going to marry her, but she just wouldn't stop talking about it."

"That's a pretty expensive way to shut someone up."

"Yeah, she ended up sleeping with one of my best friends, so that one didn't work out either."

"She cheated on you with your best friend?"

"Yep."

"Dang! And I thought I had been in some bad relationships."

"Yep."

We went out to dinner that night while Haley was with Darryl's parents. They were kind and doting grandparents that I didn't want to see leave Haley's life. They recognized the wreckage that Darryl left behind him anywhere he went so they enjoyed when I asked them to babysit so they had an opportunity to spoil the baby girl.

Bryan and I had a great time. We talked and laughed and had a couple of drinks, and when we got back to his place, we started kissing, and this time, I didn't want him to stop. Our first attempt at sex was amazing and passionate and beautiful …. Until it wasn't.

His hands moved expertly around my body and I was completely lost in the moment, feeling him that close to me. He seemed surprised I wasn't stopping him as explored slowly and cautiously, making sure

I was ok with what was happening. I was ready for it to happen and let him know that. He was kind and considerate of me and what I wanted and needed. I was totally focused on him, and the moment we were finally sharing. I looked up at his face and realized I was falling in love with him when a giant drop of sweat fell off his forehead and landed directly in my eye.

"Oh, my gosh!" I held my hand over my eye. "Shit! It really stings!"

"What's the matter?"

"Your sweat just dropped into my eyeball."

"Are you ok?"

"Yeah. I'm fine. Just go ahead and finish." I laid there holding my eye trying to get the sting to stop while he contemplated what he should do next. *For the love of God! This hurts like a son of a bitch!*

He stared at my face and the horrible look I had on it as the sweat continued to sting my eyeball and he laughed at me.

"No, seriously…. It's fine. Just go ahead and keep going."

"Jen. I can't keep going when you have that look on your face."

"Just get me a washcloth or something and it will be fine. It's just stinging."

He laughed again and rolled off me and went to get me a washcloth. I was horrified at the events that were unfolding. "I'm so sorry. We really can try again. Maybe just wear a headband this time to catch the sweat drips. Or I could wear sunglasses."

He laughed at my suggestions. "No, I don't think so."

"I'm so sorry."

"No, seriously. I'm ok."

I was embarrassed that our first attempt at sex ended with me being temporarily blinded by sweat. We talked for a little while longer and then fell asleep. We woke up at around 2:00 in the morning and tried again. Since I didn't have a pair of sunglasses or a sweatband handy, I decided to take a position on top so I wouldn't get blinded in my other eye by giant sweat drops falling from his forehead. It went much better, and this time, we both fell asleep happy and satisfied.

CHAPTER 7

I met Bryan's parents, Louse and Bernie, for the first time at Christmas. We had been dating for a few months, and we had somehow ended up in an exclusive relationship. I didn't intend for it to become exclusive and I kept telling him I didn't need a relationship to be happy. I was trying to prove to myself and to him that I could do things by myself, but life was so much more fun with him we ended up spending all our time together. He asked me if I wanted to come to his parents' house for Christmas dinner and I agreed, so long as he came and met my family the next day.

We went to their house on Christmas Eve and had a lovely time. His parents lived in an affluent area of the Twin Cities, and they had worked hard to get there. Bryan was an only child and had grown up knowing the value of a dollar. He had gotten his first job when he was 15 so he could afford things for himself.

Their house was decorated beautifully. There was a large Christmas tree in front of a wall of windows that looked onto the back yard. The dinner table was set for a formal meal with candles and flowers. The setting was lovely. Haley was given a wine glass with her meal, which instantly made me nervous.

"Do you think I could get a plastic cup for her? She's going to destroy this lovely meal and your wine glasses." They caved and gave her a sippy cup, although I felt horribly self-conscious that it ruined the look of the table. I stuck Haley's plastic cup next to me, so it was mostly out of sight throughout dinner. We talked and ate by a candlelight dinner with Christmas classics playing quietly in the background. The evening was charming, and they were kind enough to buy a few small gifts for Haley to open after dinner. On our way home, I asked Bryan if Christmas was always like that at his house.

"Yeah, it's just the three of us, so it's usually pretty quiet. My mom is an awesome cook. She puts a lot of work into dinner. We've always gone all out at Christmas. Doesn't your family do that?"

Bryan's answer came the next day when he met my family for the first time. Christmas with my family is nothing short of chaos. At that time, there were six grandchildren, all ages five and under. Tom was my oldest brother and he and Angela had been together for as long as I could remember. They started dating in high school and had met at a stoplight in our sleepy little cabin town. They had three boys, Christian, Dillon, and Landon, and the only one who didn't continually run at full speed was Landon because he wasn't even a year old yet. My other brother, Scott, was just a year younger than Tom, and he and his wife, Shereen, had two boys, Jeff and Jake. Haley was the only girl and acted like she was the princess of the group. However, when push came to shove, my little princess wasn't afraid to get dirty with the boys, either.

As the house started to fill with people, conversations started flowing which usually meant one person was yelling across the room to another person. Eight conversations were going on at once between five people and it felt a little like mayhem had exploded in the room. This was the Christmas that I loved. There was food, stories, music playing, and more laughs than I could count. Dinner is served when someone yells, "FOOD'S READY!" and people start forming a line to dish up their meal. Kids are given a place to sit so that their spilling causes minimal damage, while the adults load up their plates with ham and cheesy potatoes and seven other kinds of side dishes.

About two hours into the day, as my brothers were spouting out useless trivia facts to us all, I looked around and couldn't find Bryan. *Maybe he made a run for it.* I stepped out to the garage and found him quietly sitting on an upside-down pail, chain-smoking a pack of cigarettes.

"Are you ok?" He had a strange look on his face.

"It's a lot."

"What? My family?"

"Yeah. It's a lot! Your brother was listing out every time he's puked since 1985. Who does that?"

"Tom? Yeah, he's weirdly proud of the fact that he rarely pukes. I don't know why it's a big deal for him, but it is."

"Wow!" He took a long drag of his cigarette. "It's a lot."

I laughed at him. He had come out to a freezing garage just to get a moment of quiet from all the havoc in the house. "You'll survive. This is what my family is like. Come and have something to eat."

He looked at me incredulously. "We just finished eating."

"That was round one. Round two is about to start. That's when the alcohol and cookies and treats come out. You don't want to miss that!"

"The alcohol sounds good. I'll be there in a minute. I just need to prepare to walk into that again."

I laughed again. "Don't take too long. I don't want my family to think you're hiding from them."

As I walked back into the house, I heard him say, "I am!"

CHAPTER 8

Shortly after Christmas, I started to freak out. Things were going well. Because of how happy he made me, I began to realize there was the potential for me to be hurt again. Being a single mom who had been burned a few times makes you cautious, and there's this wall I always dragged around with me waiting for something to go wrong. There was absolutely nothing wrong with Bryan or our relationship, but I kept waiting for the bombshell that had ended every other relationship I had been in. I panicked.

"I just think I need to be alone for now. I'm really sorry, but I need to end this."

"Are you fucking kidding me? What happened?" He was dismayed at my decision to break up with him when we had a pretty solid relationship going.

"Nothing. I just think I'm better by myself. I have a lot going on with Haley, and Darryl is causing problems again. There's no energy left to put into a relationship right now."

"Do you feel like it's a lot of work? Like I'm taking up all your energy?"

"No… I don't know. Yeah, maybe. I just don't want a relationship. We have a great time together, but I wanted to have something fun and casual and it's turning into something serious and more than I wanted it to be."

"So, you're freaking out because things are going well?" He was calling me out on making such a stupid decision. My response was to dig in my heels.

"No. That's not what I said." (For the record, it was exactly what I had just said) "I said I don't want a relationship and I want to be by myself."

"Ok. I'm sorry you feel that way. I love being with you and Haley and I thought we had the potential to last. I don't want to leave, but I'm guessing I'm not going to change your mind."

He walked out, and I sat feeling sorry for myself. I had given him some pretty lame excuses for why I was breaking up with him. I had no idea why I felt like I needed to, I was simply determined to do this single mom thing by myself. I didn't need him there. I was more than capable of supporting myself and my daughter and I had an unexplained need to show that to the world. I convinced myself that it was a good idea, but I was sad to see him go.

I went over to Tom and Angela's house that night to let Haley play with their kids. The great part about us all having kids so close together was that they could keep each other entertained and get some good running around time together. I was talking to Angela about my decision to break up with Bryan.

"Why did you do that? I thought he was nice!"

"I don't know. It just didn't feel right. I'm fine with it." I knew she was going to dig deeper, and I was afraid to explore this idea with her because I wanted to stay confident that I had made the right choice.

"Did you not like him?"

"I don't know. I did. I really liked him. He was just…. I guess he was kind of boring."

She turned and looked at me and took her big sister tone with me. Since I had been raised with boys, having a sister to tell me when I was being stupid was something I was still adjusting to. "Jennifer, that is a good thing. You're so used to Darryl messing with you and causing drama, you think that's what it's supposed to look like. It's not! The kind of boring that Bryan brings you is a good thing. It means there's more time to focus on happy things rather than finding your way out of a tragedy all the time."

I thought about her words and knew she was right. She always was. Yes, Bryan was boring, but he made me laugh and we always had fun together. The day would end with us talking about all the things we had done rather than me being yelled at because I looked at some guy the wrong way or I didn't make his dinner right. Bryan never accused. He never criticized. He was supportive. He was kind. He was great with my daughter. He was dull in all the right ways. I went to sleep thinking about what Angela had said and felt just the slightest regret at the choice I had made.

The next day, when I brought Haley home from daycare, she asked me, "Is Bwyan coming to pway wiff me today?"

"No, baby. Bryan can't come over today."

Great. Not only did I hurt Bryan by irrationally breaking up with him but now it's affecting Haley. I had always been cautious about introducing guys to Haley, and I screwed up by letting him in so quickly with her. She absolutely adored him. He was excellent about using M&M's strategically. I tried to reassure myself by remembering she was young. She would eventually forget about him.

I didn't really want her to forget about him, though. He was a great guy. Maybe it was a bad idea to break up with him, but I wasn't going to go crawling back to him now. I worked hard to portray myself as a strong, independent, single mother, and I had always struggled with swallowing my pride and admitting when I was wrong.

CHAPTER 9

About two weeks later, I had to drive to Eden Prairie to pick up some paperwork from another apartment community that my company managed. I never went to that area of the Twin Cities. Eden Prairie was a haul from where I lived, so I never had a reason to really go there. None of my friends lived that far from me, and I worked close to where I lived, so a trip down to that area was highly uncharacteristic of my regular routine.

I picked up the paperwork and got back on the road to drive home. If nothing else, it was nice not to be sitting in an office during the day. Because I was never in that area, I didn't know the roads very well, and I ended up missing my exit. I found another route that would get me where I needed to be but was going to take slightly longer. *No big deal.* It was a little more time out of the office and enjoying the sunshine. Minnesotans tend to cherish the sunshine whenever they can get it, particularly in the middle of winter.

I turned up the music and kept driving now that I knew where I was going. Out of the corner of my eye, I saw a vehicle merging onto the highway from the entrance ramp, so I switched lanes to give them some space. I looked over and saw a Jeep pulling up beside me. *Are you fucking kidding me?* There was Bryan. *What is he doing in Eden Prairie in the middle of the day? He should be in downtown Minneapolis at work right now.*

He looked over and saw me and smiled. He pointed at me and then pointed to the next exit, indicating he wanted me to pull over, so I did. We pulled into a McDonald's parking lot and got out to talk to each other. It was cold, but I didn't seem to notice as I stood there talking to him.

"What are you doing down here?" He smiled at me, and I instantly missed him.

"I had to go pick up some paperwork from one of our other buildings. What are you doing here? Why aren't you at work?"

"I took a half-day off today. There's a Jeep store out here and I needed to pick up a part I couldn't find at any other store."

"I see."

"Yeah." We didn't say anything for a minute or so, and it started to get uncomfortable.

He reached over and grabbed my finger and held on for a second and then said, "I miss you."

Shit. I missed him too, but I didn't want to admit it. I had been reminding myself for the past two weeks that I didn't need him. But what if I wanted him? "I miss you, too."

"So why are we doing this? Why aren't we still together?"

"Because being a single mom is really hard and I have to …."

He cut me off this time. "Seriously? I get that you're trying to prove something to someone. You've proven it. It's done. So why not allow yourself to be happy? Why do you need to keep putting up walls? I'm not going to hurt you. I love you. I don't hurt people I love."

"But what if you stop loving me?" I hated that I asked the question because it felt like weakness, but I was finally admitting what I was really scared of.

"Then we tackle that if it ever happens and we figure out what went wrong. But nothing has gone wrong. You're just inventing something to protect yourself. You can't let fear prevent you from living your life."

"That's a bunch of bullshit. I'm not letting fear do anything. I'm …. Just …. I'm …. I don't need to …. You're …. Oh, hell…. Whatever. Yeah. Ok." He laughed at my feeble attempt to try and convince him he was wrong with everything he just said. He was absolutely right. I was making excuses so I could prevent myself from being hurt again, and in turn, hurting myself. I did love him, and I loved being with him, so why was I stopping him from being a part of my life? The damage Darryl had done was still controlling me and I didn't want Darryl to win.

After looking at my feet for a couple of minutes trying to figure out the best way to swallow my pride, I finally looked at him and knew it was pointless to keep fighting him. "Do you want to come over tonight?"

"Yes. I do."

"Haley is going to be there. She's been asking about you."

"I miss her, too."

"Ok. 7:00?"

"Yep. I'll be there." He moved in close to me, put his hand on my hip, and kissed me. I liked it, and my wall crumbled just a little bit.

CHAPTER 10

B ryan and I had been dating for just over eight months, minus the two weeks I had broken up with him. I made a conscious effort to let my vulnerabilities show around him and tried to not become defensive about little things. He was true to his word and continued to love me and didn't hurt me. It was a slow process, and he would call me out when he could tell I was testing him, but I slowly started to trust him and believe that not all relationships had to involve tragedy and heartache.

He had eventually moved in, and we had developed a solid relationship. He had a good job that paid well, and I was still managing apartment buildings to make a living and support my daughter. I continued hating the job, but it came with a nice benefit of discounted rent, so it made sense for him to move into my place when the subject finally came up. He helped around the house, played with Haley, and was the father figure she needed.

The summer was coming, and Bryan and I decided to plan a Memorial Day weekend trip. We settled on a camping trip to Jellystone Park in Warrens, Wisconsin. Jellystone was one of those places that made you feel like you were at home, camping with your family that just happened to include a thousand other people. There was candy bar Bingo in the evening, S'mores stations, and a dance at night. They had 3 on 3 basketball tournaments and 3-legged races, and of course, you could meet Yogi Bear and Boo Boo, which was always a highlight.

We rented one of their small camper cabins for the weekend. It consisted of a small room with two sets of bunk beds and a full-size bed in the front. It was literally two rooms with a light overhead, and it was perfect. There was no running water and no bathroom. You had to walk your ass all the way over to the outhouse for that or walk a little further to one of the bathroom facilities that had running water and real toilets.

This was going to be our first "family" adventure together. Bryan and I had taken a couple of getaways with just each other to go skiing in Duluth and a long weekend to Las Vegas over the winter, but this was the first time the three of us would go away and do anything.

I watched Bryan trying to build a fire. He clearly had some idea of how this was going to work, but the fire didn't seem to want to light. He kept at it, trying to build the perfect fire, only to have it smolder out again. I had talked about camping a few times and made it seem like I was an expert. The truth was I had gone camping with my family when I was seven and had recently started watching the show Survivor, so I thought I knew a lot more than I did. Regardless, he was trying to do his best to impress me since I had depicted myself as a skilled camper.

"Damn wood is wet! This fucking thing won't light."

"I think you need to build a little teepee of wood and then shove wadded up paper under it." My Survivor training had clearly taught me to make the perfect fire.

"Jen! I know how to make a fire. Just …. just…. I've got it."

"Ok, but I think it would work better if you built like a little teepee…." I held my hands in a little triangle shape to show him what I meant as though it was more helpful advice that way.

"Jen!"

"Ok…. I'm just saying a teepee would work better." I walked away and let him be and the next thing I knew he had a can of lighter fluid he was preparing to use to saturate the wood.

"What the hell is that? You can't put lighter fluid all over it. That's not how you build a fire."

"The wood is wet, and it won't light. The lighter fluid will work."

"That is not how they do it on Survivor."

"We're not on Survivor! We're at Jellystone Park in Wisconsin. Do you see Jeff Probst anywhere? And for that matter, you wouldn't last a day on Survivor. You would hate the bugs and the hot and the sand."

"I would be awesome at Survivor. I would be the lovably annoying one that plays an awesome social game but doesn't really help at camp. I would also rock the puzzle challenges."

"You wouldn't last a day."

He eventually doused the wood in lighter fluid. The wood still didn't light very well, but sort of smoldered and made a lot of smoke for the rest of the night. The next day we drove into the little town of

Warrens which consisted of a post office, and a gas station which doubled as a liquor store. We purchased some dry wood and when we brought it back, he had a fire going in no time. He got a little smile on his face when the fire was lit and said, "See! It was wet."

"I choose not to discuss this at this time." He threw a marshmallow at me as I walked away and we both laughed. He may not be good at making fires, but he makes me laugh and doesn't freak out when I nag about teepees and how good I would be at Survivor.

CHAPTER 11

O n the way home from our trip we got into a discussion about
how we have two different sets of friends. Haley was sleeping
in her car seat in the back, and I pointed out we had his friends and
we had mine, but we hadn't established our friends yet. I came up
with the idea that we should have a party.

"Should we just have a huge party and invite everyone we know
so they all get to meet each other?"

"Sure. That would be fun."

"Ok. What should we do? Should we have a theme? Like a
costume party?"

"Well, we're not 10-year-olds, so I'm saying no to the costume
party."

"Costume parties are fun but ok. How about a luau? We could
get like Tiki torches and leis and have like a huge luau. That could be
fun."

"Sure. That sounds fun."

"Ok. I'm going to plan a party." I sat and thought for a few minutes about the logistics of having a big party for all our friends. "A luau seems like it would be fun. That would make a good wedding reception." *Oh shit! Did I just say that out loud? Shit...* I tried to think of a way to cover it up before I freaked him out.

Before I could say anything else, he agreed with me. "That would actually be a pretty good wedding reception. You could have like a hut over the bar and the tiki torches and stuff. That would be really fun."

An awkward silence followed his comments for several minutes. My mind was running through the entire conversation and trying to calculate the likelihood that he was messing with me or if he was serious. I hesitantly asked, "Should we do that? Do you want to have a luau wedding reception?"

"Sure. That would be fun."

"You know we'd have to get married in order to have a wedding reception, right?"

"Yeah, that sounds like a good idea."

"Wait. So, you want to get married?"

"Sure."

Did I just propose to him? The whole conversation had taken a turn and now I had more questions than answers. "Ok. I'm going to plan a luau wedding reception then."

"Yep."

"And a wedding before it."

"Yep."

"And we'll be the ones getting married."

"Yep."

What the fuck just happened?

CHAPTER 12

When we got home, we talked about it a little more and confirmed that we were actually going to get married.

"Jen, I love you, and I love Haley, and I want to spend the rest of my life with you. So, if it makes you happy to have a luau, then we'll do that. Let's plan it." He got down on one knee and held my hand. "Does this help you know that I'm serious? You want me to really propose?"

"No. Get your ass up, you silly boy. I already proposed to you in a messed up roundabout way. Mine was first. I win." He stood up and kissed me and I hugged him tight, terrified of what we were about to do, but his arms wrapped around me made me feel safe and calm.

We spent the next several months planning our wedding, and on August 20th of that year, we did, in fact, have a luau wedding reception and a wedding before it where he and I were the participants.

Bryan was much more artistic than I was and always had a good eye for design, so he oversaw the invitations. He had them come from Haley, and she signed her little name with the backward L and an E with five lines on it. It was adorable and I loved that Bryan had thought of it. The wedding ceremony was family only and held at a small church not far from where the reception was going to take place.

We spent the night before the wedding apart from each other, and this time, on my way to the church, I didn't stop to contemplate what I was doing over a McMuffin. I was sure of my choice and didn't need to process through my decision with anyone.

I saw him in his tuxedo as I walked out of the room where I changed into my dress. He stopped, put his hand on his heart and walked over to me.

"You're absolutely beautiful."

"You're not too shabby either!"

"Aren't we supposed to avoid seeing each other? Isn't it bad luck?"

"Nope… not for us. That's only for people that are on the fence about what they're doing."

He grabbed my hand and we walked together to get pictures taken before the ceremony so that we could leave right after. I realized he didn't make me practice kissing him or call me a whore, and that the one and only comparison I made the entire day between him and my first wedding. After that, I didn't think about it. There was no comparison. This was a marriage built on love, not the appearance of it.

About 20 minutes before the ceremony was supposed to start, Haley came into the church crying hysterically. She was playing hide and seek with her cousins and decided to hide in a bush (Because when your mom is about to get married, and you're wearing a dress made of multiple layers of tulle, it makes complete sense to climb into a bush). The result of her hiding spot was a ripped-up dress, a scraped knee, and her hair had gotten all messed up. She fully believed that this was her wedding, and she was distraught that she had ripped some of the tulle that made her beautiful dress twirly.

I found scissors from the church office, cut off the outer layer, and tucked her hair back with a few bobby pins while telling her it was going to be ok in hopes she would calm down. I checked the scrapes on her knee, asked Angela for a Band-Aid, gave Haley a kiss, and informed her it was time to get married. My status as a single mom didn't stop just because I had the little task of getting married to handle.

After Bryan and I said our vows, he pulled out a small diamond ring for Haley and got down on one knee to say his vows with her. He promised to be her dad and treat her with kindness and love. He promised that he would always love her just like she was his own. My heart melted, and he proudly put the small ring on her finger. I was overjoyed at the little family we had.

We took off in his Jeep and headed to the reception where we danced and drank and ate with our friends all night. Dena was there with her hugely pregnant belly and looked like she was a balloon about to pop, but she was there to support me and didn't try to convince me to run this time. There was a grass hut over the bar, tiki torches surrounding the ballroom, and a giant appetizer buffet with shrimp, skewers of chicken and beef, fruit, and enough food to feed a football team. We walked around from table to table saying hello to people and enjoying the evening together. We danced and drank and were happy.

The highlight of the night came when Bryan and I finished our first dance to Keith Urban's "Your Everything." Bryan and Haley did their first dance together to the song "His Cheeseburger" by the Veggie Tales. While Haley's loyalty was to her precious Larry the Cucumber, Love Songs with Mr. Lunt had become a favorite, as well. She would sit on Bryan's lap and tell him she loved him as much as a cheeseburger, since to her that was the ultimate love. She smiled through the whole dance and in the end, he dipped her real low. You could have been blinded by the number of flashes that went off as everyone took pictures of the two of them in their big moment.

By the end of the night, I was sick of wearing my wedding dress and went and changed so I could be more comfortable. This time it wasn't because I was pregnant, but I walked in wearing one of Bryan's button-down shirts and a pair of jeans and no shoes. We went out to the dance floor for another dance, although he had to remind me to put my beer down before we hit the floor. While we were dancing, he leaned in and whispered, "You're just as beautiful in my shirt as you were in the dress, but I would have enjoyed taking the dress off you more."

I rested my head on his shoulder and said, "The dress had too many laces and snaps. This is easier." All the while, I was thinking, "Please let it stay like this."

PART 2

WHO WOULDN'T WANNA BE ME?

We held hands and sat near the lake,
and at night we lit a fire
and enjoyed the quiet of the stars
that were all around us.

CHAPTER 13

Married life was good. We were Mr. and Mrs. Monahan. My insecurities and wariness had slowly faded, and I enjoyed being married to someone who fully loved me in return. Bryan was hard at work in a job he loved, but I was growing restless in the career path I despised. My heart yearned to go back to teaching. The problem was that the license I had wasn't that interesting to potential employers. It was the most basic of all licenses and my resume was one in 500 others that hit the desk of the average principal. There was no specialty area on my license, as many other teachers had, and the only experience I had was as a substitute teacher. I knew I wanted more, but our life was solid the way it was, and I was nervous about throwing myself back into a college program to pursue my dream. I didn't want to upset the status quo.

The next spring, we moved out of the little apartment we were renting and bought a house in the city of Elk River, just north of Minneapolis. The house we chose had a nice big yard for Haley and plenty of kids in the neighborhood for her to play with. It was nice not to have to bring her down an elevator and sit with her every time she wanted to be outside.

Bryan loved homeownership and relished the tasks associated with taking care of our home and our yard. He would tackle little projects; changing the bathroom faucets … replacing the flooring… adding cabinets to the laundry room. He mowed the grass at least once a week just because he wanted to compete with the single guy who lived next door to us. Our neighbor, Andy, was a police officer in a neighboring city and he and Bryan would often stand outside talking about the lawn and their tools and guns and anything else that screamed testosterone.

He came in one night from one of their backyard chats and said, "You know, Andy got a new riding lawnmower."

"Uh-huh…." I could guess what was coming next.

"We probably should get one, too."

I smiled at his little boy attempt to get a new toy. "Why? So you can win The Battle of the Lawns? We already have a lawnmower. It works fine. Do you really need a riding one? Or is this just an attempt to prove we're as cool as Andy?"

"Not to prove we're cool. Just cuz… you know…. A riding lawnmower would make it easier. He's getting a sprinkler system installed next week, too. Just sayin'."

"Uh, huh…. Do you boys stand out there every night comparing the size of your dicks or is it just when one of you gets a new toy?"

He laughed, but I knew the issue wasn't going away soon. The next week, just after Andy got his new sprinkler system, Bryan bought a riding lawn mower and stepped up his game to mow the lawn two times a week just because he liked to do it.

. . . . .

Bryan had found an old pop up camper for $500 on Craigslist that he bought so we could spend more time camping. It wasn't fancy, but it had plenty of space for us, and Minnesota has some fantastic state parks we enjoyed exploring. We went on our last camping trip of the season at the end of September to Tettegouche State Park on Lake Superior. Haley stayed with Darryl's parents for the weekend. It was a perfect opportunity for them to have uninterrupted Haley time so that Bryan and I could have some time alone.

Tettegouche was our favorite Minnesota state park. The fall colors in northern Minnesota are stunning, and we hiked down to a waterfall and played around for a while. We climbed on the rocks and stopped to enjoy the view of the lake and the picturesque fall colors. We drank a few beers and played card games at our campsite, which I enjoyed consistently winning. We held hands and sat near the lake, and at night we lit a fire, without the use of lighter fluid, and enjoyed the quiet of the stars all around us.

Having sex inside of an old pop up camper is one of the least satisfying forms of sex that there is. Our camper was sturdy and comfortable to sleep in, but if you move around too much, it feels a little like being inside of a washing machine on the heavy-duty cycle. With every movement, the entire thing lurches back and forth. I could picture it tipping over and having to explain to a park ranger that my husband was pinned inside our camper because we tried to have sex. Not even fancy sex... just regular, old, missionary sex. Needless to say, we attempted it once and then decided that we would save our sexual activities for the comfort of any location that didn't have retractable legs and walls made of canvas.

On our drive home, we started to talk about having a child together and whether we were ready to add to our family. We agreed that it was something we both wanted, and the time seemed right. Being an only child, it was important to Bryan that he had a child with his DNA and his blood. It didn't mean he loved Haley any less. He still treated her like his own daughter, but there was this mythical biological parent out there that was always hovering in the distance. Darryl had found a new woman to support him and had moved in with her, so he was attempting to look like a good dad and spend time with Haley. However, the drama that followed Darryl around, and as a result entered our lives, was exhausting. The idea of having a child of his own that he didn't have to share made it more real for him.

CHAPTER 14

We got to work trying for a baby and were disappointed every month when we didn't end up pregnant. We tried timing sex with ovulation by having me pee on an ovulation stick. We tried counting the days from my period to time it right. We tried just having sex as often as possible, but with no luck. Finally, we came up with the idea of taking a long weekend away in Las Vegas. Plenty of people got drunk and accidentally pregnant there all the time, so maybe it would work for us.

We always loved Las Vegas. The people-watching was fantastic, and we found ourselves in a better mood just being around all the activity. After checking into The Paris hotel, we had drinks in our hands in no time at all. We wandered around, taking in the energy of The Strip. We ate too much food at the buffet, relaxed by the pool, and found a club to dance until the early hours of the morning. We went back to our hotel room and did what the rest of the drunks in Las Vegas were doing with the hopes of making a baby.

Bryan won a decent amount of money the first night we were there at the craps table and I spent the next few days systematically losing it all. He refused to sit too close to me when we played slots, so we were sitting a few rows away from each other when my Hot Hot Penny machine started making happy winner noises.

He looked over at me and mouthed, "Is that you?" He pointed to me and then the machine and then made the universal money gesture by rubbing his fingers and thumb together.

I proudly looked at him and smiled, "Yep!"

He cashed out his machine and came running over to where I was. "How much?"

"A thousand!!"

"You won a thousand dollars??"

"No. Pennies."

"Jen…. that's ten dollars."

"Yeah, but all the lights and noises make it seem pretty exciting! Doesn't it?"

. . . . .

Our drunken exploits in Las Vegas didn't do the trick and we still weren't pregnant the next month, so we continued with our suburban family life and all it entailed, all while regularly jumping on the baby-making train when the time seemed right. Haley was in school now, and we had lucked out with the neighborhood we moved to. There were little girls everywhere, all within a year or two of each other's age. Our house was one of the main hangouts, and I relished playing the part that my mom had when I was little. I tried to keep up the same level of snack stockpiling she did, but it shocked me how quickly a group of little girls could blow through a batch of cookies.

Bryan was using his status as the cool dad to take the girls on Jeep drives when the weather allowed for it. He took a certain delight in talking about "Jeepin' naked" in front of Haley's friends to freak them out. Haley had learned through Bryan's regular lessons that Jeepin' naked just meant that we had taken off all the doors and the top, but if a new friend came over, he would yell out "Who wants to go for a naked Jeep ride?" While the friend was trying to decide if Haley's dad was creepy and she should call her parents to come pick her up, Bryan would explain about mudding and go into more detail than any little girl cared about or could comprehend.

We kept trying for a baby, but after several more months and still nothing, I decided to have some testing done and sent Bryan to do the same. The doctor called us with the results that showed that everything with me was fine, but Bryan had a low sperm count and low motility, which would make it a challenge to get pregnant naturally.

"Are you fucking kidding me? So, what few swimmers I have are all fucked up and don't have a clue what they're supposed to be swimming toward?"

"Actually, I think it's more like they're kind of lazy and uninterested in getting anywhere quickly."

"Well, what the fuck."

I was determined to find a solution, so I started listing other options that were available to us. "We could try donor sperm?"

"What the hell is that?"

"You get sperm from a sperm bank, and they do intrauterine insemination."

"So, they shoot some other dude's jizz up into your junk? No."

"Ok, what about adoption?"

"Jen, I really want to try and have a kid that has my blood if it's at all possible. Is there anything we can try before we jump to that?"

"Well, the doctor said we could try doing IUI with your sperm. She just said that it was unlikely it would happen naturally. We'll need some doctor assistance. IUI would be where they use your sperm but put it up through my cervix, into my uterus so that your little guys don't have to swim so far. Maybe they get tired easily. I don't know."

"Ok, well, what would that be? I jerk off in a cup?"

"Yeah, pretty much."

He sat and contemplated what this would mean for a few moments and then, "Ok… let's try it."

It wasn't that easy. IUI consisted of Bryan having to take a medicine that would help to boost his sperm count and me having to give myself injections throughout the month to try to mature more eggs for his swimmers to find. It culminated with him giving me a shot in the ass with a giant needle the day before I would go in for insemination.

"I need you to give me my shot." I wasn't thrilled with it but knew it was what needed to be done if we had a chance at getting pregnant.

"Can't you do this one yourself?"

"No, it's a big ass needle, and you have to stab me in my ass cheek."

"Ok… give me the needle." I leaned over against the bathroom counter and dropped my pants so he could give me my shot.

"Ok, there you go! Time to get pregnant!"

"What was that like?"

"Kinda felt like Jell-O."

"Thanks, honey…."

CHAPTER 15

After our third attempt at insemination with Bryan's sperm, we got pregnant. I started to suspect we might be when I began to feel the familiar cramps I had when I got pregnant with Haley. I was elated when two little lines showed up on my pregnancy test.

"Hey, honey?" I had that tone in my voice that told him I needed to tell him something important.

"Yeah? Wait… what did you do?"

I laughed a little. I could already see the wheels turning in his mind, trying to figure out whether I could have taken the Jeep and broken it somehow without him knowing. "I didn't do anything, but we did something. I'm pregnant."

"Seriously?" He got up and came over to me and hugged me tightly. It felt good to finally give him some good news.

Pure joy was exuding through the room. He kissed my belly and had a smile on his face the rest of the day. He didn't do the cliché move of buying his kid a baseball glove, but I could tell that every day, the fact I was pregnant was on his mind. No more shots. No more jerking off into a cup. No more invasive ultrasounds up through my hoo-ha dilly regions. We were pregnant.

Our happiness was short-lived. About four weeks later, I had a different type of cramp that didn't feel quite right. Two days later, I noticed I was spotting when I went to the bathroom. After a trip to the doctor, they confirmed that I was having a miscarriage. There was no heartbeat and my HCG levels had fallen.

I had been hoping for a baby for so long that the miscarriage took me by surprise. Given our situation, I figured we had done the hardest part which was actually making a baby. Having something go wrong was not something I had contemplated. I was sad that after all that work, we weren't going to end up with a baby.

Bryan was devastated when I told him. As sad as I was, my heart broke for him. I had a baby that was mine, and if we could never have another one, I would be fine with that. But seeing how upset he was that we had lost the baby broke my heart.

The miscarriage didn't take care of itself, so I had to go in for a D&C procedure. I got a call a couple of weeks later from the doctor saying they had done genetic testing on the fetus and discovered that it had what's called Trisomy 18. This meant that there was an extra chromosome 18. Babies with that condition are almost always born with multiple birth defects if they're born at all. The doctor explained that many of these babies end in miscarriage by the 2nd trimester. Many other ones end in stillbirth by the 3rd trimester. The doctor also told me that the baby had been a boy. When I told Bryan about this, he was devastated.

"It was a boy?"

"Yeah. I'm sorry, honey. She said that babies with Trisomy 18 rarely live very long."

"I could have had a son?"

"You still can. We can try again."

"Great. More jerking off in a cup. You could not possibly understand how humiliating it is to have to do that. The nurse brings you to a room where there are magazines and tells you to leave your specimen on the table. It's a huge blow to my manhood that my sperm aren't cooperating, and there are barely any there to begin with. It's just humiliating."

"I know. I'm really sorry, honey." I must have said this more flippantly than I had intended because his reaction was not what I was expecting. He blew up at me.

"You treat it like it's absolutely nothing. It's nothing for you!"

"Woah! Back down. It is something for me!" His frustration was directed at me and I instantly started getting defensive. "I have to give myself shots in the belly every day. You give me a shot in the ass with a huge needle. I have vaginal ultrasounds multiple times a week. They count how many eggs I'm producing. The most romantic part about making a baby this way is that the light they use so they can see my cervix is kind of warm. You don't think this is awful for me, too?"

"But you're not the one with a problem. You come home and tell me how great you are at producing eggs, and I can't even make a normal amount of sperm. Then I have you lecturing me about not sitting in hot tubs and making jokes not to jack off for three days before my date with a cup and a copy of Playboy. It's not you that has the problem. It's me, and I hate it."

I thought about everything he was saying to me and realized I hadn't looked at it from his perspective before. I hadn't thought about what it must be like to arouse yourself in a doctor's office and then leave a cup of your semen sitting on the counter. There was nothing romantic about it for him either. It had been months since he had touched me. Months since he held my hand or rubbed my back or even made a move on me at night. Our sex life had dwindled down to a cup, a playboy, and a warm light shining between my legs.

We tried again a few months later and got pregnant a second time. This time I told him, and his response was, "Ok. Let me know how it goes." Four weeks later, I had another miscarriage. I refused to give up on having a baby. Yes, Bryan wanted a son, so part of me felt like I was doing this for him, but at the same time, I loved being pregnant. The nine months I had been pregnant with Haley were incredible. Feeling your child kick and move around inside your belly is a beautiful feeling, and my pregnancy with her had been easy. I wanted to be pregnant again and have that experience with Bryan. I wanted to have a baby that had his eyes and his artistic ability and my fabulous hair. I wanted someone we could raise together without the influence of the "biological dad" hovering in the distance. I wanted a little piece of him and a little piece of me to be a part of this world after we were gone. With Haley, I had gotten pregnant without even trying, and it was frustrating not to have it go as easy as we had hoped it would.

I knew that Dena had gone to see a doctor about her fertility when she was having trouble conceiving. Luckily, she didn't end up needing it and she had a wonderful young son named Riley. I respected her opinion and knew that she would either have some advice or be willing to listen to me complain about how hard it was. She told me the name of the doctor she had gone to and I decided it couldn't hurt to see someone new that might have a different perspective, so I called for an appointment.

We went together to see Dr. Davis, and from the beginning, this appointment was different. We weren't just looking at IUI. Insurance wouldn't cover much more of that, and Bryan couldn't stand the procedure. It was taking a toll on both of us. The closest we got to romance anymore was when he passed me the potatoes at dinner without me having to ask. It was more like we were just going through the motions than really loving each other anymore.

Dr. Davis felt that our best chance at having a baby was In Vitro Fertilization. He planned to take as many eggs as he could get from me and take Bryan's sperm and make us some babies in a dish. The benefit was that they looked at Bryan's sperm under a microscope before they combined them with my eggs. This way, they could pick out the best sperm to make us the best babies. The price tag was huge, and insurance wouldn't cover it, so we only had one shot at it.

We discussed it and I felt I needed to push a little harder than I thought I would. He reluctantly agreed to try. Looking back on it, I don't think it was so much that he didn't want a baby anymore. It was the process in which we were trying to get the baby. He desperately wanted a child of his own and would do whatever it took to get one, but he didn't approach it with the enthusiasm and determination I did. He was frustrated and just wanted to be that average couple that gets drunk one night and screws and ends up with a baby nine months later.

We went forward with the IVF procedure, and the amount of paperwork that goes into the process was crazy. We had to indicate what would happen with the embryos that weren't used. What would happen to the embryos if we ever separated? What if one of us died? If I died, was Bryan able to use the embryos in a surrogate? If he died, could I use the embryos for myself? These were all things we had never contemplated, but we had to systematically go through each of the scenarios and decide what we would like to do.

In addition to the paperwork, I had appointments several times a week. I had ultrasounds on my ovaries to make sure I had a good number of follicles that were maturing. When it was time for the procedure, he went to one room, and I went to another. They extracted my eggs, but I was given a mild sedative to help me relax, so I didn't remember much of it. While this was happening, Bryan was in a separate room with a cup and some reading materials to help him get the job done. We met up in the recovery room after we each participated in our own activities. The nurse told me I should relax for the rest of the day so I asked Bryan if we could stop by Target on the way home. The good news was that they got 18 eggs from me, which gave us a good chance of getting at least a couple of embryos.

A few days later, we got word they fertilized 12 of my eggs with Bryan's sperm. It was great news! They would pick out two of them to implant in me and then it was a waiting game from there. Our nerves were pretty shaky at this point since we knew this was our one and only shot at doing IVF. If this didn't work, I didn't know what our next step would be, but I decided not to think that far ahead. I wanted to focus on this and put all my energy into getting us a baby together.

We went in for the embryo transfer on November 8. It was not the way I had ever imagined getting pregnant, but at that point, I wasn't really shocked by anything they needed to do to get us a baby. We were brought into a dimly lit procedure room. The lighting choice seemed strange, but I guess the doctor was trying to set a calming mood in the room. There was slow 80's music playing, and we walked in while the song Hungry Eyes was on and I resisted the temptation to make a Dirty Dancing joke. There was a table in the middle of the room with stirrups so I could get nice and comfy. There was a chair near the head of the table so that Bryan could sit with me during the procedure and a little window on the side of the room. There was a bunch of busywork to get ready and they finally came and showed us a picture of our embryos prior to the transfer. Bryan gave the nurse a thumbs-up like, "Yep, those are some damn fine embryos."

The doctor asked us to hold hands as Against All Odds began playing in the background. *What in the hell? Isn't this a break-up song?* Once the doctor was ready, the nurse went to the window and brought out a small dish from their sterile room where they apparently grow babies in dishes. We held hands and prepared for our last shot at getting pregnant as we listened to Phil Collins singing about feeling empty inside. The doctor transferred the embryos into my uterus with a long catheter, and they told me to lay still for an hour with a pillow under my butt until I could go home.

We walked out into the chilly November air, with both of us aware of what was at stake. We didn't talk much about it, but as I got in the car and reclined my seat so I could stay laying down as the doctor ordered, Bryan grabbed my hand and squeezed it. He didn't look at me, but it was his way of telling me that he was nervous, even if he didn't want to admit it.

CHAPTER 16

Two weeks later, I was scheduled for a blood test to check my HCG levels and find out if we were pregnant. I couldn't wait that long. The anticipation was killing me. I rationalized that, if I were pregnant, the anxiety wasn't good for the baby. After six days, I took a home pregnancy test and it came back positive.

I found Bryan downstairs to give him the news. "Hey."

"Hey. What's up?"

"My pregnancy test came back positive."

"Cool. Do you think it will stay that way this time?"

I don't think he was trying to sound like an asshole, but it came across that way. I wanted him to be more excited and felt he should have jumped up to hug me like the first time we got pregnant, but I knew what he was really saying with his indifference: "I'm done getting excited only to be disappointed again." I didn't call him out on it because I knew it would start an argument, and I wanted to focus on something positive for the moment.

I was optimistic it would work this time. The doctors were giving me drugs to help make my uterine lining get nice and thick.

They had picked out the best eggs and the best sperm and transferred the two best embryos into my uterus. I went in every other day for blood work, and it showed that my HCG numbers were rapidly climbing. I was excited but didn't want to show Bryan how nervous I was. He had distanced himself from me again and would only ask how I was doing each day.

HCG levels are supposed to double every other day. My numbers were more than doubling with each visit I went to. Until one day they weren't. My numbers had gone up, but they weren't doubling anymore. So, another appointment was made for more blood work. Again, the numbers were climbing, but they weren't doubling. The nurse called and said the doctor would like me to come in for an ultrasound. That night, I noticed spotting again. I was devastated but didn't have the heart to tell Bryan until after my appointment the next day. I asked him to come along, but he didn't feel like he could be a part of that appointment. I could tell he was preparing himself to be disappointed again.

I went to the doctor and nervously waited until they called me back. I knew the drill: Undress from the waist down and wait on the table with the sheet over me. The doctor came in and up I went into the stirrups. The doctor warned me they didn't typically do ultrasounds this early so if there was no visible heartbeat, I shouldn't be worried. He brought the ultrasound up on the screen, and I could see the amniotic sac. *Where was the baby?* The doctor focused in on something and could see the fetus. *Heartbeat? Please, God, let there be a heartbeat.*

"Could you hold your breath, please?" I sucked in and remained very, very still so the doctor could get a better look. I've never stayed so still in all my life.

"There! There's the heartbeat." The doctor measured, and the baby and the tiny heartbeat were right on target for how far along I was.

They looked around a little more, and over to the side, the nurse pointed out a small black spot. This was the explanation for my numbers not doubling. There had been twins. One of the babies was continuing to thrive, but the other baby had stopped growing and now just looked like a little black dot inside my uterus. I asked about it and was told that my body would just reabsorb what was still there since it was tiny.

I went home to talk to Bryan and give him the good news. I've found that my mood would often reflect his and his lack of enthusiasm lately made me a little more emotionless than I had been in the past. "Well, I'm still pregnant."

"Are you going to stay that way?"

"It looks like it. There had been a twin, but the second baby stopped growing. The first baby is still strong and growing right on target."

"What kind of baby is it?" I heard the cautious tone of his voice.

"Right now, it's still a blob baby. No way to know what it is yet. They're marking me as a high-risk pregnancy because apparently I'm old to have a baby and because of our history of miscarriage and the trisomy I had before. We'll get one of those fancy 3D ultrasounds that makes the baby look like a cross between an alien and a melting wax figure. You're hoping for a boy, aren't you?"

"Uhhhhhh…. I'm not saying yes, but I'm not saying no to that."

"Yeah…. You want a boy."

CHAPTER 17

O wen Scott Monahan arrived on July 27, at 3:07 in the afternoon. He was worth every penny we spent to get him. By the time I got to the end of my pregnancy, I was miserable. My son was pushing on my bladder, I was huge, I couldn't see my feet, and every part of me that could swell was swollen. I went to my doctor in the final week and begged her to help me.

"You've got to get him out. Seriously. I'm absolutely miserable."

She looked at me and said, "You're all puffy, too."

Puffy? She just called me puffy. Was this a technical term for women who looked like me and wanted to cry just getting out of a chair?

"I'm sure you're ready to be done. I can try to strip your membranes and see if that gets things going."

"Please! Do whatever you have to do. Just get this baby out of me!"

She went to do my pelvic exam, but she was a relatively short woman, so she had to stand on the little step to reach my cervix.

"Your cervix is up really high, and I can't reach it. I need to try and get a finger in there to strip your membranes, and I just can't reach." She stepped down, took off her gloves, and kind of stared at me. I burst into tears, realizing that she wasn't going to be able to do anything to move things along.

"You seriously can't induce me yet?"

"No, I can't do it before your due date. Let me go get one of the other doctors who has really long fingers and see if he can reach."

I waited patiently as two more doctors came in and tried to reach my cervix, but the damn thing wasn't cooperating. Forget the fact that half of the clinic was coming in to give me a pelvic exam, my cervix was being a bitch and wouldn't let them reach it. They all apologized, and I burst into tears again.

My doctor stared at me crying and all puffy and finally said, "Your due date is on Monday. I'll set you up to go to the hospital on Sunday afternoon. They'll give you a gel that helps to soften your cervix. We can induce you on Monday morning."

I left with at least this small amount of hope that things would be over soon, and I'd have my son in my arms and no longer kicking my bladder.

. . . . .

Sunday came and Bryan, Haley, and I went to the hospital. They dropped me off at the front door and then went to the park while I got my gel that would finally get my monstrous child out of me. The nurse gave me the gel to help soften up my cervix, and within 10 minutes I wasn't feeling well.

I looked at her as she was giving me my instructions for coming back the next morning so I could be induced. "I don't feel very well."

"Well, you're dilated to two, and sometimes the gel starts moving things along a little bit."

"Well, can I just stay? I really don't feel well."

"No, but I'm guessing we'll see you back here this afternoon!"

If this chipper bitch knows I'm going to go into labor, why the hell is she sending me away? I walked back down to get in the Jeep where Haley and Bryan were waiting for me. Haley was going to my brother Scott's house for the night so we could be to the hospital nice and early the next day. Scott and Shereen were expecting their next baby in a few weeks, but they had no problem watching Haley for the night and they lived in a nice big house where Haley and their boys could run around and burn off some energy.

As we drove toward my brother's house, I started feeling worse. My belly was starting to hurt, and I was having real contractions. I tried to play it cool, so I didn't scare Haley.

"Bryan, I need you to get Haley to my brother's house now."

"That's where we're going. We're almost there."

"No, I need you to get her there now."

He shot me a puzzled look, and I gave him back one that said, "this is happening." The car sped up just slightly. We dropped off Haley, and I told him we needed to go right back to the hospital.

"Is it happening now?"

"I think so. My contractions are like every five minutes. I've been timing them while we were driving."

"Ok. I'm going to stop at the mall quickly."

"Are you fucking kidding me? I'm in labor. Your son is going to come out of a very small hole in my body soon. I need to go to the hospital."

"I want to buy a couple of magazines in case I have some downtime. Labor can take a while."

"Bryan, I went from no contractions to contractions every five minutes in the last half hour. It's going quick."

"Ok, I'll just run in and buy a magazine. You can wait here. It will take just a couple of minutes."

He pulled into a parking spot and went running into Barnes and Noble to look for magazines in case he got a little bored while I was trying to remove his son from my body. I was fairly salty about sitting in the mall parking lot alone while I was in labor, but I was focused on the excruciating pain rather than the absence of my husband.

I called my doctor's office and let them know that I was in labor. As I sat in the car waiting for Bryan, my phone rang, and it was the on-call doctor. She was asking me all the regular questions when I had a big contraction.

"Are you having a contraction now?"

"Yes… ahhhhh…. Yes …. whew whew whew."

"Is anyone with you?"

"No, my husband's in Barnes and Noble buying magazines."

"Ok. Ummmmm…. Will he be back soon?"

"I hope so. Mmmmmmm……. I really hope so."

"Ok, I need you to go to the hospital as soon as he's back. I can tell from the sound of your voice you're in labor."

Bryan appeared a few minutes later. I looked at him with no magazines in his hands. "What the hell were you doing? You don't even have any magazines!"

"The line was really long, so I just came back. Maybe there's a gift shop at the hospital that will have magazines. Or I could swing into like a Walgreens quick??"

"Oh my gosh! Enough with the magazines! I seriously need you to take me to the hospital."

We drove back toward where we had just come from, but I could tell he was nervous that my water would break all over his Jeep seats he had recently vacuumed. In between contractions he tried to slide a jacket underneath me just in case my water broke. My belly was gigantic, and a human was trying to work his way out of my vagina, so I managed to get the jacket half underneath me and told him that was close enough.

When we got back to the hospital, he pulled up to the front door as though he would drop me off. "What are you doing?" I asked him with confusion.

"I was going to drop you off. Walking is supposed to help move things along"

I stared at him with a look of disbelief. "I don't want you to leave me. Just park and you can walk in with me." Just then, another contraction snuck up on me. "Mmmmmmm……. Drive to the parking ramp! I'm not going in alone!"

He drove to the parking ramp, and once he found a spot, he looked at me and with a small amount of guilt in his voice said, "Well, I kinda wanted to have a cigarette."

"For the love…. Ok…. here's what's going to happen. My contractions are about four to five minutes apart. Wait until I have my next one, then jump out, have your cigarette, and you'll be back in the car before my next one hits. Deal?"

"Ok… deal."

After his smoke break and another contraction, we made our way into the hospital. The labor and delivery area was on the far end of the hospital, furthest from the parking ramp. As I walked, I bitched about how a man had clearly designed the hospital and how stupid it was to make laboring women walk that far. I had to stop half-way there while I had another contraction and noticed people moving out of my way as I clung to a wall, looking like I wanted to die. We made it back to the area I had been in less than an hour ago, and Chipper Bitch greeted us enthusiastically.

"You're back! I thought we might see you again."

"Uh-huh." I hadn't gotten past my annoyance that she had sent me away to begin with.

They put me in a triage room where they check to make sure you're really in labor. If you are, you're taken to the other wing of that floor so you could have your baby. All I could think about was that the drugs were in that other area of the maternity floor. I'm a bit of a wimp when it comes to pain, and with Haley they had given me some pretty good drugs, so I barely felt anything. I knew my labor was going fast because of the gel they had given me earlier. I also knew I only had a certain window of time to get the epidural I fiercely wanted.

As soon as the nurse left, I whispered to Bryan, "Honey…. You gotta get me out of here."

"Jen, you're in labor. We need to stay here so the baby can come."

"Yes, I know that, but you can't get the drugs on this side. You've got to get into the real labor area to get the drugs. You gotta sneak me over there." I could picture the other wing of the hospital with sunlight and soothing music and fountains of drugs you could drink from any time you had a contraction. I knew I needed to get to this beautiful haven of pain-free laboring, and it was within my reach, but I had to use my stealth moves to get there.

"Riiiiight. Ok. I think they're going to come get you in a minute."

"I don't think you understand. I need drugs. I can't do this if I don't have anything. This hurts so bad. Just take me over there. There has to be a room available."

"Jen, they'll be here in a minute to get you."

"You're not listening to me! The drugs are on the other side where the 'real' laboring women are. As long as I stay here, I'm not getting any. Just bring me over there and find me a room."

"I really don't think that's how it works."

"Bryan! Please help me! Can you just go find someone? My labor is much worse than most people. I need that epidural if I'm going to do this."

"Ok." He patted my hand and talked in a soothing voice. "I'll take you there in a minute. I'll go scope out our route to get us in." He was pacifying me so I would shut up, but I felt better now that it seemed like he was trying to sneak me over to the drug side of the maternity area.

I waited for what felt like another hour, which Bryan later told me was about four minutes until a tough-looking nurse by the name of Rhonda came and got me. She looked at me, writhing on the little bed and said, "Let's go!"

"Aren't you going to give me a wheelchair?"

"Nope. It's good for you to walk." This woman was clearly trying to torture me, and I looked to Bryan for help which he wasn't able to give.

As we started walking, I began pleading my case. "Can you tell the drug people to come to my room right away? I put in my birth plan that I don't want a natural birth. I want the drugs."

She just kept walking and told me that the drug man would be there soon. I got undressed and into the bed and hooked up to the monitor. There was a medical student working with them for the day, and we were told that he would stop in to check on me. Phil the Med Student would end up being a victim of the rampage of an irrational laboring woman that day.

"Hello. I'm Phil, and I'm a med student working here today. I wanted to come in and introduce myself and check to see how you're doing. It appears as though you're having some discomfort."

"Yes, I'm in considerable pain. Do you know where the drug man is? Whew…. Whew… whew…."

"I was told that the anesthesiologist would be here soon. If you had to rate your pain on a scale from 1 to 10, with 10 being the worst pain imaginable, what would you rate it?"

I was laying on the bed moaning, and the sound of Phil's voice was putting me on edge. "Seriously? That's what you're leading with? Phil, I'm trying to work a human out of my body right now. What do you think your pain level would be at?"

"I'm sure you're feeling some discomfort. Based on what I'm seeing, things seem to be going smoothly."

"I swear to God, Phil…. I appreciate what you're trying to do here and I'm sure you need to learn somehow, but I cannot do this right now. I cannot be your classroom at the moment. I'm trying to move a watermelon through an orange-sized hole. Could you please go get someone that can help me?"

I looked over at Bryan and said, "I don't want to do this, and the sound of his voice is irritating the shit out of me." Bryan tried to say something, but before he could, I turned back to Phil and said, "Don't stand there and ask me questions when you could be doing something useful. I want you to go find the guy who has the drugs and bring him back to my room. Is that cool with you, Phil?"

As poor Phil the Med Student walked out of my room, I heard Bryan apologize to him. I was later told that I may have been a touch harsh. It was beyond me why they would send a med student into my room alone to ask me mind-numbingly stupid questions. Rhonda was undoubtedly getting an evil laugh out of watching it all unfold.

The drug man showed up a few minutes later, but it was too late to get an epidural. He gave me some sort of shot in my spine, which did nothing to take away the pain, and less than an hour later, my son was in my arms.

Haley was brought to the hospital shortly after Owen arrived in the world because we told her she could be the first visitor to meet her brother. She was very proud as she sat on the couch and Bryan placed Owen in Haley's arms. Looking at this little family we had built made my heart happy. I had a beautiful son being held by my beautiful daughter, and my husband was overseeing the whole thing. This was a man who loved me and loved his children. I knew that this was how I wanted it to stay. Maybe it was my hormones raging inside of me, but I didn't think things could ever be less than perfect.

PART 3
THE HARD WAY

Where did we make the turn to
become this couple?
I used my words to criticize him,
never compliment him.
He didn't use his words for anything.
He just didn't talk to me anymore

CHAPTER 18

Since Owen's birth, Bryan was enthralled with being a dad. He had become a master at holding his son and soothing him when he needed it. He was an excellent father, which was a nice change from what I had experienced with Darryl after Haley was born. Bryan would hold Owen close in his arms and stroke his eyebrow and whisper to him, which always immediately calmed Owen down. Bryan couldn't get enough of his little bug. We didn't have much of a sex life, but I chalked that up to being new parents and always being tired. Every time he would kiss me, the baby would cry and off I'd go to feed him. Bryan's salary was more than enough to support us, so I spent the first year at home with Owen so I could have uninterrupted mommy-son time every day and didn't have to be in the awful job I despised.

While I was home with Owen, I decided I didn't want to manage apartment buildings anymore and finally took the leap to pursue my passion. I wanted to go back to school to get my master's degree in special education. I talked it over with Bryan, and he was supportive of the idea. I was able to do a lot of my work online, so I wouldn't be gone from the house too often. I started taking classes and quickly discovered it was an area I could be good at. I loved the information I was learning and was anxious to get done so I could get my new license and get into a classroom.

Fate had other ideas for us, though. Just after Owen's first birthday, Bryan lost his job with the company he was working for. The recession had hit the company hard, and they had started slowly selling off many of their commercial properties. Bryan admitted that he saw the writing on the wall and knew it was coming but was still highly disappointed when it happened. I begrudgingly went back to work managing apartment buildings and hated every second of it but was able to continue going to school. Bryan stayed home with Owen, so daycare wasn't needed, and he spent his days looking for a new job and hanging out with his son.

Bryan collected unemployment, and the company gave him a small severance package, so there was at least some money coming in. Things were tense, and money was tight, but I found ways to get us on little adventures here and there and keep our house running. Bryan put on a good act in front of the kids, but I could tell that it was hard on him to be unemployed. He'd been working since he was 15 years old when he got his first job at Dairy Queen and to have money be so tight was taking a toll on him and us. We didn't talk like we used to. We didn't go out. He would watch TV downstairs, and I would go up to our room and watch what I wanted to. There was a distance I didn't know how to fix.

Bryan was home for nearly a year with occasional interviews from the daily resumes he sent out. He even applied to several jobs in Texas with the idea we could move there. He got called for a couple of interviews and managed to get them on consecutive days, so we sent him to Texas to check things out. He ended up not getting either of the positions, but it was a nice break from the monotony of changing poopy diapers and watching cartoons all day.

He finally got an interview with a company based out of Nashville to manage a few medical office buildings in Minneapolis. He researched the company and went to look at what he assumed would be the building he would be working in. We talked about his answers to the possible questions and ran through some of the highlights of his career he would try to bring up during the interview. His interview went great and he was offered the job on Thursday and they asked him to start on Monday of the following week. He was like a giddy little schoolgirl after he accepted. We went out to celebrate his new job, but we were broke, so we settled for dinner at Culver's and tap beers at a local bar. Our next-door neighbor, Jadie, babysat for us and we paid her with Ben and Jerry's ice cream because we were out of cash. She thought it was funny and we paid her double the next time she babysat. We had sex for the first time in months that night. I remember thinking this new job would help him get out of his slump he had been in. It certainly put him in a better mood.

CHAPTER 19

B ryan started working at Holladay Properties on Monday, and he came home that night and told me every detail of it. He said everyone he worked with was kind and fun. I could tell that this was what he needed to feel like himself again. In the coming weeks, he was more talkative and upbeat, although the romance hadn't completely returned to our marriage like I had hoped it would. He was getting acclimated to a new job, while I stayed at my job at the apartment community so we could try and recover from the financial hole we had fallen into while he was unemployed.

In October of that year, I started student teaching which meant I had to quit my job. We would have to live off just Bryan's income, which was less than he had been making at his previous position. I didn't mind leaving my job, and his salary was decent enough to pay all the bills and have a little leftover but not much. Bryan knew how important it was for me to complete my master's degree so we agreed that now was the time to do it and we would just watch our money closely.

Christmas that year didn't have the same feel as past Christmases. Finances were so tight we borrowed a fake tree from his parents rather than getting a real one. It was a huge concession for me. There weren't enough pine scented candles in the world to make me think the plastic tree replica sitting in my living room was real. There was more bickering, and tensions were high. He wasn't helping me with the housework. I was always taking care of the baby. Haley was in her pre-teen years and seriously challenging us. There was less money than usual to buy presents. I would complain when he'd mention a gift for himself that I thought cost too much money. In the weeks leading up to Christmas, I told him I thought we should go see a marriage counselor because there was obviously something not right with our marriage. He reluctantly agreed, although it really wasn't his thing to go talk about his feelings with strangers.

Our counselor was a straightforward woman named Ruth. She liked motorcycles and didn't give us any bullshit, nor did she take any from us. When she asked what was going on in our marriage and what had brought us there, we both had different answers. I told her that Bryan was distant and was going through a midlife crisis. I explained that we never had sex anymore, and we barely did anything together. Bryan's answer was similar but focused on how much I criticized him and how he just didn't know if he was in love with me because I treated him so poorly. I immediately got defensive and started blaming him for me having to be nasty.

We clearly had some work to do. The question we had to ask ourselves was if we were willing to put in the work to make it right. I said that I was, but I would blame him for all that was wrong in our marriage in the next breath. He would say he wasn't sure he wanted to be married anymore and I would accuse him of being a coward and a quitter. We said, "for better or for worse." Walking away wasn't an option in my mind.

As much as I was unhappy in our marriage, and I could see he was just as miserable, the vulnerable side of me didn't want to quit. I didn't want another failed marriage. I didn't want to be the person that stays married for a few years and then gets divorced. I was thinking of myself and how hard it would be to be a single mother of two kids. I needed him to stay with me for that reason if nothing else.

We went to a few more sessions and tried to talk things through, but we weren't really getting anywhere. We'd reached an impasse. In the last session we had with Ruth, she asked Bryan straight out if he was willing to try.

"I don't know. I'm just not really there." I stared at him. He was actually willing to walk away from me.

"He's just being unrealistic. I don't understand what his problem is. He's working again and away from home all the time. He just needs a vacation."

"Yeah, I don't think that's it. I'm just really not there anymore."

I decided not to pull any punches and hit him where it hurts. "So, you're willing to leave your son because you don't want to try anymore? Have fun explaining that to him someday."

I could tell I had struck a nerve. "No, I don't want to leave my son. I want to leave you."

Are you fucking kidding me? Did he seriously just say that? The painful breakups I had in the past came flooding back to me as I watched my wall immediately go up. He knew I could sting with my words and, if he was planning to leave me, I was going to hit 10 times harder than he was willing to. "Well, I can promise you I'll get custody and you can be the guy who sees his son every other weekend and alternating holidays. You can either work on this, or you can leave. It's your choice."

I thought about my words that night, and I was still angry. I was angry that he wasn't willing to try. I was angry that we had gotten to this place in our lives. I was angry that I felt as though I was doing all the work.

I didn't want to admit it, but there was more to our problems than a midlife crisis. I used my words as weapons when we would talk about anything meaningful. I was unhappy with our financial status, the amount of work that my master's degree was taking, the energy that was always being sucked out of me by someone needing me for something, and the havoc that Haley's newly discovered hormones were causing. I was unhappy, and I was using him as my punching bag. I could understand why he wouldn't want to put in the work to stay in that environment.

I knew that I should go and talk to him about it and apologize, but my pride wouldn't let me. I went into our marriage knowing I was capable of doing things on my own. I had spent a lot of time making sure the world knew that. I didn't want to do this alone, though. I wanted my husband. I wanted the person who had promised me he would love me. I was right back where I had been when we first met, embarrassed to be vulnerable and tell him how much I really loved him. My insecurities had returned, and I was afraid to tell him how much I missed "us." I guess I thought that would be showing weakness and I didn't want him to see that side of me right now. We went to bed without talking about it any further, and I assumed it would just go away, and he would come back to his senses.

CHAPTER 20

B ryan had been coming home from work late for the past few weeks and had grown increasingly distant. The problems between us hadn't gone away like I hoped they would. If anything, we were further apart than we had ever been. I was sitting on the couch, trying to decide what to make for dinner and started going through some of our bills I needed to pay. For some reason, I decided to pick up the phone bill and looked through the calls.

Haley sent how many text messages? My gosh... she never gets off her phone. She doesn't talk to other humans though. Just texts....

Bryan's texts weren't nearly as high, but he seemed to be on his phone nearly all day. *My gosh.... There's a call for 54 minutes.... 78 minutes.... 62 minutes.... Who the hell is he talking to for that long? And it's always on his drive home, and it's always the same number.*

I decided to Google the number and see why he was talking to this person every day for hours at a time. A name showed up as someone who worked in one of the buildings he managed.

I called him on his way home from work and asked, "Who is Audrey Buckner?"

"What?"

"You're spending a lot of time talking to this number. I Googled it and this name showed up. Who is she?"

"No one. She's just a lady at my building that I've been trying to fix a water leak for."

"Oh, well, you're talking to her almost every day for like an hour or more at a time. Can't you just have a contractor fix the damn water leak?"

"Jen, I'm just trying to do my job. What the fuck? Are you checking my phone records now? Can I seriously not do my job without you ragging on me about it?"

"Sure, Whatever." I dropped the subject and hung up on him. But that number was in the back of my mind somewhere, nagging at me. I didn't ask him anything further about it, but somehow it felt familiar and unsettling. Did I know that name? I couldn't recall ever hearing the name Audrey Buckner before. The more I thought about it, though, I realized it was my apprehension that was familiar, not a stupid name like Audrey Buckner. I lived through this with Darryl; that was the familiarity. It was the answers that didn't quite make sense, phone numbers that were repeatedly called, vague descriptions of activities he'd been to alone. As I went to sleep, I was restless, and the name Audrey Buckner was still floating through my mind.

After tossing and turning for more than an hour, I looked at my husband asleep next to me. I could feel myself turning into my alter ego, Crazy Bitch, as I quietly crawled out of bed and did something I had never done in all the years we had been together ... I went through his phone. Like a ninja moving in for the kill, I quietly grabbed his phone off the bedside table and crept down the stairs. I looked through his messages and found what I suspected I might find. He was having an affair with Audrey Buckner.

Are you fucking kidding me? I had suspected what I was going to find, but the shock I felt was still powerful. *Oh. My. Gosh. He's seriously having an affair.* I read through everything and then walked upstairs, kicked the side of the bed to wake him up, showed him his phone, yelled, "Fuck you!" and threw the phone at him. I pride myself on having a quick wit, but in my rage, the best I could come up with was "Fuck you."

He followed me downstairs so we wouldn't wake up the kids, but we spent the remainder of the night with me yelling at him and him telling me he didn't know if he could stay married to me.

"Then why the fuck are you still here?"

"Because of Owen. Because of Haley."

"So, it has nothing to do with me? It's the kids?"

"I love them more than anything in the world, and I can't imagine them not having me here every day, but I also don't know if having me here while I'm this miserable is good. I don't know what to do."

"And you want me to tell you what to do? You want me to give you advice on whether you should leave me? You're supposed to love me. You told me you would never hurt someone that you love. You told me that you would always love me."

"I know, but things change. It's just happened over the past few years. We're not the same couple we were."

"You are no better than any other guy. I thought you were different. I opened up to you and let you in further than any other guy I've ever been with. I trusted you. I didn't think you were Darryl, but apparently you have more in common with him than I thought you did."

We sat staring at each other for the next 10 minutes, neither of us talking or knowing what else to say. I searched my brain for the solution, but I couldn't find my way out of this. My marriage was going to end because of another cheating asshole. If my wall had started to come up before, it could rival anything the Night's Watch was guarding at that point.

As I was sitting there thinking about how hurt I was that he would do this to me, I started to think about what it meant. Even though I had spent the better part of the last year criticizing everything he did, I was also losing my best friend. When something good or bad happened, he was still the first person I called. I kept reminding myself that I could do this alone. I had proven that to myself years ago. I just didn't want to. I wanted my partner. Maybe it was because it was comfortable. Maybe it was because it was what we had done for the last nine years. And maybe those were the excuses I gave not to show the pain I was feeling because of what he'd done. The truth was, I was crushed that he would cheat on me.

"I need you to give me some time before you go. I need to figure out how I'm going to support myself." He agreed to that, and I went to sleep on the couch, and he went back to our room. I couldn't look at him, much less sleep in the same room as him.

CHAPTER 21

The next morning, I woke up after getting only an hour or two of sleep and got Haley off to school and Owen to daycare. Then I sat and I thought. What had gone wrong? Where did we make the turn to become this couple? Every conversation ended with something snarky being said. We spent our time apart rather than together. We didn't go see our friends. We didn't have sex. We didn't hold hands or kiss each other. I used my words to criticize him, never compliment him. He didn't use his words for anything. He just didn't talk to me anymore about anything important. Our life had become a series of automatic motions we went through without really feeling anything toward each other. Had this all started when we were going through IVF? Did it start before that? I couldn't think of the last time we had been really happy together, but it bothered me he was willing to walk away. I didn't want to let that happen. This wasn't the same as when Darryl cheated. I truly loved Bryan, and I didn't want this to end without putting up a fight. Our attempt at counseling wasn't going to work if we didn't both have all the relevant information. Many people would say I was crazy to want him to stay with me after he cheated. Society told me that in order to be a strong woman I needed to kick his ass to the curb and stand my ground. I thought about that for a very long time before I took any action. To many, an affair is unforgivable. It's not negotiable. If you cheat, it means you leave. I rationalized my next steps with the idea that when someone in a relationship cheats, it doesn't mean that your feelings for them end. You still love them, but you're hurt by the actions of the cheater. It means that your feelings become more complicated. You have to work hard to figure out what went wrong and decide if the relationship is worth saving. Good people don't cheat because they just feel like getting some sex. Maybe the bad ones do, but those are the ones that aren't worth staying with. Darryl was my proof of that. But Bryan was a good person, and our relationship had been meandering toward divorce for a couple of years. Neither of us bothered to try to stop it, and now I was in damage control mode. Maybe my jagged edges and tough exterior had never really gone away. They had been masked by the newness of someone treating me decently, but underneath it, there was a sharp edge always ready to strike.

I called him and said I was on my way to his office. Shit wasn't going to go down like this without me getting my words heard. I told him I wanted to meet Audrey Buckner, and I expected her to be in his office when I got there. The choice to go marching down to his office was not one I was proud of, but as much as it hurt that he had an affair, I also recognized where my part in it was. I wasn't kind to him anymore, and if someone is willing to give you kindness, support your emotional needs, and listen to you complain about the miserable bitch you're married to, then I understood it. I didn't excuse it, and I didn't condone it, but I understood it. People want to feel loved, and if the person who is supposed to love you is treating you like garbage, then I understood the appeal of straying toward someone that shows you kindness. I needed to own my part in this if I wanted to be able to salvage our marriage.

He told me he didn't think that was an option for me to meet with her, and I calmly told him it was in everybody's best interest for him to make sure she was there. I was fully prepared to get what I wanted at that moment, even if it meant I had to bust into her office to get it.

An hour later, as I walked in, I wasn't sure exactly what I was going to say, but I knew that I wasn't going to let this happen. He was my husband. I wanted the chance to make things right between us. I walked into his office and she was standing there with him. I walked up, threw a right hook to her jaw, and knocked her perfectly straight, shiny white teeth out of her flawlessly lip glossed little mouth. (Ok, that didn't happen, but it sure would have felt good if I were the violent type.) Since I'm not violent by nature, I used the best weapon I had in my arsenal for the war I was about to wage. Finding the words I needed had rarely escaped me, and I suspected it wouldn't end up being a problem at that moment.

I held out my hand and introduced myself. "Hi, I'm Jennifer. I'm his wife. Are you the one he's fucking?" There was silence from this little nothing of a twit of a human being. As I looked at her, I could see what he saw in her. She was pretty. She was thin. She had medium length, shiny blonde hair, but mine was still better. I sat down at the small table in his office and waited for them to join my little meeting.

"So, let's get this started so we can all move on to more interesting things" They both sat down at the table, while I considered my next words. "First, you understand you're a whore, right?"

"That's your opinion."

"No, that's the definition of someone who knowingly sleeps with someone else's husband."

"Ok. Is that all you have to say?"

"No, I have plenty more to say to you, but I'll keep it short and to the point. You value your career above everything else? From what Bryan has told me about you in the past 12 hours, you're pretty driven?"

"Yes, my career is important to me."

"Ok, well then let me lay it out to you like this: I have a copy of every text message. I have a copy of every email you sent during work hours, most likely from your work computer. I have the transcript of what can only be described as cybersex you engaged in during the middle of the day from your work computer. I know where you work. I know which office is yours and I know who your boss is. If I ever find out you spoke to my husband again... looked at him, thought about him, tried to contact him in any way, I will turn everything I have over to your boss and let him make his own decisions about whether you're a whore or not." I stopped talking and looked her straight in the eye and waited for her response.

She started to give some sort of feeble explanation about how she was sorry …. *Blah blah blah…. Shut up, bitch.* I decided to cut her off because I honestly didn't care one bit about her excuses. I didn't care if she was going to get a divorce. I didn't care if she had good intentions. This was for Bryan and me to figure out. I didn't need her existence clouding our discussions while we tried to figure out our future, no matter what it looked like.

"You can go now. I'm going to sit here and talk to MY husband."

She stood up and walked out as I turned to look at Bryan, who had been silent during the entire time I spoke. "I think I got my point across. Did I go a little too far into Crazy Bitch territory?" He was furious with me, but there was something else in his eyes I couldn't quite place.

I knew it wasn't this woman's fault that my husband had an affair. I knew it was a decision by both of them. The difference was I didn't know her. I knew the man that I had loved for the past nine years, so it was easy to blame her and not him.

After giving himself a moment to calm down, he finally spoke. "I really can't talk about this now. I need to cool off before I can even look at you. I promise we'll talk tonight, but I'm taking the rest of the day off to do some thinking."

"Where are you going to go? Are you really going to leave here? You're not going to go be with her?" I sounded like a whiny, needy teenager, but now wasn't the time to be worried about insecurities. I had to let all that go to make the real changes I knew needed to be made.

"She loves her career more than she loves anyone else. She won't talk to me after the threat you just gave. You made sure of that."

I walked out with him. We each got into our vehicles and went our separate ways. I went home and thought about what I had said to both of them and wondered if what I had done was going to help or hurt our situation. I recognized that my actions weren't rational, but I also loved my husband, whether I was good at showing it or not.

CHAPTER 22

He came home around 2:00 that afternoon and I was waiting for him. I saw the man I had broken with my criticism walk through the door and sit down across from me in our living room. In my zeal to be a strong-willed and independent woman, I had driven away one of the most important people in my life. I knew it was time to really let my vulnerability out and, although it was one of my most difficult challenges, I had to admit when I was wrong. I hoped that he would do the same.

"How did we get here?" I asked the question hoping he would have the answers for me.

"I don't know. But we're here."

"I don't want to be here. I want a husband and a marriage and a father to my children. You're not just walking out on me. You're walking out on them, too." I wasn't trying to play the guilt card, but I knew to him it must feel that way.

"I know, and I don't want to leave them. It's just gotten so hard to live like this. It's been hard for a long time." He sat back and thought for a moment. "Well, I think you effectively let her know where her place was."

"Is she worth it? Are you really going to leave me for her?"

"You know, I don't know if I was ever going to. I was caught up in it. She's got a husband, and they're going through a bad spot, too. She listened. She understood what I was feeling. When I would talk to her about the struggles we were both having, though, I would tell her how I didn't know if I could live without my son. I would tell her how much I would miss seeing him every day. She would come back with how she wanted to make sure she got the paintings in her divorce. Her reasoning was shallow. It was never going to work, but she was comforting me when I needed to be comforted."

"I've been awful to you, haven't I? I'm sorry for that. I've been so mean the past few years with all the stress and change and uncertainty, and I've taken it all out on you."

"Yeah, but I've been awful to you, too. Just in a different way."

"Can we go back and see Ruth and try again? This time with us both on the same page? Having the same information as each other?"

"Yeah. We can do that. I don't know if we're going to recover, but I'm willing to try."

I saw him soften as I thought about everything that had just happened. "What made you change your mind?"

"You haven't had that kind of fire in you in a long time except when it was directed at me. I sat and listened to what you were saying to her, and I realized that your passion is what made me love you in the first place. I just got tired of being on the receiving end of it. I watched you direct your fire at trying to save us. You've always protected what you love. You've always used that crazy fire to protect your family, and today, I saw it being used for us, and I liked it."

"So, me unleashing my inner psycho bitch on some whore turned you on?"

He laughed. "No, it didn't turn me on. It scared the shit out of me. But I also saw how much you wanted to save us, and I don't think you really wanted to do that before. You just wanted me to do what you wanted so you could protect you. I saw your passion today, and if you're willing to put that same kind of passion and energy into saving us, I'm willing to try, too."

Our next session with Ruth was honest and real and different than any other session we had been to. I wasn't willing to say it was only me that caused our marriage to get to that point, but I owned my part of it. I acknowledged how critical I was and how harsh I was on everybody at home. I conceded that I was pushing him away without knowing I was doing it, and he owned his actions and his indifference. I recognized that I had never completely let my guard down after the disaster that Darryl had left of my life, and I had taken it out on Bryan. Even more, I don't think I ever fully dealt with my mother's death, so Ruth and I decided that I would do some individual counseling to talk through the emotions I was still harboring from that. We both admitted our part in causing hurt to the other person and, for the first time since we started seeing Ruth, we both agreed that we were willing to put in the work to try and make things right again. We were ready to love each other again even though the road back was going to be all uphill. We were willing to make the climb and admire the view once we got to the top.

PART 4

ONLY YOU CAN LOVE ME THIS WAY

*My husband planted a huge
kiss on me at midnight,
and I was reminded of how
much I loved him
and his spinning disco lights.*

CHAPTER 23

*H*e's coming home tonight. A quick scan around the room told me what I already knew. I better tidy up the house so it looked like I had done something remotely productive while he was gone. The truth was, most days after work I fed the kids and then watched Grey's Anatomy reruns after I put Owen to bed. Bryan traveled semi-often for work, but it was only for a few days at a time. A quick trip to Nashville… a couple of days in Dallas…. A conference in Las Vegas. Nothing too taxing, but the short breaks away from each other had done a lot to help build trust back into our relationship.

Bryan and I had settled into a happier place and our relationship was thriving. We had worked hard to make things right in our marriage, although it wasn't easy. We spent a lot of time in Ruth's office. She was excellent about giving us "homework" to do when we'd leave her office. Have a purposeful conversation…. Work on trusting each other…. Talk more often…. Spend time designated for just the two of you. We had kept at it and addressed the issues that had gotten our marriage to the awful place it had been in. It was not easy. In addition, I met with Ruth each week to talk about my messy past and how it was affecting my present. It felt good to finally process some of the suppressed emotions that I was holding onto. We talked about Darryl from time to time, but the focus was on dealing with my mother's death.

It had worked and our marriage had grown stronger and happier in the past six years. I loved it when he would absently grab for my hand and hold it in his, which was something he did when we first started dating. We would go to a movie and dinner on a Friday night to get some time to ourselves, and romance was beginning to return in our own special way. We've never been a mushy couple, but we've always made each other laugh, and we both agreed that when we were going through the bad stuff, we stopped laughing with each other.

On my last birthday, Bryan brought home a bottle of wine and some chocolates he had gotten from a vendor at work for Christmas. It was lucky for him my birthday is only a week before Christmas or he would have been screwed. He crossed off his name on the card and wrote "wife" and then crossed off "Merry Christmas" and wrote "Happy Birthday!" I found it hysterical. He knew I would love it, and he was right. It was perfect. It was the type of natural, quirky, and comfortable relationship we had when we first met and why we stayed together and decided to fight for each other.

In addition to finding time to spend together, we had also both found things which made us happier individually. I finished my master's degree shortly after we'd returned to counseling and had gotten a job as a special education teacher the following school year. I absolutely loved working in a school. It gave me a sense of purpose I didn't have when I was managing apartment buildings. The work I did with my students was rewarding, and it was easier to let the little things go now. I wasn't so controlling and critical of things. I had more joy in my life both at home and at work.

Bryan was still at his same job and was doing great with the company. They respected his opinion and work ethic and had rewarded him for it with a significant raise the previous year. The unfortunate whore who had been a problem in the past had quickly moved to a new office in a different building after my threat of destroying her career by exposing her propensity for hooking up with other people's husbands.

Bryan's restlessness was calmed when he started The Ballet Project a few years earlier. He had always been artistic and had used his talents in photography to work with dancers in various urban settings. The project was starting to take off and, although it didn't make him any money, it was a good outlet for him to express himself. The young dancers he worked with absolutely loved him and his goofy humor. He had a few local dance studios he regularly worked with and enjoyed putting the dancers in harsh urban locations to photograph them in their soft tutus and ballet shoes. He was able to capture the grace and athleticism of the ballerinas he worked with and his work turned out beautifully. He had a natural talent for photography and was always looking for a new location or new idea.

His Ballet Project ideas would often take over our garage on the weekends, but just as I had found my joy in teaching, he had found his joy in photography. At one point, he had come up with the idea to photograph ballerinas with water, so our garage transformed into a photography studio, draped in black plastic. The ballerinas all came to our house, and he photographed them while they threw water at each other and sprayed each other with a hose. He got some amazing photographs from the experience and the project continued to grow from there. He bragged that his photos were all done without being photoshopped, other than to touch up some of the edges and adjust the lighting, but the water itself was authentic. That was important to him, and he took a great deal of pride in the project.

What we found was that having those special things that made us happy apart, also made us happy together. He would listen to me talk about something my students had said or done that day. I would listen to him talk about the ideas he had for the Ballet Project. Having a life together was important, and we made sure we frequently did things as a couple, but we found that a healthy relationship was healthiest when we didn't need to spend every moment of every day with the other person. Having a life apart from each other was how we were able to grow into a better couple together.

I got up and walked around, picking up glasses and plates from snacks that were eaten two days earlier and was already exhausted just thinking about doing the dishes.

"OWEN! I need you to come here for a minute!"

Owen had his 8th birthday party in July, and it was epic. We had about 10 little boys over who went through Ninja Turtle Training in the yard. Bryan created a laser maze for the kids using yarn and wooden dowels pounded into the ground, and we had a bunch of other Ninja like games we played. Bryan often referred to Owen as, "The Sweetest of the Sweetest." It was a pretty accurate description. He had grown into a kind and sensitive young boy who was always willing to give a hug and snuggle with his mom at night.

"Buddy, I need you to go downstairs and pick up some of your toys. I stepped on a whole bunch of Legos earlier, and my feet didn't like it much."

"OK, well, can I have a friend come over?" This was his way of deflecting from what I had asked him to do.

"Yeah, I suppose, if you get your toys picked up."

"Ok. Thanks, Mom." He ran back downstairs, and I heard his video game startup. *What the hell happened to picking up your toys? It had been less than 30 seconds since I asked. How could he forget that quickly?* I went ahead and tackled the dishes because asking Haley to help was a futile request.

At 17-years-old Haley had mastered the art of doing nothing productive unless it involved her friends. She was a good kid, and I knew she could be a lot worse than she was, but teenagers are teenagers, and even the good ones can be a handful.

One night a few months earlier, she had gone out with some friends, and I got a call about 11:00 at night because she needed me to come pick her up.

"Mom, I think I did something stupid."

"Ok, well, what did you do?"

"I smoked some weed, and I think I'm going to die. I need you to take me to the hospital."

"Why do you need to go to the hospital? Was the weed laced with something?" Bryan's ears perked up at the mention of hospital and weed.

"I don't think so. I dunno. I just feel really weird, and I think I need you to come get me."

"Send me your location, and I'll come get you."

I got off the phone, and Bryan looked at me. "Are you fucking kidding me? She's high?"

"Apparently. She wants me to come pick her up because she thinks she's dying."

"Fucking teenagers." He went into an intense rant about how teenagers don't think before they do things. I held up my hand to stop his tirade.

"What were you doing at 17?"

He got a little smile on his face and said, "That's not relevant to this conversation."

I went and picked up Haley, and she insisted she needed to go to the hospital. "You're not dying, Haley. You're high."

"It just doesn't feel right mom. I feel really weird. I think you should take me to the hospital."

"I'm not taking you to the hospital. You feel weird because you smoked weed and you're high. We'll discuss it tomorrow when you can focus better."

"Fine. Don't take me to the hospital…. Can you at least take me to McDonald's to get french fries and cinnamon melts?"

The answer to that question was, "no." Instead, I took her home and tucked her into bed so she could sleep it off until morning. The next day, she sheepishly walked out of her room and got an earful from Bryan. He had experimented with drugs when he was a teenager, so he tried to explain why he had walked away from them and the damage they caused to his life and his goals. He ended his lecture with his favorite line, "Do as I say, not as I do." Haley rolled her eyes, but I knew she had learned a little something. The loss of her cell phone for a week helped the lesson hit home. Bryan and I talked about giving her a harsher sentence, but we both acknowledged that teenagers do stupid things, and at least she was smart enough to call her mom and not try to drive. The lesson was learned, and we all moved on.

As I continued walking around, trying to pick up the house, Haley came sauntering down the steps. She's a good girl, but she still had a mouth on her which proved she was a teenager.

"Hi, honey. Did you get your homework done?"

"Mom! When was I supposed to get my homework done? I needed a nap after school, and now I have to go to work."

"Here's an idea, honey. Maybe don't stay up until two in the morning and you'll have a little more energy to do the things that are responsibilities. "

"Yeah, ok." My words fell on deaf ears. *What did I expect? A sudden revelation after the 600th time I've told her this?*

"Ok, well, have fun, but please don't plan on going out after work. I really need you to get a start on that Spanish assignment." I was tough on her, but I had to give her credit for being a step ahead of many of her friends. She figured out when she turned 15 that if she wanted money, she needed to earn some. We weren't the type to give her everything she wanted, so she got a job to have Fun Funds. Of course, the money was usually gone within the first few days of her getting her paycheck, but she had plenty of Victoria's Secret panties to show for it, and I suppose that's an accomplishment of some sort.

CHAPTER 24

Bryan rolled into the house around 8:30, looking tired, with a pack of cigarettes in his hand.

"Hey! You're home! How was your flight?" I smiled as he walked into the kitchen, suitcase rolling behind him. It was a sight I'd seen more often the past couple of years. He leaned over and gave me a kiss.

"It was good. A little bumpy. You would have hated the take-off." Bryan knew I hated to fly, and I frequently bruised his arm during takeoff and landing. If we got stuck on a bumpy flight, there would be extra damage to his leg every time I jumped.

"Awesome. Too bad you didn't get stuck next to an old lady who shared her gum with you. Go see your son. I just put him to bed, so he's probably not asleep yet."

"My little bug. Ok." He ran up the stairs and tiptoed into his room, and I heard him and Owen going through their nighttime ritual.

I heard all the familiar questions. "How was your day, buddy?"

"It was good. We had a sub who didn't know anything. All she wanted to do all day was make us learn. We didn't get any fun time."

"Did you learn anything new?"

"Not really."

"Did you get a Puma Paw?" He always asked about the Puma Paw. It was the school's way of rewarding good behavior. Eventually, you could trade your Puma Paws in for something at the school store like a pencil or an eraser. Owen once came home with a pencil that smelled like cherries. I guess I could see some benefit in that. When you're sick of doing math, you can just sit and smell your pencil instead. The Puma Paws were always a source of contention, and I waited for the inevitable complaints that were about to begin.

"No. I didn't get one, but Levi got one, and he got a jewel on his clip chart today." *Another source of jealousy... The damn clip chart.*

"Don't worry about it, buddy. Did you try your hardest and do your best work?"

"Yeah, but I got two wrong on my spelling test." I was surprised he mentioned this since earlier Owen told me, "don't tell Dad" about the spelling test.

Bryan reassured him by saying, "As long as you're working hard and trying your best then I think you're the most fabulous boy in the 2nd grade. Should we say our prayer?"

We're not very churchy people, but Bryan has always said a prayer with Owen before bed each night. Even when he's away on a work trip, he'll Facetime Owen so they can say their prayer. On more than one occasion they've said they're prayer while Bryan was in the middle of a company dinner and had to excuse himself so he could say goodnight to his son.

After Owen was in bed, Bryan and I sat down and chatted for a bit. He looked more tired than he had after his last few trips.

"You look tired. Was it a long day?"

"I guess. Meetings all day today." He started talking about budget processes and his proposal to reduce paper at his office as I began to zone out. I loved hearing about his trips, but I also knew once he started talking about how much he hated paper, it could go on for a while.

"Sounds like it was a productive few days. Did you get a chance to go out with Fred?" Fred was his favorite work wingman. Nearly every story started with, "Fred and I were…." and continued to some elaborate story from there.

"Yeah, a few of us went to this pretty cool restaurant that has like four floors down in the heart of Nashville. I think it was called Acme Feed and Seed? I dunno. Something about horses or something like that. Anyway, it was pretty fun. Jeff started buying drinks for everyone, so we had a good time." Jeff was the senior executive managing partner of the company, which was just a fancy way of saying he was in charge. He and Bryan had a good relationship, and Bryan would often tell about going out for drinks with Jeff and Fred. The stories always brought a lot of laughs and I could tell they were usually the highlight of his business trips. He had a work posse that he regularly hung out with and they were his second family.

We sat for another half hour talking about his trip and what had gone on around the house since he'd been gone. I finally let him know I had an early morning, so I needed to head to bed. He kissed me goodnight and told me he loved me before he headed downstairs to watch The History Channel. I smiled and felt happy, realizing this is how we always wanted it to be and what we had worked so hard to get back to. Life was finally back to being less complicated, and we liked it that way.

CHAPTER 25

It was mid-October, and the school year is in full swing. By that point in the year, the students were past the "honeymoon" phase, and their personalities were starting to come out. I had a couple of real doozies on my caseload at that point. I was teaching mostly classes of students with learning disabilities, but I had a couple of sections of students with emotional / behavioral disorders. Those are the students who will look you straight in the face and tell you to fuck off. I've had chairs thrown across the room, been spit on, and had pencils, notebooks and basically anything within arm's reach thrown at me. My master's degree I was so proud of myself for getting was being put to good use by being able to effectively deflect a chair coming at me. There are moments of exhaustion and moments of hilarity.

Earlier in the year, I had a student in complete meltdown that caused his room to be evacuated. As I sat and talked with him, he walked from desk to desk, swearing and gluing his classmate's homework down to their desk. He would pick up a paper, slather it with glue and then yell, "Mother Fucker" and slam it down onto the desk. I was shocked at the action but couldn't stop laughing when I was discussing it with my department lead. It takes a lot of dedication to your cause to glue every one of those papers down to a desk.

I couldn't complain about my job because I loved every moment of it. There were times, however, when I would look at these young students and think "How could you think what you just did was a good idea?" Those were the days that made me question if I was entirely sane to have chosen the profession I did. I could tell this was going to be one of those days.

During third period, one of my students got angry because she had prepared a 32 slide presentation she wanted to share with the class on how horrible she felt the show Teen Titans on Cartoon Network was. Personally, I thought Teen Titans was funny. Owen watched it all the time, but this particular student felt it was important to share with the class her views on the show. When I suggested she could show it to me at my desk instead of interrupting math remediation time, she flipped out. I eventually had to have her removed from the class after the path of destruction she had caused.

For every student who calls me a bitch and freaks out, I have two students like Sam. The Sams of the world are why I keep doing what I do. He was a student from a couple of years earlier who really liked smoking weed. He liked it a lot. He was homeless and living between hotels and friend's couches and didn't see the point of trying to learn anything. He came to school because he got free breakfast and free lunch, but no one in his family had been successful at anything, and none of them really seemed to care about school. I spent a lot of time talking to Sam and helping him understand he could be more than the circumstances he'd been given in life. Sam needed guidance and compassion and needed to believe in himself. It took some time to get through to him, but I eventually did and saw the hard work he put into graduating on time with his class. He had started college the previous month and would update me occasionally on how classes were going.

After I had gotten my lessons ready for the next day, I made the quick drive home to enjoy the 27 minutes of silence I got before Owen was home from school. When I opened the garage door, I saw Bryan's Jeep in the garage. *What the hell? Why is he home? What about my 27 minutes of sitting downtime before the bus drops Owen off? Am I going to have to talk to someone during that time? That's MY time!*

As I walked in, I saw Bryan sitting on the couch. "You're home early. What's going on?"

"I don't know. I just wasn't feeling well today. My stomach is still hurting." He'd been complaining about his stomach for a few days, and I'd been giving him passive sympathy, but mainly ignoring him. Bryan had always been quite sensitive to discomfort in his body. That was my polite way of telling him he was being a baby sometimes. When he got a cold, he would take off all his clothes and crawl into bed for two days and ask me to bring him Hawaiian Punch. Something about the sugary goodness of Hawaiian Punch made him feel better.

I smiled and said, "Have you tried pooping? Maybe that will help." He hated when I would reject his ailments with something simple like pooping.

"Yeah, Jen. I've pooped. I'm not a 4-year-old." *Uh oh... he must really not be feeling good if he didn't have a snarky come back to my poop comment.* One of the staples of our relationship was being able to give as good as you get. His timing and ability to throw a few zingers my way was typically on the money.

I decided not to press it. "Ok, well, what do you want me to make for dinner?"

"Nothing. I'm just going to have some cereal." Cereal was always his meal when he didn't feel well and also the only meal he knew how to make that didn't go in the microwave.

I figured I could whip up something in a little bit to feed the rest of us but would try and take advantage of what was left of my dwindling 27 minutes. "Ok, well, I'm going to relax for a few minutes before Owen gets home." A minute later, Haley came walking down the steps. *Shit! Now I have to talk to two people. Seriously?*

I put on my best mom face. "Hi, honey. What are you doing home? Don't you have dance team practice tonight?"

With her best teenager attitude, she shut me down. "Nope. Are you making dinner? I'm hungry."

I was down to 18 minutes now. My time was quickly fading away.

"Can you give me a few minutes? I just need a few minutes before I start the next thing."

"Ok, well I have a football game to go to tonight, and I need to eat something before I go sooooo.... Yeah."

"Just give me a few minutes, ok?"

"Fine." And off she went back to the cave she called her room. It was her private sanctuary where adults were little more than a nuisance unless they were cleaning.

Shortly after that, Owen came in the front door. "Can I go play with my friends?" He dropped his backpack at the door and came over to give me a hug.

"Sure, buddy. Tell me two things about your day." This kid hadn't reached the awful teenage years yet, so I was taking advantage of every second until he didn't want to be around me anymore.

"Um, I had math, and I had recess. Can I go play with my friends now?"

Bryan jumped into the conversation, "Did you get a Puma Paw? *Dear Lord! NO! Don't ask about the damn Puma Paw. He'd show one to you if he got one.* The complaints about Levi getting more Puma Paws than he did started immediately.

CHAPTER 26

After dinner, Bryan was still having trouble with his belly and said he'd like to go lay down. I cleaned up the dishes, got Owen settled in to do his homework, and took out my laptop to work on some special education paperwork I needed to write. My student who had freaked out over the Teen Titans had now been suspended so maybe tomorrow would be slightly quieter. Bryan came down the stairs after his nap looking more pale than usual.

Concerned, I asked, "Are you ok? You don't look so good."

"I don't know. My belly really hurts. I'm going to the garage for a smoke." I decided not to comment that smoking a cigarette when you aren't feeling well isn't usually the best choice, but I knew it wasn't the time for my lecture.

I decided to join him in the garage to find out what was going on. "When you say your belly hurts, what are you talking about? Is it like when you had kidney stones?"

"No, it just kind of hurts. Not like I need to throw up, just like a pain in my stomach."

"Should we go to the doctor?"

"Urgent care is closed now and I'm not going to the hospital for a belly ache. I'll be fine."

I figured I could diagnose him as well as any doctor with the help of my good friend Google. *Show me where the pain is. Lower left.... Ok... not appendicitis because that's on the right. Do you have a fever? No... ok.... Is it like a sharp pain? No, a dull ache.* "Maybe you have prostate cancer. I think I heard that if you have your prostate removed you can never get an erection again. I don't know if it's actually true, but that would suck."

"What the hell is wrong with you? Why would you jump from appendicitis to prostate cancer? Let's assume it's not." He laughed and walked to the other side of the garage to nervously rearrange his tools, but I could tell he was both laughing at me and thinking in his head about prostate cancer.

"Ok, well I have some of that Percocet leftover from when I had my gallbladder out. Do you want to take one of those?"

"Sure. I'll see how I feel in the morning."

That night he was restless and out of bed several times grumbling about how his tummy hurt. I needed to sleep because I had a meeting at school with a parent in the morning so I did my best to get some rest, but I could tell this was something more than him just being a baby.

CHAPTER 27

The next morning, Bryan went to urgent care and they recommended that he go to the emergency room. I ran to the office at school to have them find someone who could cover my classes and quickly threw some notes together for whoever was going to cover me for the day. I zipped off to the hospital to find out what was wrong with my husband. I wasn't overly concerned, but I was anxious. The doctors would run tests, and I was confident they would give him something for the pain, but Bryan rarely got sick. He'd never had anything seriously wrong. Other than the time he had accidentally stepped on a nail, which had gone through his shoe and out the top of his foot, he hadn't been to the hospital since we'd met.

At the hospital, I was brought back to his room and found him lying in bed with an IV in his arm and fluids dripping.

"What's going on?" He looked more comfortable than he had been at home, although I didn't like seeing him hooked up to all the machines.

"I'm in the hospital." He smiled at me with a hazy look in his eyes that told me the pain meds were working.

"Yes, I can see that. Did they figure out what's happening? Do you have kidney stones? Is it prostate cancer?" He rolled his eyes, but they had given him some good narcotics, so he was less annoyed with my badgering than usual.

Just then, the doctor came in and explained Bryan had pancreatitis. *What the hell is that? Pancreatitis did not come up in my Google search last night.* I felt unprepared at this new disease I'd never heard of but figured it would be rude to whip out my phone and start Googling when an actual doctor was standing in front of me.

"Your lipase levels are up around 800, which is fairly high."

"Lipase?" *Another new word I would need to Google once the doctor was gone.* He explained that pancreatitis is an inflammation of the pancreas with the two most common causes being gallstones or alcoholism. He asked Bryan how often he drinks.

"Rarely. We're not big drinkers."

The doctor eyed him a little bit. "When is the last time you had a drink?"

Bryan thought back and looked to me to try to work it out. "I think it was about a month ago when our friends had a bonfire? I had maybe two beers."

The doctor continued with his information. "Typically, we would see pancreatitis as a result of gallstones or excessive alcohol use. We're going to do a CT to look for gallstones."

Great. I started calculating in my head how much of our deductible I had already used up and how much I had in my health savings account. It was another expense we weren't expecting but finding out what was causing this was more important than finances at that point.

They wheeled Bryan off to CT, so I took the opportunity to call his mom to let her know what was going on. She asked me to keep her updated. I waited around in his room for a bit and finally decided to go find a snack. Now that Bryan had some pain meds, I figured he must be starving so I bought him a Kit-Kat so he could have at least a little something in his belly. By the time I got back, the doctor was in the room explaining the treatment for pancreatitis. Bryan would be admitted to the hospital for a few days so they could keep him hydrated and give pain meds. Part of the treatment was he wouldn't be allowed anything by mouth. No food. No drinks. Not even any ice chips. I quietly slid the Kit-Kat into my purse before he noticed it. Bryan needed to rest his pancreas, so it had time to heal. The CT didn't show any gallstones, so they renewed their questions about alcohol use.

Bryan was adamant with the doctor at this point. "I really don't drink. I haven't had a drink in more than a month."

With skepticism, the doctor tried another method. "Ok, but prior to that, how often were you drinking?"

Bryan appeared to be getting irritated at this point. "I'm not an alcoholic. I rarely drink and have never been a regular drinker."

The doctor seemed to finally accept his answer and said someone would be down soon to bring him upstairs to be admitted.

The next few days were difficult to get through, mostly for Owen. He had a lot of questions about what was going on.

"Is Dad going to die?" He asked me in his tiny voice.

"No, Boo. Dad has a sickness inside his belly, and they have to let it rest so it can heal. The only way to do that is not to give him any food or water."

"He's going to starve! He IS going to die!" He seemed to be trying to put the pieces together and could only come up with one conclusion; If you're in the hospital, you're going to die.

"Nope. Not die. I'll take you to see him, and then we can go to the cafeteria for chocolate cake." I was hoping this would ease the terror of seeing his dad in the hospital.

Cautiously, he asked, "They have cake there? Can Dad eat it?"

"No. Dad can't eat the cake, which is why we would have to eat it before or after we go up to his room."

He seemed to consider this an ok compromise and decided he was comfortable with a visit to see his dad. Bryan stayed in the hospital for four days until his pancreas finally settled down. They discharged him and told him to rest and asked him to follow up with his regular doctor, which we did. An MRI was ordered, which showed no abnormalities anywhere in his belly. Idiopathic pancreatitis was the official diagnosis, so we accepted it and carried on with our lives.

CHAPTER 28

The Christmas season was again upon us. It had always been my absolute favorite time of the year. Right around Thanksgiving, I start singing, "It's the most wonderful time of the year.... Ding dong... ding dong." When we would go anywhere around that time of year, Bryan would turn the radio to the Sirius XM Christmas station, and I was always delighted. I knew the words to virtually every song that came on, even the obscure 2nd verse to most songs. Bryan would claim to be annoyed by it, but I knew he secretly found it charming because he would always tell people about it.

"She even knows the stupid second verse that no one else knows and can sing 'Oh, Christmas Tree' in Latin."

My mother loved Christmas as much as I did. It had been years since she died, but this time of year always made me miss her a little more. Before she had gotten sick, she would put all her efforts into decorating, so it looked like Christmas cheer had exploded all over the house. There were little knick-knacks all over, lights and garland on the banister, and a giant tree that filled the room. We would walk into a Christmas wonderland whenever we went to visit her. The last Christmas she was with us, she didn't have as much energy to do all the usual decorating, so I had gone over to help her. Part of me wanted to learn. She had a way of making everything lovely and she made it look effortless. The other part of me just wanted to make it feel like it was any other year full of Christmas joy.

My mom had always made Christmas special, and I did my best to do the same for my children. As we were driving to do some Christmas shopping for the kids, I mentioned I needed to text Haley not to forget that we were picking out our Christmas tree that night. She was off doing teenager things, but when Christmas tree picking came around, everyone was required to participate.

"I want a huge one this year. Let's put it in the corner where the peak is so we can get a super tall one." Picking out a Christmas tree was a family event and usually involved some sort of holiday themed headwear. I had a Rudolph hat with a nose that lit up. We had multiple variations on antler or tree headbands, and of course, there were the Santa hats that were always available. Some played music, one lit up, others were standard issue Santa hats. We would run through the rows of trees looking for the one that called to us. The kids would each find one and then yell "MOM! I think I've got a good one here!" and I'd run between them to inspect what they'd found. We'd repeat the process until we had the perfect tree.

When we got home, Bryan would make hot chocolate and grumble about how I always picked the coldest, windiest day of the year to pick out the tree. I would counter with, "Dude... we live in Minnesota." What that implied about the weather didn't need to be spoken any further. We'd turn on the Christmas music and decorate the tree together as a family.

After the tree picking ritual had concluded, Bryan pulled out Christmas lights that played music and dance to the songs. He had seen them at the store and knew I would be overcome with happiness. When it came to Christmas related joy, he had always known how to bring out my inner child. The tackier it was, the happier it made me. He knew that Christmas lights dancing and singing on our tree would make me giddy with happiness, and I thought about how far we had come in the past few years.

CHAPTER 29

We had established a New Year's Eve tradition of getting together with our good friends, Shawn and Becky, and drinking our way into the new year. Their daughter Sydney was about the same age as Haley and they had become friends when they were little. For a few years you could find the two of them in our basement, dressing up and making up dance routines. Bryan loved to tease Sydney, who he affectionately called Saggers because her pants were always too big. She had finally stood up to him when he was razzing her about being a 10-year-old drug pusher because she showed up with candy one day. She put her hands on her saggy pantsed hips, looked Bryan in the eyes and said, "Uh! I don't drink drugs!" She was clearly the furthest thing from a drug pusher that there could be, but he loved to give her a hard time. Over the years, we had developed a strong friendship, and many late nights were spent at Shawn and Becky's house around the bonfire, drinking and telling stories.

The previous summer we had been enjoying some adult beverages and talking about our girls getting close to graduation. The topic of colleges came up. Everyone had their opinion about which colleges the girls should apply to and which had the best programs.

"Did you know that UW-Madison is one of the top ten party schools in the United States?" Bryan's ability to pull random information out of his ass was legendary.

"Really?" I was surprised by the statistic. "Where did you hear that?"

"I read an article about it in Playboy."

We all stared at him as he revealed the source of his knowledge. I was the first to ask what everyone was thinking. "When were you reading Playboy?"

"At the doctor's office when we were doing IVF."

Everyone laughed as the bewilderment came to my face. "Are you fucking kidding me? Dude. Everyone says they read Playboy for the articles, but you had one job to do in that room with those magazines. You actually read the articles?"

Bryan smiled and admitted, "Well, I didn't want the nurses to think I was too fast."

Shawn backed his buddy up by letting everyone know that the concern was legitimate. Although he had never spent time in a doctor's office with a Playboy and a cup to provide his specimen, he understood that the length of time spent in that room apparently said something about Bryan's manhood. Becky and I simply rolled our eyes, less concerned about the speed in which their penises worked and went back to talking about our girls.

Becky had been my person to go to over the past few years whenever I needed someone to talk to. Dena was still involved in my life, but we now lived more than an hour away from each other, so it was more difficult to get together with her. I missed her terribly, and we tried to see each other once or twice a year, but there just wasn't always time. Becky was an excellent stand-in for Dena, although she would never take her place. Becky is as steady as they come, and I've always admired her ability to keep a level head and offer advice when it was needed or offer an ear to listen if I just needed to vent. She was organized to the point of neurotic and had an intense dislike of dirt being on her floor, and we loved her for it.

Shawn was the complement to Becky and a perfect match to Bryan. He and Bryan would spend their time smoking in the garage, complaining about how quickly a teenager can ruin a perfectly good car. They frequently went on "Man Dates" to see movies they knew neither Becky nor I had any interest in. They bounced stories off each other like they were brothers and the laughs never stopped when we got the two of them going.

Their older daughter, Bailey, had become a young mother at the age of 17. Her son, Mac, was the same age as Owen so it worked out for everyone. She was regularly at our house so our boys could play and as Owen had gotten older, we had seen her more frequently. She was one of the toughest young mothers I had ever met. From talking to her, you would never guess how hard she busted her ass to make sure her son was fed, clothed, and still involved in every sport he wanted to try. Being a basketball mom, I had always thought hockey moms could be straight-up crazy, which is a dangerous opinion to have when you live in Minnesota. Bailey made crazy look easy and practically lived out of her car during the hockey season. Over the years, as the friendship between all of us had grown, so had our traditions.

We treated them like family and considered them our closest friends. New Year's Eve had become a favorite night for us, and every year, I made special party hats with feathers and glitter and ribbons to mark the occasion. The more elaborate the hat, the better it was. This year, their house was being renovated, so we hosted the party at our place.

The only one missing was Shawn and Becky's son, Corey. He had the unfortunate position of being too big for the little boys but too young for the big girls. It was a tricky position to be in, so he found a friend's house to go to instead of being stuck with our company for the night.

Earlier in the evening, I had sent Bryan to the store for snacks before the party. He came home with no snacks but had spinning disco light bulbs for the garage lights. They were ostentatious and fantastic, and I loved them. Again, another one of those times I remembered why I stayed with him. Six years ago, I would have criticized him for spending money on something so silly and forgetting the one reason I had actually sent him to the store. Now, I recognized the thought behind it and enjoyed the weirdness of spinning disco lights flashing on our driveway. He installed the lights and excitedly called me outside to see.

As I walked outside in the freezing cold, he yelled to me, "The party's here, baaaabyyy!!!"

I laughed at his excitement and the little dance he was doing in the driveway. We broke into an impromptu disco dance in the driveway in negative 3-degree weather. When the party crew finally arrived, the outside lights were a big hit, and everyone commented on how much fun they were. Leave it to Bryan to find the tackiest accessory imaginable to remind everyone the night was a night of celebration.

Cards Against Humanity is always a hit with the special crew we had over that night, so it regularly made the agenda. As much as I prided myself on having a pretty dirty mind and being able to rock a good game of Cards Against Humanity, what was most impressive was that Sydney and Haley came in first and second place. *Are you fucking kidding me? How are their minds just as filthy as mine? They're 17. I'm old and experienced with filth.* The girls eventually took off to go find where the high school party was, and we counted down to midnight with Shawn, Becky, Bailey and our boys. The little boys managed to make it to midnight, but I could tell Owen was struggling to stay awake by the end of it. Regardless, I knew 2017 was going to be our year to do all the things we always said we would. My husband planted a huge kiss on me at midnight, and I was reminded of how much I loved him and his spinning disco lights.

After everyone left, Bryan and I spent a little time just sitting and reflecting on the fun of the night and talking about our resolutions for the next year.

"Easter Jeep Safari in Moab. For sure!"

"That's a good one. Can I just fly and meet you there? I can't imagine driving to Utah in the Jeep. It's not exactly comfortable."

"The journey is half the fun, but sure, you can meet me there.

"Keith Urban concert in another state. Maybe Maine!!"

"Yes! Keith! We have to hit another one of his concerts, and we have to make it to Maine. Put the two together, and you've got an awesome trip! Just the two of us."

"I'm doing pretty well at school, and our finances are getting back in line. How about Europe?"

"Do you think we could? That's so high on my bucket list. I would love to get to Germany."

"No, Paris! I have always wanted to see Paris."

"We could do both. Should we look into it? See if it's possible?"

I yawned and looked at him and said, "We've got a lot to do in 2017, but right now, I've got to get to sleep."

"Yeah, me too. Go get to sleep, and I'll be up in a minute." He leaned over and kissed me and whispered, "Happy 2017!" I shuffled off to bed and was asleep within a minute of my head hitting the pillow. *Good-bye 2016. Can't wait to meet you, 2017!*

CHAPTER 30

I was sitting on the couch a couple of days after our New Year's shindig preparing lessons for when the students come back to school. The first week after break is always a real treat. Kids have been hopped up on Christmas cookies and freedom for two weeks, and now we want them to sit still and learn something.

Bryan came slowly down the steps and stared at me. I looked up and saw him standing there and realized he had started losing quite a bit of weight. *How the heck did he manage that over Christmas? I think I gained five pounds and he looks like he's lost ten!*

Somewhat quietly, he said, "My stomach hurts again."

Crap. This is not good. He hated it the last time he was in the hospital. "Do we need to go back to the hospital?"

"Yeah, I think we do. It's the same as it was last time."

"Ok.... ok. Are you sure?"

"Yeah, I think so." Knowing how much he hated his last stay in the hospital, his belly had to be pretty bad if he wanted to go back.

"Haley! I need you to watch your brother. I need to take Bryan to the doctor."

She reluctantly agreed and headed downstairs to sit with her brother. We invited Mac over so Owen had someone to play with and Bailey could keep Haley company for a while.

The doctors did all the same tests as before; CT, blood work, and IV fluids. The results came back that his lipase was elevated again. It was decided he had another case of pancreatitis and they reported it was idiopathic again.

"Um, no. This time I'm not buying that story. There has to be some other cause for this. Do people just get pancreatitis over and over like this for no reason?"

The doctor explained that yes, it could happen, although it wasn't typical.

"And could this be cancer?"

"No, we're not seeing any evidence of that on the CT or the MRI you had done."

"So, he just sits here again? No food, no water, the same as before? Couldn't you do another MRI?"

Bryan piped in at this point. "I'm not staying here again. Can't I go home and wait it out there? I can just as easily not eat or drink at home as I could here."

"We can give you fluids and pain meds here. I would recommend we admit you and let your pancreas settle down a little bit."

Bryan dug in his heels and decided he wanted to go home and manage his pain there rather than sit in the hospital again watching HGTV. The doctor said he was comfortable with that, but Bryan needed to drink nothing but water and limit his food intake to bland foods only. He was discharged with a prescription for pain meds, and we were sent on our way. On the way home, Bryan told me he was hungry and wanted to stop for something to eat.

"Can you just swing into McDonald's?"

"The doctor said bland foods. I don't think McDonald's has anything bland."

"Jen, I'm starving. I need to eat something."

"Can I just make you something at home?" He started getting agitated, and I could tell he was frustrated.

"I just want something to eat. Just get me a hamburger. I'm absolutely starving."

I could tell at this point that the whole "manage your symptoms at home" plan wasn't going to go over well. I finally caved in and got him the hamburger he wanted, which he finished in a few bites. Clearly, he was hungry. When we got home, Haley and Bailey were hanging out in the living room. Bryan walked straight past them and up the stairs to go to bed.

Haley looked surprised as we walked in the door. "Is everything ok? Why is he home?" I had let her know before we left that his belly felt the same as it did the last time he had pancreatitis so he might be staying in the hospital again.

"He didn't want to be admitted."

"Did the doctor say that was ok?" She sounded concerned.

"He did. He said he needed to eat bland foods and limit his food intake. So, he insisted we stop for a hamburger at McDonald's on the way home."

Bailey asked, "Was that a good idea?"

"Probably not, but he wanted a hamburger." The look on Bailey's face was saying precisely what I was thinking; "This isn't going to go well."

CHAPTER 31

At 3:00 in the morning, I woke up to Bryan grunting and moaning on his side of the bed. He was uncomfortable, but he didn't want to admit it.

"Honey, do I need to take you back to the hospital?"

"No."

"I think I do."

"No."

"You're clearly in pain and they said you could come back if it wasn't working to manage your pain at home."

"They just leave me sitting there. They don't do anything for me. The beds are uncomfortable, and I can't get any sleep. I don't want to go back."

I had seen this behavior in my students frequently, so I decided to try and use my special ed techniques on him. In my calmest teacher voice, I said, "I can understand how frustrating that must be. I wouldn't want to do that either. I'm just thinking they can help make you more comfortable, though. They were able to give you pain meds that helped last time, right? Maybe we should take a trip back and just see what they recommend."

He contemplated this for a little while. "Let me see if I can get comfortable. Give me an hour, and if I'm still in this much pain we'll go back."

At 4:00 a.m., we headed back to the hospital and he was admitted.

CHAPTER 32

B ryan's 2nd hospital stay was similar to the first one except they had more people stopping by to check on him. I had taken the day off and was in his room when his doctor came by to do rounds.

"All indications are that this is another round of idiopathic pancreatitis. The plan is to make you NPO and treat it as we did last time."

"Ok. That seems like it worked last time." He was clearly more comfortable now that he'd gotten some pain meds. "I want to get out of here, though, so as soon as it seems as though things are under control, I want to leave."

"Hold on." My inner protectiveness was starting to perk up. I was annoyed that everyone was just accepting this is what his life was going to be. "I find it odd that a person would have idiopathic pancreatitis twice in three months. That doesn't seem logical to me. Idiopathic would indicate that there's no cause. People don't just get pancreatitis repeatedly with no cause. There has to be more to this."

"The most common causes are gallstones or excessive alcohol use. When is the last time you had something to drink?"

"No, we're not going down that path again. We already told you he's not an alcoholic. He rarely drinks. He had one beer on New Year's Eve. His scans showed that he doesn't have gallstones. There has to be some sort of other tests you can run."

"We could do an endoscopic ultrasound where they go down the throat and look around, but since his pancreas is inflamed right now from pancreatitis, it isn't a good time to do it. We need to wait until his pancreas has settled down before we take a look."

"Ok. Let's do that. When can you do it?"

"We would typically wait six to eight weeks after he's discharged to do that procedure."

"No. I want it done sooner than that. This is ridiculous. You need to try and figure out what's wrong with him so we're not back in the hospital every three months. He has nothing but time while he sits here, and you're telling me there's absolutely nothing else that can be done?"

"Not until we do the endoscopic ultrasound."

"Fine. How do we get that scheduled?"

"I'll have someone contact you to get it set up."

After the doctor left, I looked over at Bryan and saw a little smirk on his face.

"What?"

"Nothing. I just like watching you do your thing. You're like one of those birds .…. A chicken hawk! Yeah, you're like a chicken hawk."

"Well, for fuck's sake. Do something!"

"Yep… chicken hawk". This would be his new name for me going forward.

CHAPTER 33

B ryan's endoscopic ultrasound was scheduled for January 26. I had pushed hard enough that I was able to get it sooner than the six to eight weeks the doctor wanted to wait. The night before his scan, we were woken at 2:30 in the morning to our carbon monoxide detectors going off. *Are you fucking kidding me?* We evacuated the house and called 911, and there we sat in the freezing cold with the kids and the dog and the cats in the car waiting for the police to arrive. The firefighter that came, walked through the house and tested the carbon monoxide levels and said they were fine.

"Honestly, where you have your carbon monoxide detectors located, you would have been dead by the time they went off if there really was carbon monoxide in your house."

"Seriously? We had someone install them for us a few years ago, and this is where they had placed them."

"Yeah, you need to put them closer to the floor. They shouldn't be on the ceiling."

We got the kids back to their beds, crawled back into ours and laughed at how ridiculous we must have all looked sitting in our cars with all the damn animals. Bryan rolled over and said, "We have to leave for the hospital in like two hours. I think it's an omen."

"Yeah, that I don't get enough sleep," I said as I rolled over and tried to get comfortable again.

. . . . .

Bryan's procedure was at the hospital where I had given birth to Owen, so I was trying to reminisce while we were sitting there waiting for him to be called back. The waiting room was packed full of people waiting for same day surgery procedures, and we were lucky to find two seats together. They finally called Bryan's name, and we went to a little room where he got undressed and into one of their attractive gowns. I was told that his procedure would take about an hour, and they would page me when it was time to come back to the recovery room to see him. There were little monitors all over the room where you could track the progress of the patient by their initials; if they were in pre-op, in the procedure, first recovery, second recovery, and so on.

I made myself busy by going to find a snack and browsing through the gift shop, which was about the size of a bathroom. There were no magazines, and I laughed thinking back to the day Owen was born and Bryan's unreasonable search for magazines. I decided to go see the babies in the Baby Center, but after trucking myself all the way there, there weren't any babies to look at, so I headed back to the waiting room. I read a book, played games on my phone, called my dad, called his mom, and found various ways to keep myself busy. It had been over two hours, so I went and checked the TV and Bryan was listed as still being in his procedure.

I was starting to get annoyed and pretty bored, so I decided to find the lady at the desk to try to get some details. "Is Bryan Monahan still in his procedure?"

"His progress will be up on the monitor so you can check there to see where he is."

"Yes, I've looked at that. It says he's still in his procedure, but I was told that it would take about an hour and it's been more than two."

"I'm sorry, ma'am, but we only have the information available to us."

"Could you please find someone to tell me what's going on? Did he have some sort of complication?" I watched a lot of Grey's Anatomy, so every bad outcome that had ever been on the show started seeping into my brain. I instantly started thinking about Denny Duquette and started to panic. When I panic, I start getting pretty pushy, and I realized this lady was about to become part of my wrath if she didn't have a more concrete answer for me soon.

"Sometimes the doctors are just running behind schedule, but I will try and find out for you."

I tried to sit down and play some more games on my phone, but I was starting to worry it was taking so long. My thought circles were spinning about what could have gone wrong, and my anxiety started to increase. Finally, my pager buzzed, and I walked over to the door where a pleasant nurse was waiting for me.

"Are you Jennifer?"

"Yes, I am."

"Bryan's out of his procedure. I can take you back to see him now."

When I got to Bryan's room, he was sound asleep and snoring. The nurse, who was quite cheerful, explained that Bryan had gotten a lot of anesthesia because the procedure went longer than expected.

"Oh. Ok. Did they find anything wrong with him?"

"The doctor was going to come talk to you after his next procedure. I know that he poked around in there quite a bit, so they gave him quite a bit of anesthesia."

I tried holding Bryan's hand and talking to him a little bit, but he was completely out of it. Another nurse stopped by and looked at his chart. She explained that it might take him a while to wake up because of all the anesthesia they had given him. I started to notice that a few of the nurses were looking at his chart and talking to each other outside the door.

"Is something going on with my husband?"

"Oh, he just got quite a bit of anesthesia so the doctor could do a real thorough look. He's going to come talk to you in just a little while."

Yeah, I've heard that before. What the hell? Everyone was being weirdly upbeat with me and enthusiastically telling me that the doctor would be in to see me soon. Every time they came to look at his chart, they would point to something and then talk between themselves. Something was not right. My Spidey Sense was tingling and telling me that something bad was about to happen. Maybe the carbon monoxide detectors really were an omen.

The doctor finally came to see me and closed the curtain. He explained that when they were doing the procedure, Bryan was obviously in some discomfort and kept wiggling around, so they gave him extra sedative. When they were looking around, they found a mass in his pancreas that was suspicious, so they biopsied it. He further explained that he had the pathologist that was there that day come look at what they found, and it was highly suspicious of pancreatic cancer.

"Ok. Pancreatic Cancer. So, he has cancer?"

Suddenly, I was back in my early 20's. It was the day of my college graduation and my parents were taking us all out to Outback Steakhouse to celebrate. I guess I thought when you graduate from college, the most appropriate way to get your party on was with a Bloomin' Onion, some steak, and a few beers. As we sat around the table, drinking and laughing, talking about whether I would survive in the real world, Angela asked my mom how her doctor's appointment had gone that day. After some prompting, my mom hesitantly let us know that she had ovarian cancer. The laughter at the table stopped and we all stared at her, contemplating what this would mean.

"It's just a little spot on my ovary and they're going to go in there and take it all out. It's going to be fine."

I snapped back to the present and heard the doctor saying, "We need to wait for the biopsy to come back, but the location of the mass would be highly suspicious of it, yes. There are a couple of blood tests I can run that could give us a better indication. The first is a CA19-9, which is a tumor marker commonly associated with pancreatic cancer."

I was drawing on my Grey's Anatomy training and not recalling anything about pancreatic cancer. "Is it curable?"

"It's an aggressive form of cancer."

"But it's treatable, right?"

"You're going to want to meet with an oncologist, but it's an aggressive form of cancer. It looks as though the mass is close to the portal vein, but it didn't appear to have invaded it at this point. I'm guessing this is not something you were expecting?"

"No. Uhhhhh…. No. I wasn't expecting this. We had asked his doctor in the hospital if it could be cancer and they said no." I looked over at Bryan, happily snoring, and realized I was going to have to tell him all of this since the doctor had to go to another procedure.

The nurses checked back on him frequently, while I busily consulted Google about pancreatic cancer. The results of his blood work showed the tumor marker the doctor mentioned was slightly elevated, which was another indication that this was pancreatic cancer. I asked if it was okay for me to step out for a few minutes to make a phone call. They assured me they would contact me on my cell phone if Bryan woke up.

I went and sat in the Jeep in total shock. Pancreatic Cancer. I was stunned at the results of his procedure. I assumed it would be something simple. Something they could give him a pill for. I had no idea what to do, so I did the only thing I could think of; I called Becky.

"Hey. Do you have a second?"

"Sure. What's up? How was the procedure?"

I couldn't get the words out. All she could hear was silence as she patiently waited for me to be able to find the words. "They think it's pancreatic cancer. I can't do this, Becky. I can't watch someone else die of cancer. All I can think about is watching my mom die from ovarian cancer and how it took everything from her…. Her dignity, her independence, her spirit... I can't watch this. I just can't do it again." My mind was spinning. My thoughts were bouncing between images of my mom laying in her hospice bed and Bryan's face looking to me for help.

"Ok. Let's slow down. What did the doctor say?" I recounted for her what the doctor had told me and she, being the methodical and cautious person she is, said, "Ok, so they didn't say it's for sure cancer. Let's just wait for the test results."

"The blood work came back with an elevated tumor marker and they said the mass in his pancreas is pretty suspicious. If it walks like a duck and talks like a duck…."

"Let's just see what the biopsy shows before we overreact. Take this one step at a time. When will you get the biopsy results back?"

"They said in a few days. Probably by Monday."

"Ok, so we wait until Monday. How can I help? What do you need?"

"A cure for pancreatic cancer."

CHAPTER 34

I had finally gotten Bryan home, and we spoke in the Jeep for only a couple of minutes. He was still out of it and kept nodding off on our way home. I got him into bed and spent the rest of the night quietly thinking about what the doctor said. Every search I did, no matter how I worded it, showed the same result: Pancreatic cancer is deadly.

The next morning Bryan woke up and rolled over and looked at me. I wasn't sure how much of our conversation from the previous night he remembered. He passed out pretty quickly after we got home.

"So.... cancer?" He clearly remembered enough of what I had told him.

"Yeah, cancer."

"Pancreatic cancer?"

"Yeah. You picked like the shittiest kind of cancer to get. You couldn't get regular cancer. You had to get pancreatic cancer." I looked at him, and the pain in his eyes said it all: He was terrified. "I got in touch with your boss yesterday and called you in sick to work."

"You did? What did you tell her?"

"I just said that they had to poke around in your belly a little more than they thought they were going to so you would need today to recover."

"Was she cool with that?"

"Yeah, she said it was fine. It's Friday, so that gives us through the weekend to get things figured out."

"Why do they think it's cancer?" I explained about the tumor marker and its location. I had been up all night reading up on survival statistics, treatment options, reading medical journals, alternative treatments, learning about clinical trials. I knew I had to tell him the one thing I had been dreading telling him.

"So, it sounds like pancreatic cancer is pretty aggressive."

"What do you mean by that?"

"I mean the survivability of it isn't good."

"Just tell me."

"9%."

He sat up and looked and raised his voice slightly. "9%?!?! That's how many people survive it?" I could see his mind spinning as he thought about the statistic.

"That's the five-year survival rate, yes."

He laid back down, thinking about that number for a while. "How bad did you yell at the doctor?"

"I didn't yell! I think I was too stunned to yell. I've made a list. I even used a good pen."

"Of course, you did…."

I took out my paper I had been scribbling notes on. "We need an oncologist and a surgeon, and we need someone who knows what they're doing. I'm going to get you an appointment at Mayo. Living in Minnesota has to have some sort of benefit, and we have a world class hospital in our backyard. I'll call and you get you an appointment after the kids go to school." All the advice Becky had given me about waiting until Monday had gone straight out the window. I wasn't willing to wait. I needed to get a jump on this. When my mom found out she was sick, she and my dad had gone along with whatever the doctor's told them, no matter how long it took. Everything had always worked out for them, so they had no reason to believe it wouldn't then. I, on the other hand, had learned the hard way you have to get aggressive if you want to see results. I wasn't willing to sit back and wait. I didn't want Bryan's cancer to end the way my mom's had.

A few hours later, Bryan came downstairs and found me on the phone with the Mayo appointment line. "Yes, pancreatic cancer. Yes, it was confirmed by biopsy." Ok, so that was a little bit of a lie, but I figured if by some miracle it came back that he didn't have pancreatic cancer, I could always cancel the appointment.

Bryan sat down across from me and listened as I went around in circles with the appointment person on the other end of the line.

"No, I'm not willing to wait that long. I need him an appointment next week.... I'm sorry, but my husband has cancer, and I have no intention of letting him die, so I need an appointment next week.... Then I'll take an appointment with gastro... You're telling me that of all the doctors you have down there, the soonest you can get him in is four weeks from now? No."

I was acting like a child who wasn't getting what they wanted at the toy store, but I didn't care at that point. "That's fine. I'll hold." I looked over at Bryan and he was staring at me. I mouthed to him,

"What?" He looked at me and said, "Chicken Hawk" and walked out to the garage to have a smoke.

I joined him in the garage after my phone call and let him know that he had an appointment at Mayo on Tuesday of the following week. They told us to plan to spend two to three days there.

"No, Jen…. I have people coming into town next week from Nashville and we have meetings with HCP. Shelly is flying in for the meetings. I can't take off next week."

"Bryan, you're going to Mayo on Tuesday."

"Ok, well, you heard me say the part about Shelly coming into town? I need to be back for a meeting on Wednesday."

"No, you're going to Mayo and we're going to spend two to three days there getting you looked at and…."

"Jen…"

"Bryan! Don't even start. You're going to Mayo." He looked at me as though he wanted to say something, but I stopped him before he could start. "This isn't me being a bitch and saying you can't go hang out with your friends because I need help with the laundry. You're going to Mayo so they can save your life. You've got the fucking Death Star growing smack in the middle of your belly, and I'm going to go find someone who can blow the shit out of that thing. This is non-negotiable. I'll call your boss myself if I need to. You're going."

He looked at me for an uncomfortable amount of time and finally said, "Fine."

CHAPTER 35

We had gotten the results from the biopsy on Monday, and it was what we expected; adenocarcinoma of the pancreas. I had already prepared myself, so there was no need for the shock and awe that is usually associated with a diagnosis like that. I called my dad and my brothers and Bryan called his mom to let them know the bad news. Everyone was very comforting, and both Angela and Shereen let me know they would help in whatever way they could. Bryan's mom was rightfully upset to find out that her only son had a disease with a five-year survival rate as low as it was. It got exhausting to have to tell everyone all the information, but we had a lot of friends that would need to be told what was going on, so Facebook seemed to be the easiest way to keep the masses updated without having to relive the same conversation a hundred times. Bryan and I chose the words carefully but wanted to let people know that we intended to do everything in our power to beat the 9% survival rate that we had heard about. My first Facebook post came a few days after his endoscopic ultrasound.

There are certain words you never want to hear. As I waited for Bryan in the recovery room on Thursday after his procedure, I sensed something wasn't right as all the nurses talked hush hush in the hallway and then came into his room with too big smiles on their faces. When the doctor finally came to speak to me, he said the word I had prepared myself to hear... cancer. And not just regular old cancer.... pancreatic cancer. After some great advice from a great friend, I knew we only had one choice. ATTACK! I can't watch someone I love dwindle away to nothing. I'm not going to relive what I went through losing my mom to this horrible disease. I can't allow my children to experience that gut-wrenching pain I felt when I lost her. We must attack!

As Bryan pointed out, Deadpool summed it up nicely. "Cancer is a shit show. Like Yakov Smirnoff opening for the Spin Doctors at the Iowa State Fair kind of shit show." Given that the Deadpool indestructible treatment is not available in our area, and his face is too pretty for that, we head to Mayo on Tuesday. Bryan is a self-proclaimed asshole and is channeling all that energy toward kicking cancer's ass. He's strong, but we're both an emotional mess right now, so we've outlawed all Lifetime movies at home and are sticking to anything from the Marvel Universe.

I'll keep everyone updated when we know more, but just know that prayers, positive thoughts and the love of our friends and family are appreciated right now.

The response from our Facebook family was overwhelming. Bryan and I were touched by the number of people that sent messages and called him. He had let his boss know prior to me posting and his company immediately started talking about how they could help him.

Friends began offering to send food, which I found strangely comforting at a time of crisis. Our refrigerator quickly filled with sandwich meats and cheeses, lasagna and good old Minnesota hot dishes. We felt loved and prepared to head to Mayo to begin the fight.

CHAPTER 36

G oing to the Mayo Clinic in Rochester is an experience. It feels a little like the first time you walk into Disney World, except there aren't any rides and no one is dressed up in a costume or trying to sell you a balloon in the shape of Mickey Mouse. We took the 2-hour drive to Rochester from our home in Elk River and got there a little earlier than expected. We checked ourselves into the hotel that would be our base for the next few days and took a few minutes to unwind before the craziness started.

Bryan's first appointment was blood work at the Hilton building, so I went to get the trusty map I had printed out before we left. I had circled all the buildings we would need to go to. While I was digging through my bag to find my map, Bryan exclaimed, "Hey! They've got an app that tells you everywhere you need to go!"

"Cool. I have a map that shows us that, too."

"Yeah, but the app is on my phone and shows me where to go and tells me when all my appointments are."

"Yes, but I have color-coded my paper map according to when each appointment is." After a blank stare, he went back to downloading his app.

Mayo is made up of multiple buildings that have tunnels connecting many of them. You can get to most places without ever going outside, which is a benefit with our ugly Minnesota winters. If you take the tunnels, the walk is pretty extensive, so since we were coming from our hotel, we decided to drive to our first appointment and find a parking spot outside. When we walked into the first building, it was like an organized chaos of people waiting in lines and being called to different doors in the area. It was a huge open room with people waiting in chairs throughout. Bryan finally got up to the front of the line.

"Mayo clinic number?"

"Uhhhhh.... I don't know. Do I have one of those?"

"Do you have an appointment?"

"Yes, I'm supposed to get blood work at the Hilton Building?"

"That's where you are. Last name?"

I proudly pulled out my printed and color-coded itinerary that matched up to the color coding on the map I had printed out and found his mayo number printed at the top. "Here... is this it?" I looked smugly at Bryan as I handed over my papers. He simply looked away, refusing to acknowledge his defeat.

"You're going to want to remember that number. You will need it for every appointment you check into. I have you checked in. Go ahead and have a seat and someone will call you back in a few minutes."

We found a seat near the back of the room, and he was called back within a few minutes. It was like a well-orchestrated dance, and I was impressed by the efficiency of how quickly they got people back to see someone. His entire appointment took less than 15 minutes from beginning to end.

We had extra time before his next appointment, so we walked around in the tunnels area and found some little shops to wander through. There were restaurants and coffee shops, and we found a candy store that sold chocolate pecan turtles, so we got a few to bring home to the kids. We got Haley a bracelet and a little squishy fidget toy for Owen. He would be disappointed that it wasn't a video game, but maybe we could get him off the TV long enough to enjoy something that wasn't electronic.

Bryan's next appointment was a CT in the Eisenberg Building. This appointment went just as smoothly as the Hilton Building. His appointment took a little longer than the last one because he was getting a CT with contrast. When he came out, we headed to find some lunch even though I had eaten all the candy we had gotten for the kids.

Rochester is a city that looks like it could be big, but it feels like a small town. The Mayo campus is in the heart of the city and is massive and beautiful and modern, but Rochester also has a water tower in the shape of a giant corn cob, so it all feels kind of confusing. We went and found a restaurant and sat down to eat. Bryan's appetite was less than it had been in the past, but he managed to get a few bites of a hamburger and some fries.

Our last appointment for the day was with gastroenterology. We were brought to a little room and asked to wait. Bryan was nervous about what his options were, but he was in good spirits. As we waited for the doctor to come in, I could tell that he was quietly listening for footsteps in the hallway to stop outside our room to announce the doctor's arrival. Finally, we heard the clicky shoes of an important person approaching. The door opened and a man wearing the nicest shoes I had ever seen entered. He sat down and talked with Bryan about what had brought us there, what the scans showed, and what the next steps would look like. In the end, he suggested that it would be better for us to meet with oncology and a surgeon to see if his tumor was removable through surgery.

He explained that they would typically do what is called a Whipple procedure to remove the cancer from his pancreas. *Whipple! Finally, something I recognized from Grey's Anatomy.* I felt like I finally knew something that was going on. *Dr. Bailey did these all the time!* He also explained that Bryan's mass was fairly small, only about 2 centimeters, so that was working in our favor.

We waited for someone to come talk to us about an appointment with Medical Oncology and, as it happened, they were able to get us in the next day. We went back to our hotel room and called the kids and talked about the events of the day. Bryan was tired and needed a good night's rest if we were going to go through another day of appointments again.

That night, we got into bed and I put my head on his shoulder. We were both feeling the weight of what was happening around us. It was a lot to take in. I had lived in Minnesota my entire life, and had certainly seen the Mayo campus before, but the energy that surrounds it when it's full of people getting from one appointment to the next was something I hadn't experienced before. We fell asleep that night, exhausted and overwhelmed with my head still on his shoulder. It was a clear violation of the "no touching while sleeping" rule I had established after the first time we had slept together, but that night I didn't care. I wanted to stay as close as possible.

CHAPTER 37

The next day we had some breakfast and then got ready for his next round of appointments. We walked in from a different side of the campus, and the building just smelled of importance. Giant sculptures were hanging from the ceiling in various colors, and I commented that they were what I imagined his tumor looked like.

"Giant sparkly balls with glitter?" He looked at me like I was a little nuts, but also saw the amusement in picturing his tumor as giant glitter balls.

"Yep! Except maybe not that happy looking."

"I have a feeling it's not that happy looking either."

"Yeah, but it's shaped like that…. At least in my imagination."

As you walk through the campus, it becomes apparent when you've switched from one building to the next because they all have a different theme. One building is marble and shiny and open and sunny with a grand piano in the lobby. When you pass into the next building, it's dark wood and cozy and warm feeling. It depends on where you are what type of feeling you have, but it's an absolute maze. We had to stop several times to find the building we were looking for.

When we got to medical oncology in the Gonda building, we settled in and waited until it was our turn. The room was a sea of old and young waiting to have their lives rescued from cancer. It was the most depressing place we had been at Mayo so far. I couldn't help but think about what Doctor Clicky Shoes told us yesterday; 2 centimeters is tiny. That's not even an inch. They have to be able to do something to get that tumor out of there. Most people with pancreatic cancer aren't diagnosed until they're a Stage 4 and live less than six months. Bryan was found at Stage 2. That had to be a good thing for him. I thought about how small 2 centimeters was. *They could go in with a melon baller and rip that thing out of there!*

When it was finally our turn, we were brought back to another room. The hallways looked like Las Vegas with little lights outside every room indicating what point of the process the person in the room was at. Were they waiting for a doctor? Was the nurse still in the room? Do they need labs? Again, it was highly choreographed chaos. After what seemed like a very long time, the jolliest doctor I had ever met walked in. He had a thick German accent which immediately perked Bryan up. Bryan's grandparents had been raised in Germany and he had dreams of going there someday. He was semi-fluent in German, so he used a few phrases to make a connection with our delightful German doctor. Bryan was excellent at doing things like that. He could find the smallest detail to connect with someone.

Dr. Schneider went through what we already knew. He had called in their surgeon who specialized in the pancreas to meet with Bryan after we finished with Dr. Schneider. He explained that typically they have better results if they do neoadjuvant chemotherapy, which meant they wanted to do chemo first and then decide if surgery was an option. He described the chemotherapy he would recommend and confirmed that we could do his treatments a little closer to home.

"Where do you live? The Cities?"

"Yes, we live in Elk River… Just north of Minneapolis." I answered for Bryan since I could tell he was slightly overwhelmed with information.

"Ok, so where would you go for treatment?"

"I was looking at Minnesota Oncology in Coon Rapids, but I suppose he could go anywhere."

"I would recommend Dr. Laudi if you go to Coon Rapids. He's excellent. There are other good ones, too, but Laudi is very thorough and is a great guy. I can send my notes to him. I would recommend Folfirinox, though. It's a tough one, but you're young and should be able to tolerate it."

I whipped out the Captain America notebook that Becky gave us before we left. Captain America is tough. We are tough. The notebook seemed appropriate. After talking with us for quite a while, he excused himself to go find Dr. Kirkland, the surgeon.

Bryan looked at me, and I could see the excitement in his eyes. "That all sounds pretty good. The chemo doesn't sound great, but surgery sounds like it's an option. You said that's the only cure, right?"

"Yep. From everything I've read that's the only cure. I think Dr. Schneider said that, too. By the way, nice job working some German into the conversation."

He smiled and we waited. Then we waited some more. And waited some more. And after that, we waited some more. After more than an hour and my climbing frustration about to boil over, I decided I was going to go find someone and give them a firm teacher style behavior correction.

"Jen, you can't go do that."

"This is ridiculous. We've been waiting for more than an hour."

"I know, but you're not going to yell at the surgeon." He rarely took that type of firm tone with me.

"Why not? He needs to treat people with respect."

"Because he's the one that's going to save my life."

I stared at him for a few moments, weighing the risks and benefits of chewing out the doctor who was supposed to cut open my husband's belly and remove the cancerous mass that was killing him. I reluctantly conceded. "Fine. I'm not happy about it, though. Just because he's the all-powerful surgeon doesn't mean he can treat us like shit."

Several minutes later, a short man wearing a fancy suit came swooping into the room with a half-assed apology about making us wait. We both sat forward, full of hope, and listened to what he had to say.

"I've looked at your scans, and your tumor is fairly small. It's in the neck of the pancreas. Typically, we would do a Whipple procedure where we remove a portion of the pancreas, a portion of your small intestine, gall bladder and the bile duct. It's a complicated procedure and has a lengthy recovery time. Unfortunately, when I look at your scans, the tumor is pressing against the portal vein and has caused a blood clot. The clot is fairly extensive so I wouldn't be able to get to the tumor surgically."

I think he just said that he can't operate on Bryan. Is that what he just said? "Did you say you can't operate?"

"That's correct. The tumor is inaccessible because of the blood clot. What I would recommend is to go forward with neoadjuvant chemotherapy. We tend to have better results when we do it that way. We have lower rates of recurrence. I would also recommend a blood thinner to try to resolve the clot that is preventing us from getting at the tumor. Come back and see me after six to eight rounds of chemo and we'll scan you again and see if there's anything we can do. I'll have someone call you, and we'll schedule an appointment for three to four months from now."

He swooped back out and left us sitting there stunned. Bryan looked at me and said, "That didn't sound like good news. Did that sound like good news to you?"

"I don't think so. I'm not really sure. It sounded more like 'It's not good news right now but let's try a few things and see if things change.' Does that sound right to you?"

"Yeah, I guess. Let's get going home."

CHAPTER 38

On our drive home that night, we were both quiet. There was no need to stay in Rochester for another night, and we wanted to get home and see the kids. We didn't speak for the first half-hour of the drive. I could see his wheels turning, and I knew I needed just to let him work his way through whatever was in his head.

After some time, he finally said, "I don't want to die."

"I don't want you to die either. If I wanted that, I would have killed you years ago."

"Right? So, what am I going to do? Should I get another opinion?"

"You can. It never hurts to do that, but from what they said, Fancy Suit Dude is the best there is when it comes to the pancreas. If he says he can't get to it right now, then he can't get to it."

"I just can't believe they can't go in there and take the stupid thing out."

"I think they can, but it sounds like you'd bleed to death, so that's probably not a good option."

"Yeah. I wouldn't like that." More silence followed.

"The chemo scares me. I don't know what it's going to be like."

"Well, I can tell you what my mom's was like from what I remember if you think that would help."

"No, it's been so long. I'm sure that things have changed a lot since then."

"Do you want me to Google for you? Find out what the side effects are?"

"Yeah. It's better to be prepared, right?"

I got on my phone and started looking for the side effects of Folfirinox. "Well, you're not going to lose your hair! So, that's good!"

"I can handle hair loss. What are the other side effects?"

"Nausea, vomiting, fatigue, taste changes…." I went on and on spewing out what was listed as side effects.

"Stop. I don't want to hear this anymore."

I put my phone down and we drove for another half hour in silence. Finally, after we'd called all the people that didn't deserve to get updated by Facebook, I made another post so that the text messages and phone calls from people asking how things went would stop.

Mayo update: Not the best of days, but just like Princess Leia, we have hope. We went early yesterday for blood work and CT. His blood work shows that his CA 19-9 is at 106. This is lower than when we were at North Memorial but could just be because different labs test differently. Mayo is probably a more accurate reading. Bryan was thrilled that Mayo has an app that gives you all the information you need, so his dream of a paperless society is closer to reality.

We finally met with Dr. Wears A Fancy Suit this afternoon. As it sits right now, the tumor is inoperable because of its location. It is in the neck of the pancreas and is cutting off blood flow to a particular vein. This has caused a large blood clot.

The plan is to meet with vascular medicine and oncology next week. He'll go on blood thinners and then start 6-8 rounds of some pretty nasty chemo. When I asked them if they're confident this will work, his assistant said that Dr. Wears A Fancy Suit wouldn't do it if he didn't think it would work. On a more positive note, Bryan has a bit of an appetite and was able to eat some dinner, and he's currently driving us home, so I don't have to listen to him complain about my driving.

Right now, we need many prayers that the blood clot will disappear, and the chemo will shrink the tumor so that surgery will be an option. I'm hoping that the chemo doesn't completely take him out of commission.... hope worked out pretty well for Princess Leia and the damn Death Star was destroyed, so I'm going to go with that.

Again, we got a lot of responses and Bryan felt better knowing that there was an army of people behind us sending positive thoughts and saying prayers. We needed hope at that moment. We had honestly believed that with his tumor being so small and finding his cancer at stage two they would be able to operate. What we found was much different and the kind words from all our friends encouraged him. He felt ready to fight.

CHAPTER 39

We were able to get an appointment with Dr. Laudi the following week after a few strings were pulled by the friend of a friend who worked there. Dr. Laudi was a dream of a doctor. He was kind and caring and explained all of Bryan's results to us thoroughly.

As we sat there, listening to the barrage of information being thrown at us, it was obvious that Bryan was getting overwhelmed. Listening to the way his life was about to change was staggering. I could see him trying to dig deep to find the strength to fight the way everyone was screaming at him to, but it was easier said than done. As Dr. Laudi walked out of the room, Bryan looked at me and tears filled his eyes.

"I'm scared, Jen. I don't know if I can do this."

"I'm going to be there with you every step of the way." I hugged him as more tears came to his eyes. "I know it's scary, honey. We're going to do this together. I'm not giving up on you."

Dr. Laudi's assistant, Lacey, walked in and found Bryan in a puddle of tears. I looked at her and said, "He's just having a bit of a moment. It's a lot to take in."

Lacey understood and told us, "We have lots of moments in these rooms. If there's anything you need, you can call me. That's what I'm here for." I knew she meant it and I was happy to put my husband in such capable hands.

Leaving the office, I felt like there was a concrete plan of attack and Dr. Laudi seemed optimistic that it would work. He put in orders for Bryan to get a port installed so he could receive his chemotherapy through that. It was scheduled for Friday of that week. The plan was to have him start chemo immediately after the procedure. In addition to the port, he was going to get a celiac plexus block which deadens some of the nerves that provides pain to the belly and would help ease some of his discomfort.

The day of the port install, as tends to happen in hospitals, the plan didn't go as smoothly as we had hoped. His doctor, who looked exactly like Matthew Broderick but talked about as fast as one of those sloths on Zootopia, came in to speak with us and explained that he was a bit behind schedule. By the time Ferris Bueller was finally ready for him, it was too late for Bryan to get any chemo that day.

When I spoke with the scheduler at Minnesota Oncology, I was told that he could start chemo the following week, but I was anxious and let my emotions get the best of me. "No, he needs to get in for chemo before that. Every minute he sits here not being treated, that tumor is growing."

"I understand, but we need at least five hours for his treatment. Even if we tried to rush it, and he was able to get over here right away, it would be nearly 7:00 by the time he was done today."

"Ok, so what are his other options? I'm not going to make him wait another week. My expectation is that you all take this as seriously as I am. This is my husband, and he's not going to die if I have anything to say about it."

"Yes, ma'am, I am taking it seriously, but I just can't get him in today."

I heard Bryan's words in my head saying, "These are the people that are going to save my life. Stop pissing them off." I tried to soften and let my guard down a little. "I understand that. I honestly do. I hope you can understand that we're frightened and overwhelmed, and we want to get him started as soon as possible. Please... Is there anything else that can be done?"

"Let me call the hospital and see if we can get him there this weekend."

"I appreciate that. Thank you so much." I received a call back a few minutes later that Bryan was able to do his first infusion treatment at the hospital on Sunday. I thanked the scheduler repeatedly and let Bryan know that his first round of chemo would be in two days. He was starting to come out of his anesthesia and munching on the Lorna Doone cookies the hospital stocks, so he happily agreed to the plan I had put in place for him.

I asked him how he was feeling, and he looked at me and said, "Awesome sauce and a bag of chips, baby!" The celiac plexus block seemed to have worked and the narcotics they had given him were making things much more fun than it had been the past few days.

CHAPTER 40

Treatment for pancreatic cancer sucks. There's just no way around it. It sucks. Bryan's first round of treatment was using the combination of drugs that make up Folfirinox. Dr. Laudi had agreed with Dr. Schneider's suggestion and explained that it's a tough treatment, but it's effective. Bryan went in once every two weeks for treatment. Unfortunately, by the time he just started to feel better from the first round of chemo, it was time to start the next one. This drug didn't make him lose his hair, but after sitting in the chair getting poisoned for five hours, he would come home with a small backpack that had another 40 hours' worth of medication in it. It was like a little ball of poison he brought home and it made him sick.... Like praying on your knees on the bathroom floor for it to end kind of sick.

Even though Bryan had experimented with more than one illicit drug as a teen, he was very anti-drugs as an adult. He had told me how he had seen what his life was becoming and walked away from all his friends one day so he could get away from the parties and the drugs. When I brought up the idea of smoking weed, he immediately shot it down.

"No. I'm not going to smoke weed."

"I've done a lot of reading on this and everything I've seen says it helps with nausea and the general ookiness you're feeling."

"I don't want to do drugs. They're giving me pain meds. I'll just stick with that."

"Ok, but I want you to keep the idea open." I was never very good at the drug thing when I was young. I knew plenty of people who smoked it, but I was pretty naive when it came to drugs, so I did my best impression of someone who knew what they were talking about. I talked to a friend of mine from college who was much more worldly than I was, and he said he knew someone that could probably get us some weed if we wanted it. I figured it would be better to have some on hand just in case. He was happy to help, and a few days later brought me a small baggie of weed.

After Bryan's next round of chemo, he was feeling miserable. He came home with his poison ball and spent the next two days in bed until it was time to bring him back in to get disconnected and have his line flushed. When we got home, he was still feeling miserable, so I gently brought up the idea of smoking some weed again. This time he was slightly more open to the idea.

"So, how does it help?"

"I'm not sure what the technical reasons are, but I know it helps with nausea. Are you still nauseous?"

"Yes. A lot."

"I know it helps to stimulate your appetite, too. Let's just give it a try and see if it helps. If you don't like it, we won't do it again."

"Fine. You're like a drug pusher now. What's up with that? I thought I was the one with the drug issues when I was young."

"I'm just trying to do what I can to help you, and this might help."

The kids were both in bed, so Bryan went out to the garage to smoke some weed. He took a few small hits on the bat I had gotten him, and then he went in to watch some TV. I was getting pretty tired, so I went and laid down in our bed. About 20 minutes later I laughed when Bryan came into our bedroom with a box of Girl Scout cookies and sat on the edge of the bed and ate the entire thing while blankly staring at the TV show I was watching.

"So, I guess the weed is helping?"

"Huh? Yeah, I dunno. Maybe."

"I guess all that stuff about stimulating your appetite was pretty accurate?"

"These Girl Scout cookies are good. Seriously. You wanna try one?"

"No, you can go ahead and keep those for yourself. Maybe you should head to bed."

"Hmmm? Yeah, ok."

CHAPTER 41

The company Bryan worked for was incredibly accommodating. As soon as he told them about his cancer diagnosis, they got him a new laptop so he could work from home on the days he wasn't feeling well. His boss, Kirsten, was sympathetic to our situation, and she and Bryan got along great. Jeff regularly called to check on Bryan and shoot the shit whenever they both had some extra time. They both reached out frequently and truly treated him like family.

By his third round of Folfirinox, Bryan had worked out a routine where he would work from home on the Monday and Tuesday after getting disconnected from his bag and would work half days for the rest of that week to give the ooky some time to wear off. I came home from work after that cycle and found him sitting at the kitchen table, laptop open, on the phone having a serious discussion about some larger items he was hoping to get included in his next budget. My husband was impressive when he started talking business. He knew his profession well, and I could picture him in his dress shirt and tie as I listened to him talking to the big wigs of his company. I quietly walked into the kitchen so as not to interrupt his important work call. However, when I looked a little closer, I found that Bryan was wearing Batman onesie pajamas with a bright yellow cape that attached to the back with Velcro. I burst out laughing. Haley had bought him the pajamas two years ago for Christmas. I loved that he was still hard at work. He liked the normalcy that work offered him, but the Batman pajamas made his belly comfortable with no waistband tugging at him, and I guess the cape made him feel powerful. Regardless, he was digging in and giving it his all even through the poison he got every two weeks.

. . . . .

April 8th was always a difficult day for me. It's the day I lost my mom. As Bryan was fighting his cancer, I took that day to find some quiet time for myself to reflect on everything that was going on around us. My mom was the greatest influence in my life, and it got me to thinking about how she had influenced me even after her death. When she died, I could not understand why. Why would someone so kind, who didn't have a single malicious bone in her body, be taken from me? How could she, of all people, get such an awful disease? Someone who never hurt anyone, lived for holding her grandbabies, always made sure everyone had a snack, always put others before herself... why? It didn't make sense.

A few days before the anniversary of her death, I was talking to Angela and she said, "I'm really impressed with how you guys have attacked this."

It started me wondering ... had I not lost my mother to cancer, would I know how to fight the way we were fighting now? Would I have had the foresight to immediately start calling the best doctors within 200 miles of me? Or would I have, like my mom did, just accept that things take time and the doctors would eventually get in touch with us? Would I be searching for clinical trials? Filling out applications for studies? Finding alternative pain medication? Reading case studies in medical journals? Would I be studying test results and researching what every term meant so I could understand?

Maybe I had to lose my mom so I knew how to fight so my kids wouldn't lose their dad. Maybe I had to lose her and get to my lowest point so I could be stronger now. Maybe we needed an angel in Heaven fighting for us. Maybe there was a reason.

The more I thought about that idea, I found some comfort in knowing that maybe - just maybe - there was a reason for her death, and I could use that to help my family fight the fight they needed to. They were all looking to me to guide them through the fear and uncertainty. All those years of being angry at her death had brought me to this moment. The anger floated away and was replaced with a feeling of calm determination. I was going to help them through this because I had been there, and I knew how.

CHAPTER 42

After Bryan had completed all of his rounds of chemo, we headed back to Mayo to meet with Dr. Wears a Fancy Suit and our delightful German doctor. Our appointment happened to be on the last day of school, so an added bonus for me was that I wouldn't have to be involved in the craziness of 1200 middle school students who were so close to the sweet, sweet taste of freedom that they got a little crazy. I would be 100 miles away listening to my husband complain about how the contrast dye for his CT made him vomit.

The doctors both agreed that the treatment was working, but the collateral veins hadn't gone away, so surgery still wasn't an option. The irony was that the way the blood clot and collaterals formed also saved his life. He could have died from the blood clot well before he went on the blood thinners.

We went home and made an appointment to see Dr. Laudi. Yes, Mayo is a world-class hospital, but we trusted Dr. Laudi to always do what was best for Bryan. Every time we met with him, we felt like he was giving us his undivided attention and we were thankful we were able to get him on Bryan's case. He explained the collateral veins better so that we understood why Bryan wasn't surgical.

"So, when they do road construction and have to close down the road, the cars need to find a way around the construction, right?"

"Sure. Like a detour." Bryan was trying to make sense of it, and a more simplified explanation was helping.

"Right, like a detour. The major road, in this case, the portal vein, is blocked because your tumor is pressing on it. The blood needs to find a detour so smaller veins formed to allow the blood to flow. Unfortunately, because of the way they formed, it's making it impossible to get to the tumor."

"Can't they cut around the veins"

"No. Imagine that you have a bowl of hot spaghetti noodles. Now, drop a scoop of ice cream into those noodles. The ice cream will melt, right? The ice cream will sink in around the noodles. That ice cream is your tumor. You'd have to scrape every speck of ice cream off every single noodle to be able to call you cancer free. If we can't get all of it, there's no point in doing the surgery because it will just come back."

"Well, do collateral veins go away?" I was trying to find hope in what we were being told.

"It's hard to say. That's what we're hoping will happen with the blood thinners."

Dr. Laudi decided that chemoradiation was the next step to try and shrink the tumor. Bryan met with a straightforward, no bullshit radiation doctor the next week and he explained the process. He would go in every day for five weeks so they could cook the shit out of his tumor. I had finally found someone who shared my vision of destroying the Death Star that was still residing in his belly.

Every day when he would leave, I would sing the song "Radioactive" by Imagine Dragons to him and then make a little explosion sign with my hands indicating what we were hoping was happening inside his belly. The radiation didn't have the same kind of nausea and vomiting effects as chemo did, but it really drained him. Bryan started going to bed around 8:00 every night which was highly unusual for him. He had always been a night owl and I was the early to bed, early to rise kind of girl. Now, he was going to bed hours before me, and I was still waking up before him.

Bryan napped a lot throughout the day, which meant I needed Haley to watch her brother when I had errands to run. One particular weekend, Bryan was sleeping, and Haley was at work, but I needed to run to the store so I asked Owen if he would be ok by himself for 20 minutes while I ran and got what I needed. He assured me he would be fine. He was nearly 10-years-old and was getting good at helping me around the house when I needed him.

When I returned from the store, I saw Owen standing in the front window of the house frantically waving at me. He looked genuinely worried, so I hustled to park the car in the garage so I could get inside. I ran in without grabbing the groceries to find out what was wrong. *Is Bryan sick? Did a pipe burst? Did the dog die? What happened that he could be this concerned in the 20 minutes I had been gone.*

"What's the matter, boo? Is dad ok?"

"We have a problem!"

"What happened?" My heart was racing fearing the worst.

Owen brought me to the kitchen. "Ants! We have ants on the kitchen counter! We need to move fast, or they'll deplete our food supply."

Are you fucking kidding me? This kid just scared the shit out of me. When did he start using words like "deplete" and what kind of ants are these? I imagined walking into a scene from War of the Worlds and was relieved to find two tiny ants crawling on my counter which I smooshed with my thumb. Problem solved. Thank God I got to them before our food was depleted.

CHAPTER 43

That summer was lame. We didn't go on any camping trips, and we always went on at least three or four each summer to some of our favorite places. Our pop-up camper had seen better days, but it was comfortable, and we loved taking the kids on adventures in it. We often teamed up with Shawn and Becky and their crew for a weekend camping extravaganza. There had been a plan to go to Yellowstone that summer, but instead, we settled for daily trips to the Tumor Cooker. I could tell that Bryan was getting frustrated with the fatigue that accompanied radiation therapy, which prevented us from doing much. He had been down the past few weeks, and I wanted to do something to cheer him up.

The perfect plan started to take shape because of the group I affectionately referred to as The Jeep Guys. I was often chastised for this since not all of them had Jeeps, but it was a group of guys with big trucks that liked to go off-roading together and talk about the dirt they got on their vehicles. They would look at the dirt, admire the dirt, talk about other places there was dirt, and then take pictures of each other driving on the dirt. Of course, it was more about the camaraderie than it was actually about the dirt, but I loved to tease them about it. One of them had gotten in touch with me about wanting to get a group together to surprise Bryan with some Jeep love. It slowly evolved into a surprise party on the 4th of July to help him remember what it was that he was fighting for. I invited a few of our other friends who weren't part of The Jeep Guys but knew the extra faces would make the party even better.

I spent a week quietly cleaning up the house and the yard and making small changes I hoped weren't noticed. I made hamburger patties in secret and stored them in the bottom of the vegetable drawer of the fridge. I had hamburger buns hidden under the bed. I had bought paper plates and soda and had them stored around the house, hoping he wouldn't see.

The day of the party was a gorgeous day. The plan was for everyone to meet up at Menards near our house and then pull into the neighborhood like a little Jeep parade to surprise him. The problem was that I had to figure out a way to get Bryan outside at the right moment.

Bryan came down the stairs to find me cleaning up the kitchen. "Hey, honey? I'm going to go for a Jeep drive. It's a beautiful day out, and I took the doors and top off."

Oh shit! He wants to leave, and the party is starting in 20 minutes. "Umm…. Could you just wait a little bit? I need some help first."

"What do you need help with?"

"Umm…. I wanted to …. Umm…. I wanted to clean the grill."

"Ok. Well, do you really need my help with that?"

"Yeah, uhhh…. Bailey is coming over with Mac."

"Ok, I'll be back in a little bit. I just really want to go for a ride. I haven't been on one in a while, and I'm feeling pretty good today."

"Yeah, but Bailey is coming. Could you just wait?"

"For Bailey?"

"Yeah."

"Why?"

"I don't know. Because she's coming over to see us. She should be here soon, so could you wait?"

"I've met Bailey before. She's here all the time. I'll see her when I get back."

"No, I need you to help me carry those chair cushions to the back yard."

"I already did that. Seriously, Jen. I'm just going to be gone for a little while."

"No. I need you to wait until Bailey gets here."

"What the hell? I just want to go on a quick Jeep drive. I haven't felt good in weeks, and I actually feel good enough to get out of the house a little."

"Well, I could go with you? If you just wait until I finish cleaning the grill?"

"Seriously? Fine ... whatever. I'll wait for fucking Bailey to get here who I see like every other day. I'm going to go lay down."

He walked away with stompy feet, and I was stuck in a predicament. I had pissed him off enough that he was now up in our room pouting and I needed to get him outside in a few more minutes. I was going to have to enlist the help of the kids.

"Owen!" I whispered for some help. "I need you to go outside and pretend like you need to show Dad something."

"Well, what am I showing him?"

"Nothing, you just need to pretend.

"Well, should I go make something to show him?

"No, buddy. We don't have that kind of time."

"Haley, you go stand watch for the Jeep parade."

"I'm on it!" She ran outside to stand guard. Haley loved the excitement of the party and was all about pulling a surprise out for Bryan to help him feel better. His cancer had hit her pretty hard and she had really pitched in to make things work the past few weeks.

Owen piped up, "Should I go make a fort?"

"What?"

"So that I have something to show him. I could make a fort for us."

"No, honey. I just need you to pretend so that dad goes outside. Don't worry about it, bud. I'll just figure something out."

Just then I got a text message from Bailey that the Jeep parade was starting. They would be to our house in a few minutes. I needed to get Bryan outside.

"Bryan! Could you come here?"

"No. I'm resting."

"Honey, I need you to come down here. Owen wants to show you something."

"I'll see it later. I'm not coming down."

I walked up the stairs and found him lying on our bed, arms crossed, flat on his back. "Could you please come downstairs? I want to show you something outside."

"No. I'm not coming. I wanted to go on a Jeep drive, and I have to stay and see Bailey. Seriously. I'm not coming down."

"Bryan, you are acting like a child."

"I don't care."

Just then I got another text message from Bailey that they were turning the corner to come down the street. "Bryan, stop acting like a child. Get out of bed and walk down the stairs."

"Fine. Whatever. I've met Bailey before."

"Yes, I know that. Get your ass downstairs."

We walked outside just in time. As Bryan walked out the front door, 20 vehicles pulled up in front of the house honking their horns and yelling out their windows.

"What the hell is this?" There was a look of confusion on his face. "Hey, that's Larry! What's going on? Is that Greg? Why are Jess and Alanna here? And Josh?" All our friends started jumping out of their vehicles and walked up to the house with smiles on their faces. Lawn chairs started coming out of the backs of their vehicles, coolers full of drinks were carried up to the house. There were platters of food in hand, and a few lawn games were brought out. People congregated in our driveway all while Bryan still had a stunned look on his face.

"Did you do this?" He turned and looked at me, grinning from ear to ear.

"I had a little help from The Jeep Guys."

"Oh my gosh! I can't believe this. I'm in complete shock!"

As the group gathered, I told the story of my husband having a toddler-sized tantrum when he wasn't allowed to go drive his Jeep just 20 minutes before the party was supposed to start. Everyone laughed and razzed him a little about listening to his wife and we got the party started. The grill was fired up, the music was turned on, and tables were put out with all the food that people had brought. We had an amazing party for him with people laughing, telling stories, playing games and eating lots of food. It was perfect.

Later that night, after Bryan got to drive his Jeep to the 4th of July fireworks, he admitted that he really needed the escape that the party gave him. He had been feeling down the past few weeks like he never got out to see anyone or do anything other than go to radiation appointments, back to work and then to sleep. This was a medicine that wasn't prescribed by any doctor but one that had healing benefits that couldn't be described. It kicked his fight back into gear and reminded him about the joys of living.

Chapter 44

Bryan finished his radiation appointments in early August and we took a much-needed weekend away to Duluth for some rest and relaxation. Luckily, my Aunt Kay lived in Duluth and we could sit on her lakeshore for hours, talking and throwing rocks into the water. The area was always deserted so we were able to get some quiet time to ourselves.

As we were sitting there, enjoying the sunshine, the solitude, and the sound of the waves, I hesitantly asked him, "Do you think it worked?"

"I don't know. I'm cautious, but I'm hoping it did something."

"Me too. I'm just worried that it spread. You've been so tired lately. I'm worried that the chemo and radiation weren't enough."

"Well, all we can do is wait and hear what he says next week."

"I'm so exhausted living the cancer life. I know I'm not the one who actually has cancer, but I'm tired all the time just trying to manage all of it and the school year hasn't even started yet. I can't imagine how tired I'll be once I have lesson plans and grading and parent meetings to deal with. I can barely keep my eyes open most of the time as it is. I just hope it actually did something and we can get a little break."

"Yeah, me too." He paused for a moment. "Wanna see who can throw their rock the farthest?"

"I'll kick your ass."

"You've never beat me before."

"Yeah, but now you're all cancery and shit and the radiation has weakened you. It's my opportunity to win. I gotta find a good rock that can get some distance."

"Loser buys the ice cream?"

"Let's do it. 1….2….3!" For the first time ever, I beat him, and he bought the ice cream.

CHAPTER 45

The next week Bryan went in for a scan to see if the radiation had done anything. We were both nervous about what we would hear. A few days later, we were in the office waiting patiently for Dr. Laudi.

"Hello! How are you both doing?"

"Great! Hopefully great. Are we great?" Bryan was as nervous as I had ever seen him. He had been through so much; we were just hoping that we'd hear some good news.

"Yes. You are great. Your scans are clean."

We looked at each other. With disbelief in his voice, he asked, "What? Completely clean? It's gone?"

"It's gone, or at least it appears that it's gone. When I compare the scan from February with the scan from last week, I can see where your tumor used to be, and when I look at that same spot, there is no tumor."

"So, the radiation got rid of it? Are you fu….uhhhh…. Are you kidding me?" He was thrilled to hear this news, and I was speechless, which is something that didn't happen to me often.

Dr. Laudi had a big smile on his face as he gave us the news. "Yes, it looks as though the radiation did the job. Now, let me explain it to you like this. You clean your floor so it's spotless. You use all your best cleaners because your mother-in-law is coming over. She comes in and looks at your floor, and you say it's spotless. How can you prove to your mother in law that there is not one speck of dust on that floor? You can't. In other words, there could be microscopic parts of the disease left. But right now, we would call this NED or no evidence of disease. We would consider you to be in complete remission."

I typically never stop talking. I always had an opinion to share. I had a snipey come back for everything. I embraced sarcasm like a beloved toy, and I was speechless. It was the best news we could have heard. I looked at Dr. Laudi as we got up to leave and could only say, "Thank you." It looked as though he was going to be part of the 9% and we were hopeful it would stay that way.

Bryan and I walked out, and the smiles on both our faces were from ear to ear. It was better news than we could have hoped for. We knew that he would need to come back frequently for check-ups and blood work to make sure his cancer didn't come back, but this was amazing news. It was like a giant weight had lifted, and I could tell that he felt free. We took the kids out to celebrate at a local restaurant that had great cheeseburgers, video games, and laser tag. For the first time in months, Bryan played laser tag with Owen like he was a kid again. He was running, assuming his sniper position and acting like a fool as he dodged Owen's attacks. I came in last, only slightly behind Haley. She and I had no hope of winning, but laser tag had always been something our family did together, and that night, we played with giant smiles on our faces. For the first time in a very long time, we were playing without Death trying to play against us.

PART 5

BREAK ON ME

Finally, I was able to squeak out,
"Bryan? I'm scared."
He was instantly across the room,
holding me as the tears came to my eyes.

CHAPTER 46

In December of that year, I went in and got my first mammogram. Bryan's remission had made me very aware of how important it was to advocate for my own health. My doctor had been on my case about getting a mammogram for a year or two. Since I'd always been healthy, I had been putting it off. I did regular breast exams and had never felt anything weird or concerning. After the scare with Bryan, I knew that advocating for your own health was an important piece of staying alive.

I went in for the appointment, not knowing exactly what to expect. When she came and got me from the waiting room, the nurse was wearing her winter jacket. I thought that was weird, but hey, some people get chilly easily. She brought me through the whole clinic and out the back door. *Where the hell are we going?* Outside was the Boob-Mobile. I think it had a nicer name than that, but all I could think about was the little Bookmobile that would show up at the end of our road when I was a child that you could check out library books from. This seemed like the same thing, but for boobs.

I was brought inside and was pleasantly surprised that it was quite warm. With the nurse bundled up like she was walking into a sub-zero blizzard, my nipples had started tightening up just thinking about it. I was given the lay of the land and told to undress from the waist up. The tech that performed my mammogram was wonderful and didn't make it feel weird at all as they smashed my boob into the giant boob press.

As I was about to leave, she said, "I want you to remember that the doctors don't have anything to compare your results to so if you get a 'second look' appointment, don't be freaked out. It just means there's a questionable area, but it could be anything. It does not always mean it's cancer."

I appreciated this bit of advice and tried not to worry about it. The next week I got a call saying that my results came back fine and there was no need to go back in even for the second look. My mammogram was clean, and I was relieved.

CHAPTER 47

Since my mom's cancer had developed at a fairly young age, I had always heard about this mythical "cancer gene" that she had told me about. She had mentioned that several people in our family had gotten cancer, and my grandmother died from ovarian cancer a few years after my mom. I did some digging on the issue and found out that there really were certain genes that made a person more likely to get certain types of cancer. I made an appointment with my doctor so I could get the needed referral to get genetic testing done.

The day of my appointment was routine. I was asked a lot of questions about my family health history to determine which type of test was needed. When did your mother die? What did she die of? Is your father still living? Do you have any siblings? How did your grandparents die and at what age? It was pretty routine stuff. I was told that my results would take a few weeks, and I set up an appointment for a follow-up to get the results and then completely put the entire experience out of my mind.

In the middle of February, I was taking a minute to just breathe after all the craziness that had been going on in our house the past few weeks. Haley had gotten her tonsils out, Bryan still had follow-up appointments to go to, Owen had activities he needed to be driven to; things were crazy at home and there weren't enough of me to make sure everyone got where they needed to be. I decided to sit down and just let my brain breathe for a minute when suddenly, I remembered that I had missed my follow up appointment with the genetic counselor. *Crap! I hope they don't charge me for that appointment since I was a no show.* I decided to call and clear things up.

"Hi, I had a follow-up appointment last week and I completely forgot to go to it."

"Do you want to reschedule it?"

"No, not really. It's just to get some test results and I don't want to have to take more time off work if they're just going to tell me there's nothing wrong with me."

"Ok, could I get your name and date of birth?" I gave her the pertinent information to pull up my chart, and she looked for the name of the doctor I had seen back in January.

"Ok, let me see if the doctor is available to talk to you. She can advise you what to do." I waited patiently to be transferred to the genetic counselor I had met with a month ago.

"Hello, this is Linnea."

"Hi, this is Jennifer Monahan. I was supposed to have a follow-up appointment with you to get some test results. I completely forgot about it. I'm so sorry. I really don't want to take another day off work just for you to tell me I'm fine, so could you just give me my test results over the phone?"

"Let me pull up your chart here. Monahan? Ok, I've got you here. We do like to see patients come into the office so we can discuss the results with them."

"I completely understand that, but if you're just going to tell me I'm fine, I really don't want to take another day off of work."

"I do have some appointments later in the day if that would work better for you."

"I have to get home to my son right after work so someone's there when he gets off the bus. Can't you just give me my results over the phone? It seems like a long way out of my way to just be told that I'm fine."

"Well, we really do prefer to see patients in the office when we give test results."

Wait a minute.... Maybe I'm not fine. "Uhhhhh.... You're not going to tell me I'm fine, are you? Did my results come back with something bad?"

"Well...." She hesitated for several moments and finally said, "I can give you the results over the phone if you're sure you're ok with that. I just want to make sure you know you can come in if you'd like to. I'd be happy to go over everything in person."

"Yes, please give them to me over the phone."

The doctor went on to explain that I had the BRCA-1 gene mutation. This gave me a 65% chance of getting breast cancer and nearly 70% chance of getting ovarian cancer. She further explained that they'd like to put me on a high-risk protocol for both ovarian and breast cancers which would mean I got ultrasounds of my ovaries and a mammogram every six months.

"Well, luckily, I just had a mammogram, so I'm not worried about that."

"That's good. Let's get you set up for an ultrasound to make sure everything is ok there."

I called Bryan to tell him about it. "Well, it sounds like they have a good plan to keep an eye on everything."

"Yeah, I'm not so worried about my breasts. I do regular self-exams. I've never felt anything funky when I was doing those, and I just had a mammogram, so I'm more worried about my ovaries, especially since that's what my mom and grandma died from."

"Ok, so what's the scoop? How do they monitor you?"

I told him about the high-risk protocol and we both agreed that it seemed like a reasonable plan to keep monitoring me.

"They said when I'm done having babies, I should have a complete hysterectomy."

"Ok. That makes sense."

"Are we done having babies?"

"Uhhhh…. Yeah. I think we passed that window a while ago."

"Cool. We'll save money on tampons!

"Awesome. Does that mean I can finally get that winch for the Jeep?"

"How much do you think tampons actually cost?"

CHAPTER 48

I was able to get an appointment the next day to see my favorite dildo look alike: the vaginal ultrasound. The results all came back normal, which put my mind at ease a little bit. The next week I went in to meet with Dr. Case at the University of Minnesota who would be explaining to me about the additional testing I needed. She was very thorough with me and explained the different ways that breast cancer can manifest itself. I had always assumed it was just a lump that I was looking for, but there were also other signs such as dimpling, fullness, tender breasts, and so on.

"Have you noticed any changes?"

"No, not really. Well, I guess my boobs have been a little sore lately, but they always get sore when I'm about to get my period. I'm pretty excited to get that hysterectomy! One less thing to deal with every month."

"Exactly! Go ahead and move up to the table, and I'll do a quick breast exam."

I jumped onto the table and explained, as I always do, how ticklish I am so she should be prepared for me to jump a lot. While she was doing the exam on my left side she asked if I had been sore or tender on that side.

"Yeah, but I really think it's just my period. It happens every month."

She wanted me to have a breast MRI done just to be safe and as part of the protocol she was putting me on. She explained the procedure and brought me to the front desk to make an appointment for the breast MRI.

I've gotten MRI's before. I've never particularly enjoyed them, but they've never been a big deal. You lay on a table. They move you into the tube. You lie still. It's over. A breast MRI is the most uncomfortable thing I had ever done in my life up to that point.

I arrived at my appointment at the breast center full of cheer and optimism. *This should be no big deal. A quick little picture of my boobs so they have a comparison for future scans. No biggie!*

I was brought into a little changing room that looked like the lounge room at a spa. I was told to undress and put on one of the robes that were available. It was very tranquil and relaxing. There were little potted plants, diffusers showering the room in pleasant smells, the lights were dim, and soft music was playing in the background. I forgot that I was somewhere called "The Breast Center."

A nurse eventually came to get me for the big event. It wasn't like a normal MRI. First, you lay face down on the table and there are two holes you're supposed to put your boobs in. The table is kind of at an angle, so as you're lying there, there's a metal bar that's supporting you. Because your boobs are in the holes, you're putting all your weight on your sternum, which is incredibly uncomfortable. There was a little pillow in the middle of the table similar to what you would see on a massage table. I was asked to put my hands above my head and lie as still as possible as they moved me into the machine.

The nurses and technicians were wonderful about telling me what was going to happen. "We're going to start in just a minute, Jennifer. You'll hear the machine making a lot of noises and then I need to try not to move around a lot. We'll get a better image if you stay relatively still."

I was slowly moved into the MRI machine, and soon I heard it start whirring and thumping. Err Err Err Err…. I tried my best to lay very still, but it eventually started getting hot in there. My face was still smooshed into the pillow. *Ok, don't move. Try and lay still. This will be over soon.* Err err err… The machine kept going. Occasionally, the MRI overlord would come on a speaker like the Wizard of Oz. "You're doing great, Jennifer! We've just got one more scan."

For the love of God! My nose itches. I now had sweat dripping down my face I couldn't itch away because I was supposed to be lying still. The bar I was laying on was digging into my breastbone, and my arms were starting to cramp from laying with them up over my head for so long. Err err err….

"Excuse me? Are we almost done? My arms are starting to cramp and my face itches."

"We need you to lay very still if you can. We're on the last scan. It will be just a few more minutes."

Ok… a few more minutes. Count. It was a way I had always distracted myself. If I knew I had to wait a certain number of minutes, I would count slowly and distract myself by trying to time it out to the amount of time they said. I started counting in my head.

1….2….3…. I finally counted to eight minutes and asked again, "I'm really uncomfortable. Are we almost done?"

The scans were over shortly after that. I was moved out of the machine and was told someone would contact me with the results in the next couple of days.

The very next day, I received a phone call, which I enthusiastically answered. "Hello?"

"Is this Jennifer?"

"Yes, it is!"

"This is Julia From the U of M breast center." *That was quick! They really know how to treat a girl at the boob spa.*

"The doctor took a look at the results from your MRI, and he'd like you to come in for a biopsy."

"Oh… why?"

"Well, there's a spot on your MRI that looked suspicious, so the doctor would like to get a biopsy."

"Oh…. uhhhhh…. A spot? Like a bad spot?"

"At this point, we just want to confirm this area from your MRI on your left breast. I have appointments available tomorrow if you're able to come in?"

"Ok…. ummmm…… I teach classes in the morning. Could I come in the afternoon?"

"Absolutely!" We got a time set up, and that night I took off all my clothes and looked at myself in the mirror. *Ok, what was it that Dr. Case had said? It's not always a lump? Where was that stupid card she had given me that showed all the boobs on it?* It had different pictures of what breast cancer can look like in different women.

"Bryan?" I yelled to him from the bathroom.

"Yeah?"

"Have you seen my boob card?"

"What?"

"My boob card. It was on the seat of the car, and I brought it in and put it in the mail basket. I'm trying to compare my boobs to the boobs on the boob card."

"Sounds like a fun card. Want me to help??" Since he'd gone into remission, the sexuality had slowly returned to our marriage. He was much friskier and clearly had more energy than he had in the past year.

"Actually, yeah. Come here and feel my boob."

"Cool!" He walked into the bathroom and found me standing like Superman with my hands on my hips and no shirt on.

"Does one of them feel bigger to you?"

He grabbed both my boobs and made a honking noise because he thought he was funny. I laughed and said, "Seriously? Are you 12? I honestly want you to tell me. Does one of them look or feel bigger?

"I suppose so, but aren't boobs like feet? One of them is always slightly bigger?"

"I don't think so. I don't know. I've never noticed it. The doctor wants me to come in for a biopsy tomorrow afternoon. There was something that showed up on my MRI that they want to look at."

"Oh." He sat down on the edge of the bathtub and looked at me.

"I'm guessing it's nothing. When I had my mammogram, the lady told me that when they don't have a baseline comparison, they're always a little more careful."

"But don't you have a baseline with the mammogram?"

"Yeah, but that's a mammogram. This was an MRI." I had no idea if that was true, but I was trying to rationalize why they wanted me to come back in because there was no way I could have breast cancer. It would be an unthinkable cruel joke for me to get breast cancer when Bryan had just gone into remission. Bryan seemed to go along with this idea and gave my boobs one more squeeze as he walked out the door.

CHAPTER 49

The next day I went to my appointment for the biopsy with the same enthusiasm I previously had. I couldn't imagine that this could be breast cancer. I'd had enough cancer in my life, so I figured this had to be something else. The doctor explained the breast biopsy procedure. They would numb my boob and then using ultrasound would take several samples in the area that they had seen on the MRI.

"Cool. Sounds like a good plan." I accidentally got a look at the needle they would use for the biopsy and I nearly had a panic attack right there. It was a big ass needle! I focused my attention on the ultrasound rather than looking at the devices they were going to use. After years of trying to get pregnant and weekly ultrasounds for that process, I felt like I was pretty good at understanding what I was seeing on ultrasound. The doctor found the area he was looking for and put a marker in so they could find it more easily in the future.

Wow! They are really taking good care of me! I guess this BRCA-1 gene is a bigger deal than I thought it was.

The doctor explained what he was going to do. He would insert the needle into the area he was targeting. I would hear a click as he took a core sample of the breast tissue he was looking at. He said they would try and get five or six samples so they could look at them under the microscope.

I could see the needle go in on the ultrasound screen and then "CLICK!" It startled me and made me jump.

"I'm sorry. The noise scared me."

"It's ok. Just try and lay still on this next one."

Ok, focus your attention on the screen. There's the needle…. Prepare for the click. "CLICK!" And once again, I jumped.

"I'm sorry. I don't know why I can't figure out that noise is about to happen."

"How about if I count, '1….2…. 3' and then say 'click' when I'm about to click it?"

"Yeah, let's try that."

That process seemed to work a little better, and I was able to stay still for the remainder of the core samples they were taking.

After the procedure was over, and they had removed several biopsy samples, I sat up and the doctor explained what would happen from there. Another doctor would look at the samples and get back to me with the results.

"Ok. That sounds good. Should I be worried?"

"If these results were to come back negative, we would assume it was a false reading, and we would redo the test while you were in the breast MRI so we could be more precise with the biopsy."

Oh, shit. Did he just say I was going to have to go back into the breast MRI machine? That thing is my nemesis. I hate that thing. Wait…. What did he just say?

"Wait… what?"

"The area in your breast is highly suspicious for breast cancer. I would assume that the results would show it is. If we received a negative result, we would want to take a closer look at the area, and the only way to do that is by performing the biopsy under MRI so we can pinpoint the area more precisely."

Did he just say I have breast cancer? "No… I just had a mammogram. It didn't show anything."

"There are several types of cancer that don't present as a lump. This is more of a thickening of the breast tissue, so it doesn't show up well on a mammogram. We'll know more once we have the results from the biopsy."

The doctor left the room, and the nurse told me I could get dressed as she was going over some information on what to expect in the next few days. There would be some bruising. It might be tender after the numbing medication wore off. My head was spinning, and I needed to talk to Bryan. I wasn't even focusing on what she was saying about the giant bruise that was about to show up on my boob. *Breast cancer. No. That can't be right. I don't have breast cancer. Bryan had pancreatic cancer, but he's in remission. We couldn't both have cancer. That's too many kinds of fucked up to be real.*

I got to the car and immediately called Bryan. I explained to him what they said.

"Are you fucking kidding me? So, you have breast cancer?"

"I guess… I don't know…. They didn't say that I did, but they said that the area they biopsied was pretty classic looking breast cancer. I just don't think that could be right."

"Well, let's wait until we get the results and see what they say."

"Ok…. I'm going to get home to Owen. Haley is there with him now and I'm sure she's ignoring him. I'll see you when you get home."

That night Bryan and I didn't talk about it at all. We just carried on with our activities as though everything was normal. I didn't sleep well that night, but the next day I was back at work as though nothing was different.

CHAPTER 50

I received a call two days later handing down the verdict: Invasive lobular carcinoma. The doctor who did my biopsy had been right. This was the kind of breast cancer that doesn't form a lump, so it was lucky I had gone for my breast MRI when I did. The fact that my left boob had been sore and slightly larger than the other one for some time was an indication it had been growing for a while.

The nurse further explained that my breast cancer was ER / PR positive and HER2 negative. It meant that my specific type of cancer feeds on estrogen and progesterone, so I would likely begin taking a medication that blocked those hormones. She said that someone would contact me about setting up an appointment with a surgeon and an oncologist, but it looked as though a mastectomy was in my future.

This posed a huge problem for me. In times of crisis, I go into a particular mode. I become the planner, the scheduler, the researcher, and the protector. As Bryan liked to call me, I'm a chicken hawk when it comes to other people's illnesses, but this was me. This was my crisis and my illness. I didn't know how to handle the situation.

I went to work the next day and tried to keep my mind off the vile mass growing in my boob until I was able to get a plan in place. I didn't want to wait. I knew how important it was to move quickly as I did with Bryan's cancer. Now it was my own cancer, and I needed to be proactive and push to get this taken care of. I called Dr. Laudi's office and left a message with Lacey. I'd talked to her enough times over the past year about Bryan, so I felt like I knew her pretty well. I received a return call when I was in the middle of class. and I didn't want my students to know what was going on yet. Luckily, I had just assigned them to a group activity, so they were busy talking amongst themselves and were most likely not paying any attention to me.

"Hey, Jen. It's Lacey. What's going on?"

"Hey Lacey, I'm in the middle of a class surrounded by middle school kids, so I need you to catch what I'm throwing down without me having to say it."

"Ummm… ok."

"I found out I have BRCA-1 so I went and had an MRI that showed a spot which I had biopsied. The biopsy didn't come back the way I wanted it to. I need a surgeon, a reconstructive surgeon, and Dr. Laudi's services. Can you help me out?"

"I got ya, Jen. Are we talking about breast cancer?"

"Yes."

"Ok, we would normally send people to Dr. Harrison, who is upstairs in our building. She will have a plastic surgeon she routinely works with that she can refer you to. I'll have scheduling get in touch with you, and we'll get you in to see Dr. Laudi."

"Perfect. Thank you, Lacey."

"I've got you, Jen. Don't worry."

I hung up and felt better that the beginnings of a plan were in place. Lacey and Dr. Laudi had never let me down when it came to Bryan, so I knew they had my back when it was my turn to be the patient.

During the last class of the day when I had prep time, I was called to the principal's office to meet with him and one of the assistant principals. This was the time of year when they started staffing for next year. I had to the school two years earlier, and I wasn't worried about my performance. I had consistently had good observations, and I got along well with the other people in my department. My mind wasn't really focused on what was happening at school, but I knew I was still doing a good job. If anything, going to school and working with my students was a nice escape from the other chaos that was happening in my life right now.

"Hi, Jennifer. Come on in and have a seat." I assumed we would be going over the results of my last observation and then discussing what kinds of classes I would like to teach next year.

"We think you've done a great job this year. I know you've got a lot of things happening in your personal life and you've done a good job of putting those things to the side. Unfortunately, we're going to have to probationary cut you. Our numbers have changed for next year, and we'll be eliminating your position."

I just sort of stared at him, stunned at what I was hearing. *This can't possibly be happening.* I hadn't told anyone about my breast cancer diagnosis because I had only found out the day before, but this couldn't come at a worse time.

"Wow... Ok ... well ... am I still eligible to apply for other positions in the district?"

"Of course. Just let me know if you'd like me to make a call for you or give you a letter of recommendation. We'd love to have you stay, but our numbers are just going to be different and, unfortunately, you have the least seniority of all the teachers in your department."

"Ok. Ummm ... yeah, a letter of recommendation would be great. I'd really appreciate that."

I walked out of the room and back to my classroom and was completely stunned. The school district had excellent health insurance, and I was not looking forward to having to job hunt when I was going to be getting my boobs cut off soon. I needed to slow down and take this one step at a time.

I called Bryan at work and let him know. "Hey, you busy?"

"Nope. What's up?"

"I just got cut from my position for next year."

"Are you fucking kidding me?"

"No. Their numbers for next year have changed, and I'm low man on the totem pole, so I'm out."

"Wow. Are you ok?"

"Yeah, I guess. I'll find another job. I was just hoping to be able to concentrate on one thing at a time, but I guess not. I'll start looking for a new position. I'm not worried about finding a job for next year. Special ed teachers are always needed. It's just that all the good jobs will be posting soon, and I'll need to start applying for them when I should be worried about breast cancer."

"I'm sorry, honey. I know you liked it there."

"Yeah, I have some pretty awesome students here. I'm going to miss them, but I guess there's not much I can do about it."

"Want me to make you dinner tonight?"

"I appreciate you trying to make me feel better, but I don't think cereal is what I need right now."

"I was going to order pizza."

"If that's what you consider 'making dinner' then, if my cancer doesn't turn out the way we want it to, I need you to remarry quickly after I'm gone. The children will starve."

He laughed because he knew it was true. "You going to be ok?"

"Yeah, I'll be fine. I always land on my feet. I just didn't want the added distraction. I'll talk to you about it tonight. See you at home."

. . . . .

I had regularly updated people on Bryan's cancer using Facebook. We kept our posts straightforward and optimistic and continued throwing in Star Wars references, including, at one point, comparing Bryan to Han Solo being encased in carbonite. Keeping our sense of humor was what had continued to propel us through the difficult parts of his cancer. That night, Bryan looked at me and said, "You want to do an update?"

"There's nothing to update. Your scans have been coming back clean. Maybe after your next blood work I will."

"Ok, but I'm not talking about me. I'm talking about you."

"Why?" I couldn't figure out what he was referring to at first, and then it hit me. "Oh, because I have breast cancer?" It still felt surreal to say it out loud.

"Yeah, you deserve to have the same amount of support I did. Besides, some of those hot dishes were really good. Maybe people will bring us food again!"

"I can make you a hot dish. I don't need people bringing us food."

"Right. Except that you're going to be having surgery to remove your breasts and the kids and I might want to eat while you're recovering."

"I'll still be able to cook. It will be fine."

"You just sit and think on that for a while and decide whether that seems realistic."

I realized he was right, so I sat down and found the courage to write a Facebook post that updated people on what was going on with me. It felt weird, but even if I didn't need people making a fuss over me, Bryan and the kids still needed some support while I was out of commission getting my boobs removed. I sat down and posted about the continued drama that seemed to follow us around.

For the past year and a half, you've all been listening to me ramble on about Bryan's cancer status.... whether he's eating, his tumor marker levels, how much weight he's lost.... all the good stuff. Well, now it's my turn.

Many of you know that I recently tested positive for the BRCA-1 gene mutation. After hearing this, I stepped things into high gear and started my due diligence and high-risk testing schedule. I had my blood drawn, had an ultrasound to check for ovarian cancer, and got a breast MRI.... possibly the most uncomfortable thing I've ever done up to this point in my life. Unfortunately, they found a spot on my MRI that I had biopsied and the results were what the doctors expected; breast cancer... Invasive Lobular Carcinoma. I'm scheduled with a surgeon for this Friday to get a bilateral mastectomy on the books and am meeting with oncology on Tuesday. (Silver lining.... they suck fat out of your stomach when they reconstruct your breasts, so that's a plus! I'll have a skinny waist and a killer rack!)

Bryan and I are not sure why the universe has chosen us as the ass end of its cruel joke... I mean, really, what are the odds of both parents in a family getting cancer at the same time? I refuse to dwell on the Why Me aspect of this, though.

My family doesn't function well without me. I once went to the mailbox and stopped to talk to the neighbor for five minutes and when I came in, all three of them were in a little line needing me for something, so I won't let this keep me down for long.

I have confidence that this has been caught early and some Heavenly intervention came from my mother, as this type of breast cancer is difficult to pick up on mammogram.... it doesn't form a lump. It's more of a "thickening," so the BRCA status combined with the MRI is how they found it. I may have to rely on Bryan to do my Facebook updates for a while, but I'll make him promise to throw in some Star Wars references. I apologize in advance for his lack of witty analogies and underlying sarcasm.

I hit submit and let the world in on my secret. I hated it being out there, but I knew that Bryan was right. The messages and comments started pouring in from people as dismayed as we were that this could be happening. Bryan and I had vowed to maintain our sense of humor through his cancer and we would through mine. I've always been uncomfortable with mushy stuff, so Dena nailed it when she sent me a message that simply said, "WTF?" accompanied by a clip of the Imperial Death March. She knew how to make me laugh through my fears, which is what I was determined to do.

CHAPTER 51

The next week I took a day off to go meet with my surgeon and Dr. Laudi. Dr. Harrison was incredibly thorough and very kind. She said she had done many of these surgeries, and I was completely confident in her abilities. She went through what the surgery would entail and talked to me about sentinel lymph nodes.

"We're going to inject some radioactive dye into you on the day of your surgery. While we're in surgery, the blood flow from your breast will go into what we call sentinel lymph nodes. This is the first place the blood flows, so if there is cancer in the lymph nodes, this would be where it would go first. We can tell which ones the sentinel lymph nodes are by using the dye they'll give you about an hour before your scheduled surgery time. Once I remove the sentinel lymph nodes, I'll have the pathologist look at them while you're still under. If he sees even one spec of cancer in any of them, I'll remove all the lymph nodes on that side. I'll do the same things on the other side."

"Ok. That makes sense. Will I be able to power the Flux Capacitor after they inject me with the radioactive dye?"

Bryan stepped in and corrected me. "That's plutonium. Radioactive material would more likely turn you into the Hulk."

"I think plutonium is radioactive, though. Isn't it?

"You might be right, but if we're talking about the Flux Capacitor, then you would specifically need Plutonium, not just any radioactive material. She's not injecting you with plutonium."

I nodded in agreement. "That's a good point. Nice catch, honey. Regardless, if the big lymph nodes have cancer, then there's the possibility it's spread to other areas, correct?"

The doctor had quietly watched us debate our nerdy superhero/time travel issue and seemed happy that we were back on track. "Correct. Because of your BRCA status, I would recommend that we take both breasts at that time. If we don't, it is likely that your cancer will come back in the other breast at some point."

"Yep. I agree. Take whatever body parts I don't need."

"Ok, I'm glad we agree on that. Let's talk about your nipples."

"My nipples?"

"Yes, I can do a nipple sparing procedure, but to be safe, I would recommend that we take your nipples, as well."

"You're going to remove my nipples. What will be there?" I looked at Bryan to gauge his reaction. How was he going to feel about a fake boobed, nippleless wife? He was listening intently and didn't seem phased by the nipple removal like I was.

"Well, you can talk to the plastic surgeon about that. They have different ways to give you new nipples, but I would recommend that to be safe, we take your nipples."

"Ok. I'm not going to have nipples. At least not functional ones."

"That's correct. Have you picked out a plastic surgeon yet?"

"No, I was hoping you had someone you could refer me to."

"Dr. Carlson is excellent. I've worked with him numerous times, and he operates at Mercy. I can have my scheduler coordinate with his office so we can get you in there sooner than later. If you have any questions, make sure you call. Sound good?"

"Yes, thank you. I appreciate you meeting with me so quickly."

She's going to remove my nipples. I'm losing both of my boobs, and now I'm not going to have any nipples. I don't know why this affected me so much, but it really upset me. I realized that nipples aren't all that useful after you're done having babies, but it was the idea that there would just be nothing there once the surgery was over and I had recovered. *What else could they take away from me?*

Next, we went to Dr. Laudi's office, which was a little surreal. We had done this routine with Bryan so many times, it felt strange to have the roles reversed. When our favorite nurse, Angel, brought us back, Bryan went to step on the scale as he had always done until we both realized we were there to have me looked at. I got to sit in the "good chair" this time, and Bryan sat in the uncomfortable "spouse chair" that I had spent the last year complaining about.

"That chair sucks, huh?"

"I'd rather have the patient chair only because then you wouldn't be going through this."

Angel made the "awwwww" response that Bryan was looking for and I rolled my eyes. *Kiss ass....*

Dr. Laudi came in a few minutes later and went through everything we knew. ER positive ... that's good. PR positive ... that's good. HER2 negative.... Also, good. He was going to do a test called an Oncotype that told them whether I would benefit from chemo or not. Essentially, it showed how likely my cancer was to come back after surgery, assuming they were able to get clean margins and cancer hadn't spread to my lymph nodes. He also set me up with a PET scan prior to surgery. I could tell that he was being thorough with me, and I appreciated that more than he could ever know.

I was able to get an appointment a few days later with the plastic surgeon Dr. Harrison had referred me to. He was the epitome of what you think of when you imagine a plastic surgeon. Good looking.... Cocky .... Liked the sound of his own voice.... But talented, thorough, and understanding. He went through all the options with me for reconstruction, and I was happy to hear that he could go straight to implant. I wouldn't have to have tissue expanders, which from what I had read, were pretty miserable. He told me they would place the implant after the surgeon was done removing all the breast tissue, and then I would have drains in for a few weeks after my surgery.

"What am I supposed to do with the drains? Drain them?"

"Yes. That's why they're called drains."

"How do I do that? And what do I drain into?"

"We'll explain it all to you once the drains are in place, but they're easy. You just squeeze a little bulb and the fluid that's building up will drain out."

"That sounds nasty."

"Nope. It will be great. You won't have any problems with it."

Dr. Carlson had an assistant who worked with him named Jillian that would handle most of my follow up care. I met her briefly that afternoon while he was discussing the procedure with me. My head was spinning with all the information, but one thing I picked up on was that every person who worked in that office was good looking. Maybe it's a cliché that people that work in a plastic surgeon's office are all pretty, but this office was full of the prettiest people I had ever met. It was finally like I really was in an episode of Grey's Anatomy. Dr. Carlson asked one of the pretty people to go get his "box of boobs," so I could see what the implants were like. She came in with a big box of implants for me to look at so I understood what would be going into my body.

He went through the different sizes and how he didn't know for sure what he would put in until he got in there on the day of surgery. I made it clear to him that my boobs had gotten much larger than I needed them to be after all the weight I gained, and had still not lost, while I was pregnant with Owen. I suggested that a smaller volume would be perfectly fine with me and my boob grabbing husband.

We talked a little about nipples and, although I would have to wait a few months for my incisions to heal, he could eventually make me new, origami nipples. He explained how they use the equivalent of a cookie cutter to make areolas and then fold and tuck the existing skin to make non-functioning, look-alike nipples. As freaked out as I was to be losing the little item that made my boob feel like a boob, no one would know when I was cold by looking at my chest ever again. After a little more discussion of my procedure and recovery time, I went home to make dinner for my family as though nothing strange had happened that day.

CHAPTER 52

My surgery was scheduled for April 18. I finally let my school know that I had breast cancer and would be gone for anywhere from three to six weeks depending on how my recovery went and the extent of my cancer once they got in there. They assured me I had nothing to worry about, and my classes would be covered while I was out.

The day of my surgery finally came, and I was nervous, but I put on a good show for the kids that morning. I got them both off to school, told them I loved them and squeezed them each 10 different times. Bryan and I had a little time before we had to leave for the hospital, so I puttered around the house and took a couple of last looks at my nipples just to remember what they looked like. It finally hit me while I was standing and looking at myself in the mirror. *I have breast cancer.* It was so easy to forget about the severity of what was going on when I spent all my time planning and researching. It had more of a job feeling to it that way, and I was smart enough to realize that I had returned to the method of avoidance I had used after my mom died. But, standing naked in front of the mirror, looking at the body I had known for 45 years and realizing it was about to completely change hit me like a ton of bricks. I was scared. What if something went wrong during surgery? What if the cancer was more extensive than what they thought? What if I die?

I walked out of the bathroom. Bryan was sitting in the living room, playing a game on his phone, and I just looked at him for several moments from the top of the steps. Finally, I was able to choke out, "Bryan?" He looked up at me. "I'm scared." And the flood gates opened. He was across the room, holding me as the tears came to my eyes.

"It's ok. Everything is going to be ok. I'm going to be there with you."

"But what if something goes wrong?"

"It won't. Your doctor is talented. She's done these hundreds of times before. "

"I'm not going to have nipples anymore."

"I know. Nipples are overrated."

"What if I'm left one boobed because they can't do the reconstruction?"

"Symmetry is overrated, too. You'll be beautiful no matter what."

"I know it's just my boobs. It's not like I'm having heart surgery or brain surgery or something, but things go wrong in surgery. There was an episode of Grey's Anatomy…."

"You're not on Grey's Anatomy."

"Yeah, but in this one episode…."

"The character who was played by an actor died. I get it. You're not going to die. We need you too much. You're too important to us for anything to happen to you."

"Promise me that if something happens, you'll take care of the kids?"

"I promise."

"And you won't let Haley go live with Darryl? She can stay living here?"

"She's my daughter. She's not going anywhere."

"Promise me you'll make them more than cereal for dinner?"

"I can't promise that, but I'll try. I'll make reservations."

"You're not funny. I have notebooks for each of the kids that have letters I wrote to them. Owen's is green and Haley's is purple. I have them in the drawer on my side of the bed."

"How did I know you would write them letters? I'll make sure they get them if anything happens, but nothing is going to happen."

"You don't watch Grey's Anatomy. You don't know."

"Ok." He kissed my forehead. "You ready to get going?"

"Yeah, I'm ready."

CHAPTER 53

B ryan drove me to the hospital, and we listened to Eye of the Tiger on the way there to prepare to kick cancer's ass. Eye of the Tiger was the fight song we used anytime we needed to get pumped up to tackle a difficult task or we needed courage to accomplish something. I always had Haley listen to it before basketball tournaments, and it had become a tradition over the years. There was an unfortunate incident when she was about to shoot a free throw, and I made a classic "Oh my gosh! Is that your mom?" kind of move. The ref had just handed her the ball, the gym had gone silent, and I yelled, "Eye of the tiger, baby! You got this. Eye of the tiger." She looked over at me and slowly mouthed, "Shut ... up." Still, Eye of the Tiger meant we were ready to fight, and I knew that this was a time to fight.

We didn't stop at the mall to pick up any magazines on this trip. As we walked to the surgery check in area, he grabbed my hand and held it tight to let me know he was still there. As I waited to be called back, I made it clear to him that it would be silly for him to sit there for five hours while I was unconscious. When my dad arrived, I told him the same thing. While I appreciated the support, I didn't want them both just sitting there all day. I didn't have to be to the hospital until 10:00 and I wasn't able to eat anything that morning, so I made Bryan promise he would bring me a McMuffin when he brought the kids to visit me that night. They both left when I was called back, and I got to the business of getting my boobs and that nasty cancer removed.

There was a great deal of busy work to get me ready. I got undressed and placed my clothing in the little green bag that was provided. I had to wipe myself clean from neck to waist with a warm cloth that looked like it belonged on the bottom of a Swiffer and left me all sticky. Dr. Carlson came in to visit with me and drew on me with a purple marker. A special team was brought in to put in my IV since it had to be placed in a specific area of my arm. And finally, I was brought down to an area of the hospital to have the radioactive dye injected into me so they could identify the sentinel lymph nodes while I was in surgery.

I was happily oblivious to the intense pain about to be bestowed upon me as they wheeled me down the hall on my little bed. Based on the number of signs warning people that radioactive material was being used in the area, I was pretty sure I actually might turn into the Hulk or Spiderman after this procedure. The nurse wasn't allowed to come in the room with me, so I was alone with the torture lady that would inject me. She took out a giant needle she suggested I not look at, but it was too late.

"Where the hell are you going to stick that?"

"I have to place the needle just above your nipple in the areola so that the material gets to your lymph nodes."

"Are you kidding me? You're going to stick that needle into my nipple? Do you have like some numbing cream or something?"

"No. Unfortunately, we don't."

I took a long slow breath. *Eye of the tiger, baby.* "Ok. Let's do it."

She prepared the materials she had to use on me, and the next thing I knew, she was putting a huge ass needle into my nipple. "Mother fu.... Son of a bitch. That hurts. I'm sorry. Holy shit that hurts." I was instantly sweating and hot from the pain. "Oh my gosh. Is it almost done? Shit!!"

"Yes, just another couple of seconds and we'll be done with this one."

She took out the needle, and I relaxed a little bit. "That hurt like a son of a bitch. Wow!"

"Yeah, most people don't particularly like it."

She pulled out another needle and started getting things ready again. "Wait... We're doing it again? Why?"

"Well, we have to do the other side now. I'm sorry. I know it's not pleasant."

"Pleasant is not even close. This is torture. Why do you need to do the other side? I don't have cancer there."

"The doctor has orders to do both sides. I'm guessing she's going to check the lymph nodes on both sides just to be safe."

"Ok, so we have to do that whole torture routine again?"

"Yes, I'm sorry. Are you ready?"

I took another deep breath and thought of how I was anything but ready. "Ok. Let's do it." And again, I was sweating and hot from the pain. "Son of a .... That hurts!"

CHAPTER 54

I woke up from surgery in my room and remembered very little of anything before that. I looked at my nurse and said, "Do I still have two boobs?"

She was very kind and gently said, "Yes, you do! They were able to put implants on both sides."

"Ok, so I'm still symmetrical?"

She laughed. "Yes, you're still symmetrical."

I was fairly groggy and didn't really know what was going on, but Bryan brought the kids and my dad to see me that evening. True to his word, he walked in with a McMuffin for me.

"Hey, guys! You came to visit me! You remembered my McMuffin!!"

Owen was at my side, "Yeah, we stopped at McDonald's on the way here."

"Ohhhhh…. That was really nice of Dad, wasn't it? Did he get you something to eat?"

"Yeah, I got a cheeseburger and a chocolate shake."

"Awesome."

Bryan chimed in, "Absolutely! You want your food?"

"Yes, I'm starving." He handed me the McDonald's bag, and I dozed off holding it in my hand.

"Jen? Hey…. You want to eat your McMuffin?"

"Hmm? Yeah. I'm going to eat it now. That sounds good." I sat there holding the bag that contained my beloved McMuffin, but I didn't have the energy or the coherence to open it and actually eat anything.

Just then, the nurse walked in and saw me cradling my McMuffin and said, "Oh, honey. I'm sorry, but the doctor put you on a liquid diet."

In my semi-conscious state, I heard Bryan say, "Uh-oh."

I was half yelling and half crying as I expressed my displeasure at the fact I couldn't eat the food my husband had brought me. "What the hell? Why can't I have a McMuffin? All I wanted was something to eat. I've been looking forward to it all day. Who the hell puts someone on a liquid diet because they have their boobs removed? That's stupid. What the hell am I supposed to eat? Am I supposed to sit here and starve? Is that going to make my boobs heal faster?" I didn't care if I was acting like a child. The idea that I couldn't eat was incredibly upsetting even though I was a long way from being able to put the food into my mouth and chew.

The nurse finished checking my IV bag and asked me a few questions about my pain level, and I yelled at her as she walked out of the room. "People should be allowed to have McMuffins when someone cuts off their boobs!"

Bryan was at my side trying to make me feel better about the situation. "Ok, honey. Maybe I can bring you something to eat tomorrow."

I started falling back asleep and remember mumbling. "I don't want to eat tomorrow. I want to eat now. I'm going to watch Survivor now. It's Survivor Wednesday. We need to have popcorn."

"Honey, it's like 5:30. Survivor isn't on yet."

"Oh, yeah. Ok, I'm going to watch it when it's on. I think I need to sleep now. Can you ask everyone to leave? I'm really tired."

"Ok. Ummmmm…. Sure. We can all go and let you rest. Buddy, you want to come give Mom a hug? It's ok. You won't hurt her."

"Bye, Mom. I'm sorry you couldn't eat your McMuffin. I love you." He gently gave me a hug while I struggled to stay awake to say goodbye to him.

Haley came over next to give me a hug. "Bye, mom. I hope you get some rest and get something to eat. Love you."

Finally, my dad came and gave me a hug. "Hey, dad. I don't have boobs anymore, and they won't let me eat real food."

"Yeah, that's not a good day."

As they walked out of the room, I heard my dad say, "She really wanted that McMuffin, didn't she?"

Bryan replied, "Yeah, it's best we just go so we don't anger the beast again."

CHAPTER 55

I woke up at about 1:00 in the morning and realized I didn't get to watch Survivor, which made me cry. At some point, I had apparently ordered myself some chicken broth, which was still sitting next to me on the little tray next to my bed. I decided to check Facebook and see what Bryan had posted about my surgery. He had done an excellent job of keeping people updated as to what was going on. He had even included some Star Wars references which I was impressed with.

I decided to listen to my voicemail and found out I had been called to interview for a teaching position at one of the high schools in the district I was currently working in. It was a great position, so I decided to call them back to let them know I would be interested in interviewing. The only problem was that I had just had a double mastectomy and was pretty high on the painkillers they were giving me.

"Hi, this is Jennifer Monahan. You had left me a message about ummmm.... Interviewing for a teaching position tomorrow. Or today? I don't know what day it is. I'm really sorry that I didn't call you back but.... Uhhhhhh.... Yeah.... I had a double mastectomy today because I have breast cancer and stuff, so I was unconscious when you called. But, I'm awake now and .... yeah... I'd.... ummmm.... I'd really like to interview still, but I don't think they'll let me out of the hospital to come in unless I brought my I.V. bag with me or something. Hehehehe .... That would be a pretty bad interview with an IV bag attached to me. I don't know if I could wear clothes or if I'd have to interview in my hospital gown and it's an ugly green color. Maybe I could do a phone interview? I think I'm going to be here for a couple more days so if you could call me, I'll tell my doctor not to come in while I'm interviewing. Thanks! Have a good night! Bye!"

. . . . .

I was still pretty groggy when I started getting visits from various people on the medical team. First thing in the morning, as I was trying to recall through the haze in my brain how badly I had embarrassed myself the night before, in walked a gorgeous blonde, wearing 3-inch heels and leather pants. She sort of swooped into the room, her hair flowing behind her like a galloping horse, and said, "Hey. How are you feeling this morning?" My hair was matted to my head, I had drain tubes coming out of my armpits, I couldn't lift my arms over my head to comb my hair, my pee was blue from the radioactive dye, and I desperately needed a shower from all the sweating I had done overnight. In addition, I had no way to get deodorant on because I couldn't lift my arms high enough to do it. *Who the hell is this chick coming in here looking all fantastic with her leather pants and heels?* She made a little small talk while I searched my memory to figure out who she was. She asked to see my incisions and I figured, well, everybody else has taken a look at them so she might as well, too.

When she started talking about my implants and my drain tubes and showing me how to strip them, I figured out that she was Dr. Carlson's assistant, Jillian. *Of course, she had to come in here looking fabulous at 7:00 in the morning when I feel like this.* She was incredibly kind, and I couldn't blame her for looking like a Victoria's Secret model, although it made me feel a little worse about myself at that moment. I had hoped I would feel a little prettier than I did at that point. Unfortunately, a double mastectomy leaves you feeling quite unattractive, so you remind yourself that it's just one of those things you need to deal with if you want to stay alive.

Dr. Harrison came in to see me and told me they were able to get clean margins on everything. My tumor was just under two centimeters, and no lymph nodes were involved that they could see. She had sent the few sentinel lymph nodes she removed to pathology and would give me the final report when I went in for my checkup in another week.

Shockingly, the principal's secretary I had left a drug-induced, rambling message for called me that morning and said they would set me up with a phone interview for 1:00 that afternoon. She gave me some sort of pep talk for interviewing when I had just had surgery, but I explained that I was really interested in the job and would like the chance to be considered.

When my nurse came in to check on me, I told her I needed to have a quiet room so I could interview that afternoon. She offered to put a sign on the door so no one would come in and she gave me the smallest dose of my pain meds so I could be moderately coherent. She was a little surprised that I wanted to do the interview from my hospital bed, but a teacher wants to teach, and I didn't want to have to keep looking for jobs. I was hopeful this interview would provide the results I wanted.

At precisely 1:00 I was called by the interview team. I happily participated in a phone interview for what I was hoping would be a great job and allow me to stay in the district where I already had a couple of years under my belt. It turned out to be the worst interview I have ever had. I'm usually really good at interviewing, but I was still pretty hopped up on painkillers and pretty beat up, so I had a hard time answering a lot of the questions. Not only was I not able to put an intelligent sentence together, I started to fall asleep during part of one of my answers. Mid-sentence, as I was trying to explain my philosophy on working with students with high behavioral needs, which is something I excel at, I started to nod off. One of the interviewers said my name and I snapped back, but the damage had been done. Would anyone want to hire a person who repeatedly told the interview team she was high and then fell asleep mid-sentence? Yeah, I didn't get the job.

While I was in the hospital, Bryan was on the other side of the skyway getting a checkup scan for his cancer. He had continued to stay in remission and wasn't currently on any meds, but I had noticed that his tumor marker was slowly starting to climb. I watched his blood work like a hawk and, although the numbers hadn't gotten out of the normal range yet, it was strange that they would slowly be moving upward when they had previously been so low. I asked him to request a scan to see if something was changing. After his scan, he came over to get me and bring me home. He was looking tired and said that he'd started to have more belly pain the past few days.

"Yeah, I don't know. I'm just pretty run down right now."

"Ok, let's get me discharged and home to my bed. I don't want to stay here another night."

We stopped at McDonald's on our way home so I could finally get my McMuffin. It was delicious and satisfying and I inhaled it like a rottweiler who hadn't eaten in a week. The hospital had finally taken me off my liquid diet, but the food at the hospital was less than satisfying and I ended up eating only the strawberry shortcake with each meal. That beautiful and tasty McMuffin was like a gift from the heavens as we drove toward Elk River. Bryan finally asked me if I needed some special alone time as I moaned, "Oh, my gosh... this is soooooo gooood.... mmmmmmmm."

I was finally able to shower after a couple of days, but washing my hair was a challenge because it was still hard to lift my hands over my head. I managed to get some soap in my hair and swirl it around a little bit, but just standing in the warm water felt heavenly. After my shower, I had to ask Bryan to brush my hair for me. To this day, I can't decide which was more painful: Healing from a double mastectomy or having my husband whack at my head with a hairbrush as though he was trying to find his way through the jungle with a machete.

CHAPTER 56

The next week, I had an appointment with Dr. Laudi to go over the results of my pathology and discuss the plan for me going forward. To be more efficient, we had Bryan double up with me so he could get the results of his scan at the same time.

"Everything looks good. Your tumor was just under two centimeters so we wouldn't typically do any chemotherapy when the tumor is so small. We also have the results of the Oncotype. The way it works is they test slices of your tumor and report back a score from 1 to 100 that tells how likely your tumor is to come back. The lower your number, the less likely it is to come back, and the less beneficial chemotherapy would be for you. Your number was the lowest I've ever seen. It was a 5."

"Seriously? So that's good?"

"Yes, it means that the risks and side effects of chemotherapy don't outweigh the benefits you would receive from it, so we won't do any chemotherapy. Now, your tumor feeds on estrogen so we'll give you an aromatase inhibitor that blocks your estrogen, so your tumor has nothing to feed on. You're getting a hysterectomy this summer?"

"That's the plan, yes."

"Ok, so until then we can give you Tamoxifen. It's medicine we give to pre-menopausal women. After your hysterectomy, we'll switch you to Arimidex. The side effects include hot flashes and maybe some moodiness." He looked at Bryan and gave him that knowing look like, "Be prepared, dude. Shit's about to go down!"

"Ok, but no chemo? No radiation?"

"No, you were fortunate. This was caught very early, and you have the best possible result we could ask for."

I was stunned. As soon as I was diagnosed, I started comparing myself to my mother. She was about the same age as I was when she was diagnosed. I was so used to cancer equating to death, I didn't really know what it meant to be cancer free. News like this, that my cancer was completely gone, was hard for me to fathom. I was elated at the news, but it was short-lived.

"Now let's have you switch chairs."

I got up and moved to the spouse chair while Bryan took his place up in the patient chair so he could hear the results of his scan. I was trying to balance the excitement of my news, with knowing that something bad was looming for Bryan. If everything had been fine, they would have just called us rather than have him double up his appointment with mine.

"Your situation is a little more difficult."

"Yeah, I guessed."

"Your tumor appears to have come back in the same spot it was last time. That tells me that the radiation killed most of it, but there was likely a small amount of tumor there that wasn't detectable on your PET scan from August of last year."

He continued talking to Bryan about treatment options, what would give him the best chance to extend his life the longest, but he made it clear that anything they did at this point was not curative. It was only meant to extend his life.

"Ok, and the chemo you're giving me? Is it the Folfirinox again?"

"No, we'll give you Gemcitabine and Abraxane. The most common side effect is hair loss, some nausea, but less than it was with Folfirinox. It's an effective treatment. The hope is to hold the cancer in place, so it doesn't spread. Your tumor is still small, and we're not seeing any evidence it's spread anywhere else."

"How much time am I looking at? Just give it to me."

He paused and thought about his words before he spoke. "It's hard to say. Everybody responds differently, so it really depends on how you respond to this treatment. Some people can stay on it for years. Unfortunately, your cancer is very aggressive, and recurrent pancreatic cancer is difficult to treat. If I had to give a number, I would say maybe six months to a year."

We left Dr. Laudi's office completely conflicted. This was a joyful time for me because I had just heard that I was going to live and not have to do any chemo or radiation. My cancer journey was concluding with taking a pill every day for the next five years. But simultaneously, we just heard that Bryan was not going to survive his cancer journey. It was the shittiest possible position to be in, and the conflicting emotions were difficult to reconcile for both of us. I didn't know how to process what we were told. I had been given a gift of knowing that my cancer had a 5% chance of coming back, all while Bryan had a 9% chance of living.

"So that's good news for you!" Bryan broke the silence after we'd been driving for a few minutes.

"It is, but I can't really feel happy about it right now."

"Yeah, but hey…. At least one of us will be alive to take care of the kids. Assuming you don't get hit by a bus or something."

"Yeah, I'd rather we had good news for both of us, though."

"Yeah, me too. This fucking sucks."

"It sounds like they can keep you on chemo for quite a while, though. They can keep things in place that way, so it doesn't spread."

"Yeah, but this life sucks, Jen. The chemo sucks. Feeling like this sucks. My belly is in constant pain. I've learned to live with it, and I typically keep it hidden from all of you, but I'm always in pain. I'm tired, and I'm going to get more tired once the chemo starts. I don't want to live the rest of my life like this."

"I know. I'm really sorry, honey. I truly am."

"If I'm looking at the possibility of only six to 12 months to live, I need to go live. I need to look back and say I did things. That my life wasn't sitting in an office every day, going over budgets and reading contracts. I need more than that. I want to really live. "

"Hand me your phone."

"Why?"

"Just hand me your phone."

He reluctantly handed it over, and I found the number of his boss in it and called.

"Hey! How was the doctor's appointment?" Kirsten answered the phone, assuming it was Bryan calling. She had continued to be supportive and kind and had been Bryan's confidante at all work-related functions for the past few years. She and the whole company had been excellent to him, and I knew that the conversation I was about to have was necessary, but that didn't make it easier.

"Hey, Kirsten. This is Jen. Bryan's wife."

Bryan whispered to me, "What are you doing??" I held up my hand to tell him to be quiet.

"Oh, hey, Jen. Wait. What's going on? Is everything ok?"

"No, we were just at the oncologist, and Bryan got some hard numbers we didn't like hearing. His cancer has returned, and there are fewer options for him when it comes to recurrent pancreatic cancer."

"Oh, I'm so sorry, Jen. I'm really so sorry."

"I appreciate that. However, with the news we got today, we need to make some changes. So, I hereby respectfully give Bryan's two-week notice on his behalf. He'll be using the remaining time he has left to live his life without having to sit behind a desk every day. I'm sorry, but this is what he needs right now."

I looked over at Bryan. He had tears in his eyes and a look of sadness on his face, but he didn't stop me. "Tell her I'll call her on Monday."

"Bryan said he'll call you Monday and get things figured out with you, but this is just something he really needs to do right now."

"I get it. I agree. This is absolutely what is best for him."

"Thanks for understanding. He'll talk to you on Monday after he's had some time to process this." I hung up the phone, and we didn't talk about it. He reached over, grabbed my hand, and we drove the rest of the way in silence.

. . . . .

People had been calling and texting wanting an update on both of us, so I took to Facebook again to keep everyone in the loop on our situation.

Welcome to Adventures in Cancer with the Monahan Family.... it's a long one, so if you want the update you better dig in and get some snacks!

Let's start with the good....

I met with my surgeon, plastic surgeon and oncologist. The surgeons both said that everything looks great after my surgery. Everything is healing nicely. I don't remember my boobs being quite this lumpy before, but my surgeon is going to go in and fix all that after my incisions have healed. Let me just say, boobs are not pretty after they've been hacked up 10 ways from Sunday, so I won't be posing for Playboy anytime soon.

The oncologist gave even better news. They do a test on slices of the tumor that tells them the likelihood of the cancer coming back. Since I've always tried to be an overachiever, he said my number was the best he'd ever seen.

I'm still home from work for another week. I'm insanely bored most days, so you'd think I'd be productive, but naps are just too enticing. I can't completely use my arms yet, so laundry isn't really happening. If you run into one of us at the grocery store and we smell a little funky, you'll know why.

I will not be doing any chemo or radiation. I'm on a drug that suppresses my estrogen because that's what the tumor feeds on and I'll be on that for about five years which will let me experience the fun of menopause! I'm excited! I really can't complain about any of this because I know I got the best bad situation that I could possibly get. I really am incredibly thankful for that and all the kindness that so many people have shown us. It's been overwhelming how kind our friends and family are.

Now let's move on to the not so good news...

After I met with my oncologist, which also happens to be Bryan's oncologist, he asked Bryan and me to switch chairs. (It's very efficient to double up our appointments!) Bryan's belly pain just hasn't gone away. At his last check-up, we noticed that his tumor marker was slowly creeping up. More imagine was ordered and after an MRI and PET scan, it appears that Bryan's cancer is back.

His tumor is tiny.... only a half cm, but it's still in that same pesky location so it looks like the doctors just can't get to it.... the blood clot really did some damage to that area. The plan is an endoscopic ultrasound to confirm what they're 95% sure they already know, meet with another surgeon to see if he has any brilliant ideas, and get genetic testing to see if he could qualify for a targeted therapy similar to what they're doing with my estrogen medicine.

We haven't given up and all hope is not lost. Where is Obi-Wan when you need him? He's our only hope! (That was Bryan's line and I actually laughed out loud when he said it... Bryan is such a gomer and Obi-Wan is just the coolest) We always knew there was a possibility of it coming back. It looks like more chemotherapy is in his future. It's not great news, but we are continuing to move forward, stay positive, and continue to fight the fight he needs to right now.

. . . . .

That night Bryan got a message from Boss Man Jeff to call him if he was feeling up to it. Bryan called him back, and I heard him saying he hated to leave the company. They'd been so good to him throughout the entire time he'd been sick. They'd been kind and understanding with his treatments, and he was grateful for that, but this was something he needed to do. He needed to start crossing things off his bucket list and spending time with his family. Jeff understood and told Bryan that he would be missed and reminded him of all the good things he had done in his position with the company. He let Bryan know if there was anything he needed, he just needed to ask.

When he hung up the phone, he had tears in his eyes again. Of all the decisions he needed to make during his cancer journey, this was by far the hardest. He liked the normalcy that his job offered him, but now wasn't the time for normal. Now was the time to step outside the box and put his mark on the world.

PART 6
DAYS GO BY

I knew this was a night
I never wanted to forget
and I tried to memorize the sounds
and smells of the moment.

CHAPTER 57

B ryan stayed at his job until they could find a replacement for him. By the middle of June, he was officially done working. I was off for the summer from school, so we did a few projects around the house, and I would sit with him on his chemo days to keep him company. The new chemo wasn't nearly as bad as the first one he had done, but his hair started slowly falling out.

"It's ok. I've got a nice shaped head."

"You look like Lex Luthor."

"I'd prefer to be compared to Professor X. He's badass."

"Yes, but Lex Luthor is an evil genius. That sums you up better. Wait... young Professor X or old Professor X?"

"Young professor X, cuz I'm totally in good shape like him."

"Ok. But still, I think you're leaning more toward evil genius."

· · · · ·

Earlier that year, Bryan's mom had recognized that Bryan was on borrowed time and had generously offered to take us to Europe.

We happily accepted her kindness. The kids knew that Bryan's cancer had come back, and Haley understood what that meant. I wasn't so sure that Owen did, but I reminded him often how important it was to make special memories with Dad. Owen would ask frequently if he and Bryan could do things together, even if they were small. I had found him a counselor to help with some of the anxiety that came with having two parents battling cancer and it seemed to be helping him to talk through some of it.

Bryan was excited to start crossing things off his bucket list, and our trip to Europe was a pretty significant item for him. It was the one and only time I saw him make a list of things he needed to pack before we went on a trip. Normally, I would have spreadsheets and checklists and pack little meals for everyone for the plane and Bryan would throw a few shirts and pants in a bag just before we left for the airport. This time he was excited and made a packing list a week before we left. He created the list on his phone, so he didn't have to use paper, but still, it was an improvement over his normal routine.

We left for a two-week trip to Europe on July 5th because I insisted on being in the United States on the 4th of July. Somewhere in the back of our minds, we knew that this was his one and only chance to see Europe and we crammed as much into it as we could. We had four days in Munich with a day trip to Salzburg, three days in Dusseldorf where Bryan's grandfather grew up, four days in Paris, three days in London and then back home.

The first night we were in Germany we drove into Munich to go to Marienplatz and take it all in. There was something magical about being there and drinking in the culture and the history of a place we had always dreamed of going. We soaked up Munich with its old buildings and beautiful countryside. Bryan put his German language skills to good use while I stood there and pointed at things and talked loudly in English as though that would help people understand me.

"Jen, yelling at them doesn't help anyone understand what you're saying."

"Well, it makes me feel like it's helping. I learned how to say 'No.' That seems to be working for me."

"Didn't you try and of those language apps I sent you before we left?"

"No. I have you to translate for me. Why would I need to learn German?"

He sighed and rolled his eyes at me and I went back to pointing at things. This was effective until one day when he was tired, and I had to run into a store by myself to buy some snacks. The cashier started talking to me in German and I just smiled and held out my hands with all the money I had in my palms and let her pick what I owed. I had no idea if they were ripping me off or if I paid the correct amount for the Pringles and ice cream I bought. As I ran out the door, I yelled, "Deutsch danke!" feeling pretty satisfied with my accomplishment. Bryan later told me I yelled, "German Thanks" at them, but I figured it was close enough.

While we were there, we took a tour of a concentration camp, which Bryan was very excited for. We had rented a car in Germany so that he could drive on the Autobahn and as we drove toward the Dachau Concentration Camp, I kept seeing signs for Ausfahrt. I finally mentioned to Bryan that the city of Ausfahrt must be huge. Everywhere we went it seemed there was a sign pointing toward Ausfahrt.

He looked at me with a look of amazement on his face at my sheer stupidity. "That means 'exit.' Did you notice you always see the sign for ausfahrt at the exit ramp?"

"Huh! Look at that…. I guess I just assumed it was some really big city or like an amusement park or something. Like when we're at Disney and there are signs everywhere telling what attractions are at that exit."

He very quietly whispered, "Wow!" and then kept driving to the ausfahrt that led to Dachau.

We were able to get a guided tour of Dachau, but the tour wasn't recommended for children as young as Owen, so I stayed back with him while Bryan, Haley, and Louise took the tour.

"Jen, I don't want you to miss this!"

"Seriously, I'm fine. This was what you wanted to see and I'm not about to let you miss it. Just tell me about it when you get back."

Haley later told me that the tour was emotional for Louise and she got teary during several parts of the tour realizing that she likely had family that had gone through a facility similar to it. She didn't say too much about it on our way back to the hotel, but I could tell that it was impactful for both her and Bryan.

We took a day trip to Neuschwanstein Castle and took in some of the country on our way. Louise bought Haley an authentic German beer while we were there and Haley gobbled it up, making me suspect that maybe this wasn't actually her "first beer ever" as she claimed it was. We drove through tiny little German towns and spent a day in Berchtesgaden to take a tour of Hitler's Eagle's Nest. Bryan indulged his fascination of World War II the whole day and talked about how amazing the tour was. On the way back, we stopped in Salzburg so I could dance through Mirabell Garden and pretend I was one of the Von Trapp kids in The Sound of Music. For me, that was a lifelong dream come true.

After Munich, we headed north to Dusseldorf where Bryan's grandfather had lived as a child. We stopped in Rothenburg ob der

Tauber on our way and explored the medieval city. The charming cobblestone streets and little shops were fun to explore. It was a bit of a maze, but with every turn, there was a store where you could purchase some sort of sword or shield. The sheer volume of weaponry that could be purchased there had Owen spinning.

The drive to Dusseldorf was long, and we took several stops to get out and walk around, stretch our legs, get some snacks and use the bathroom. I was absolutely fascinated when I came across a toilet seat that would clean itself. As soon as you flushed, the toilet seat started slowly spinning and a mechanism attached to it would clean the seat. I tried to convince Bryan to get one for our house and he laughed. I frequently brought up that toilet seat during the rest of the drive.

Once we arrived in Dusseldorf, Bryan and Louise went for a whole day to discover the area where Bryan's grandfather had been born. They explored the little village Louise's dad had lived in as a child and found the 800-year-old church where he had been baptized. They went and spoke to some people in the church about getting some details on family history and it was a productive day for them. Bryan had always been fascinated by history and having the chance to learn about his own history put a huge smile on his face. The kids and I took that day to swim in the pool and recuperate a little. We strolled through old city streets and toured a chocolate factory in Cologne. When Bryan and Louise got back that evening, he recounted the details of everything they'd seen and showed me some of the 200 pictures he'd taken. It was an emotional day for both of them to go on that journey together.

We spent our last night in Germany in Wiesbaden, a short distance from Frankfurt so we could catch a train to France in the morning. Bryan spent the night talking about Jason Bourne and how it looked like a scene from one of the Bourne movies. He and I wandered around for a little bit and took in the vibe of the city while the kids and Louise rested in our hotel room. We roamed aimlessly, taking it all in, holding hands as we walked through a little foreign town surrounded by people and music and the festivities of a summer night in Germany.

As we sat on our balcony that evening, I knew that this was a night I never wanted to forget, and I tried to memorize the sounds and smells of the moment. As we watched the city below us, Bryan absently said, "I could totally be Jason Bourne." I rolled my eyes and laughed. *Sure you could, honey. You absolutely could be Jason Bourne.*

CHAPTER 58

When we got to France, Bryan expected me to be able to communicate in French as well as he spoke German because I had taken two years of high school French. All I knew how to say was "Where is the toilet" and "I don't speak French." My skills were limited compared to his, and our first experience in France was being scammed by the cab driver that brought us to our hotel. It wasn't a great way to start, but things significantly improved from there.

We went to visit the Eiffel Tower and I heard Haley gasp as we got our first view of it. This was a dream for both of us. We took the elevator up to the top, and as we admired the city below, Bryan and I looked at each other. He smiled at me and said, "We're on the Eiffel Tower right now! What the fuck?"

Our family was strangely proud of the fact that we'd played laser tag in 17 different states, so now that we were in France, we took the opportunity to bring our game international. It turns out that laser tag in France is no different than laser tag in America. It was one of those things we needed to do so we ran and hid and shot each other with French laser guns.

We were in France on Bastille Day, so there was an added layer of celebration going on while we were there, which made it even more special. We watched fireworks on the bank of the Seine River, and we toured the Louvre while I talked about The Davinci Code and kept saying things like, "So dark the con of man." Haley got to see the Mona Lisa and Owen and Bryan watched the military parade with Louise that was going down the Champs Elysee. Bryan lit up while we all watched a military flyover that started the festivities.

The next day, France won the World Cup, and the party really got started. Our sleepy little French streets turned into a madhouse of people running and celebrating and singing songs in French that we didn't understand. It was an amazing experience to be there for that type of celebration. We yelled and danced in the streets with the French people and pretended we knew what everyone was saying.

By the time we got to London, we were all exhausted, and I was particularly run down. I had been having a difficult time getting up in the morning but assumed it was just part of the busy schedule we were keeping. I took a shower the first evening we were there, and when I got out, I noticed that my right breast was bright red. It looked as though my breast was severely sunburned, and there was a distinct line where the redness stopped. Upon a closer look, my incision had split open and appeared to be infected.

"Hey, Bryan! Could you come here?"

"In the bathroom?"

"Yeah, I need you to look at something."

"Uhhhh…. Do I have to?"

"Yes, just come here."

He came in so I could show him my boob and his response was, "That's nasty. It looks really infected. Didn't you feel it? It looks like it hurts."

"I don't have any feeling in either of my boobs, so no, I couldn't feel it. It looks pretty bad, though, right?"

"It doesn't look good. You should probably call your doctor about it."

I called my plastic surgeon's office, and Jillian called me back in a matter of minutes and asked me to send her a picture of what my breast looked like. She called me again a few minutes after I had sent the email.

"I need you to come in so I can get a better look at what's going on and get you on some antibiotics. That looks pretty infected."

"Well, that's not going to happen. I'm in London."

"Like London, London?"

"Yeah. We're still on our trip."

"Ok, I need you to go to a hospital and have it looked at. When do you get back?"

"Two more days."

"Ok, come in as soon as you're back. He's going to want to probably take out the implant and culture it and clean it out really well."

"Am I going to lose my implant?"

"I can't say yet. It's possible."

"Shit. Ok. I'll head to the hospital." I hung up the phone and called Bryan back into the bathroom since that was the only place we could talk without the kids hearing us. I didn't want to alarm them or make them worry. The next day we were going to the London Eye and exploring the city, so I didn't want to cause any drama if I didn't need to.

"They want me to go to the hospital. I'll go first thing in the morning. You guys are going on that double-decker bus tour tomorrow?"

"Yeah. You aren't going to be able to go?"

"I doubt it. I guess I'm going to be checking out the international health care system."

The next morning, I took a cab to the hospital where I waited three hours to see a doctor. When I checked in and tried to explain that I only had American insurance, I was informed it was free unless I needed to be admitted. *Wooo! That's the first free thing we've done this entire trip! Score!* The doctor finally came out to get me and brought me back to a room. I explained to him what was going on, and he said he wanted to take a look at my breast. He stepped out so I could undress and when he came back, he had a woman with him that he explained was a chaperone to help me feel more comfortable.

"Dude, everyone and their sister has seen my boobs at this point. I'm not worried about it, but I appreciate the thought."

The chaperone chimed in with the sweetest British accent, "So basically, you're just like a stripper?"

I stared at her with my mouth open, trying to decide if the British are hysterically funny or incredibly rude. I finally laughed at the absurdity of someone who sounded just like Mary Poppins calling me a stripper and said, "Yeah, I guess I'm sort of like a stripper."

"From the top up! Just the top!"

She certainly knew how to lighten the mood. The doctor looked at my incision and agreed that my breast was very much infected. There was some discussion of removing the implant, but he thought he would leave that to my plastic surgeon since I was leaving to go home in another day. He put me on an antibiotic I later found out was not available in the United States, but it cleared up my infection like a champ.

Bryan and I spent the last night we were in Europe strategically packing up all the souvenirs we had amassed, including a five-pound bag of Gummy Bears for Bailey that I'd been dragging around since the drive to Dusseldorf. I carefully packed up the wooden sword Owen had gotten in Rothenburg and Haley had gotten several t-shirts and a necklace in France. We had accumulated little trinkets and memories along the way that needed to be protected to make the trip home. After we'd spent an hour packing our suitcase like we were playing a game of Tetris, we went to sit on the steps in front of our hotel, watching the cars drive on the wrong side of the street and listening to the sounds of a bustling city.

Going into it, we knew this trip would be challenging. Finding common interests for a 10-year-old, an 18-year-old, two 40-something cancer patients, and a 72-year-old is a tough nut to crack. Despite the challenging combination of ages and interests, we had pushed on through exhaustion, infections, missed exits, long train rides, and misunderstood languages. We had marveled at the beauty of the country, the history that surrounded us, the unfamiliar language, and rest stop toilet seats that self-cleaned when you flushed. This would have been the trip of a lifetime, even if Bryan weren't dying. Given our current situation, these were memories we would always cherish.

CHAPTER 59

We got home late Thursday night, and I went straight to my plastic surgeon the next day to have my breast looked at. The antibiotic had done an excellent job of beginning to clear up the infection, but Dr. Carlson still wanted to remove the implant and clean everything up and reclose the incision. My procedure was scheduled for Monday, and I was able to keep my implant, but I recognized how close I was to being one boobed.

My hysterectomy was two days later, and my surgical oncologist agreed to go forward with it even though I had just come off a raging infection. She felt that an infection that was nearly gone from my boob wouldn't compromise the hysterectomy so on Wednesday, the week after we returned from Europe, I went back into surgery to have my uterus, ovaries, and cervix removed. Surprisingly, it was an outpatient procedure, so I was sent home that night loaded up on pain meds.

My hysterectomy was not nearly as difficult to recover from as my mastectomy had been. I took a few days to just lie around the house, but I was basically back to my old routine within a few days. The doctor did give me a restriction on vacuuming and carrying laundry baskets, so I took full advantage of that.

One of the unfortunate problems with us both having cancer was the differing side effects we were both experiencing. After my hysterectomy, and with the estrogen-blocking medication I was taking, I would have hot flashes. Bad hot flashes. I looked as though I had just run a marathon while wearing a wool coat in the middle of a desert in July. I had sweat dripping down my face and soaking through my shirts. I slept with as little clothes as possible and had two fans pointing at me.

On the other hand, Bryan had lost over 50 pounds because of his cancer and was freezing at night. He slept with three blankets, his Batman pajamas, and a beanie on his little bald head just to stay warm. We would laugh at how ridiculous it must have looked. Me, laying there, yelling, "For the love of God! It's so fucking hot!" And he, curled up in a ball, shivering, "Uh huh…. Could you get me another blanket?"

Bryan resumed chemo the same week as my hysterectomy, so we were both pretty run down and most days we would rock-paper-scissors our decision as to who got to be sick that day. It was mostly effective, but at times we had to rely on Owen and Haley to help us with small tasks, which they happily did. Haley was being incredibly helpful with her brother and would take him for ice cream or to a friend's house to keep him occupied so that Bryan and I could get some rest when we needed it. Given our current situations, it ended up being quite frequently.

CHAPTER 60

With both of us having cancer, it was astonishing how quickly our hospital bills added up. I had good insurance, but the deductible was high, so we had a lot of out of pocket expenses. Bryan was no longer working, and there was a six-month waiting period for him to receive Social Security Disability benefits, which I thought was ridiculous. I understood the idea behind it. They needed to make sure he was actually disabled so that everyone didn't just start taking social security disability benefits but having absolutely zero income from him for six months was going to really hurt us.

Shawn and Becky threw us a benefit on Saturday, August 4th, at their home. I had a small amount of guilt about having a party where they were trying to raise us money when we had just spent two weeks in Europe, but Bryan pointed out that his mother paid for the majority of that trip.

The benefit, which Becky and I named, "Cancer Wars: The Monahans Strike Back," was a huge success. Bryan had Photoshopped each of us, including the kids, onto a Star Wars poster, and it looked awesome when it was shared on Facebook. Fred and Jeff came into town from Nashville which made Bryan happy to be able to catch up with the work family he genuinely missed. There were games and prizes and food and raffle tickets, and Becky did a fantastic job of putting it all together. I was astounded by the turnout. We're relatively quiet people, but the number of friends that came out and showed their support was touching and shocking. Even friends from high school that Bryan and I hadn't seen in years were there. It was amazing.

Feeling the love from all the people that came to our benefit was a beautiful feeling and we were humbled by all the love and support. Shawn and Becky's kindness in opening their home to support us and all of the work they put into this huge, magnificent party told me they really were my family, even if it wasn't by blood.

When the last of the guests had left, I finally sat down as a warm summer breeze was blowing and opened a beer and took it all in. Shawn walked out of the house with a little box and said, "How much do you think is in there?"

I had no idea how to even begin to guess the amount, so I said, "I heard that there was like $200 just from raffle tickets." We had hoped we'd raise enough to pay down a few doctor bills that month and maybe have a little leftover to get the kids some school clothes.

Shawn looked at me with wide eyes and said, "You're going to piss yourself when you hear how much we raised."

He opened the little box, and the total amount was more than enough to take care of all of our expenses that month. The money was used primarily for bills, but Bryan indulged in a new TV for our family room since, as he put it, "I've got nothing to do but watch TV in between puking from my chemo sessions." It was an extravagance that, for once, I didn't hesitate on.

CHAPTER 61

B ryan's bucket list was extensive and varied. It included everything from going to the Badlands in South Dakota to swimming with sharks to taking his son for ice cream and teaching him how to be a gentleman. On August 11, I received a strange message from one of Bryan's Jeep friends. There was an organization called Burning Wish that had recently started up and was taking applicants for people to go to Burning Man. Bryan just needed to apply to make it all happen. When I told him about it, his eyes lit up.

"Seriously? I've been wanting to go there since I was like 20-years-old, but it's always been too expensive for me to go."

"Then you should go! Let's apply!"

"Do you think we could actually do that? If I get chosen?"

"We'll make it happen."

"Well, what should I do?"

"Oh, for the love… just apply!! Here…. Stop talking and go putter around the garage for a while." I sat on the steps of the garage and five minutes later I had finished his application and written out a mushy story about how much this would mean to him and how important it was for him to go to Burning Man. "Ok... that's done!"

"You applied for me?"

"Yep! You'll get chosen, so let's figure this out."

"Should we wait? I don't want to get my hopes up and then not get chosen."

"Yes, but by then, it will be too late to get everything ready to go. Burning Man starts in three weeks."

"Oh, seriously?? I didn't realize that. Well.... Uhhhhh.... Ok.... What do I need to do?"

We sat and figured out some logistics. If they chose him, that would take care of his tickets into Burning Man as well as his camping while he was there. He just needed to get there. We put a few things on hold until we heard something back, but two days later he was informed that he was going to Burning Man.

"Holy shit!! Are you fucking kidding me??? This is so awesome!!"! He was excited at being able to cross off this major bucket list item. We started to really plan details at that point.

"Ok, so you want to drive, right?"

"I think I need to. How else would I get there?"

"I dunno... ok... so driving. Will the Jeep make it? It's getting up there in miles."

"Yeah, we've got a Jeep outing this weekend so I'll take it with me, and the guys can help me with a tune up before I go. It should be fine."

"Ok, can you sleep in the camper while you're there? We haven't used that thing at all the last two seasons. It's probably got a little mouse town that's developed with a little mouse grocery store and a mouse movie theater. I don't even want to look in it."

"I've opened it a few times, and it's fine. Yeah, that will work. I need somewhere to sleep when I'm there. They're setting me up with a group I can join so I won't be completely by myself. I suppose I could sleep in the back of the Jeep, but that doesn't sound very comfortable."

"That's good. Ok, let's find a route for you. You have two options. The southern route, which is Minnesota, South Dakota, Wyoming, Utah, to Nevada or you can take the northern route, through North Dakota, Montana, south through Idaho and then to Burning Man. Which would you prefer?"

"Let's say southern on the way there and northern on the way back."

I looked at the map to check out where good stopping points would be. "Oooh! You're going to go right past those salt flats you've always wanted to see!"

"For real? I've always wanted to go there."

"Isn't it like a giant flat area that's covered in salt?"

"Yeah, something like that."

"Could I just pour some salt on the floor and have you look at that? It's salt."

"It's a natural wonder that is disappearing. I watched a thing about it."

"It is not one of the natural wonders. The Grand Canyon is a natural wonder. The Great Barrier Reef…. Mount Everest. What you're talking about is salt."

"Yeah, but I want to see it, and if I'm going to drive right past it, I might as well stop."

"Good point. Go for it. I'll be honest with you…. I don't really know much about Burning Man. What exactly is it?" I Googled it on my phone while he was trying to explain to me what it was. I started scanning through one of the articles that popped up. *Ok, it's in a desert. Lots of music. Lots of art. That seems like his thing. Multiple places to get alcohol. What the heck is Illumination Village? Or someplace called The Hive? Woah! Hold up!* "There's an orgy tent? Seriously?" *What had I agreed to?*

He laughed. "I have no intention of going to the orgy tent."

"You better not. I don't know why that's even a thing. Is that what this is? Just a bunch of people getting high and getting sex?"

"I'm sure there are some people that do that. I honestly want to go just so I can experience it. Maybe if it were 20 years ago, I would have more interest in the orgy tent or some of the drugs but there's art, there's music. It's meeting people from different parts of the world and coming together for a common purpose. It's letting go of your hate and your ick. There are thousands of people just enjoying each other's company."

"Yeah, I bet they ...."

He held up his hand. "Enjoying each other's company with their clothes on. There are these huge art installations you can walk through and see. And yes, there are a lot of drugs and a lot of parties. But I have cancer, and I have no intention of doing anything that causes any of the three D's."

"What's that?"

"Death, Disease or Divorce."

I accepted his answer, and for just a split second, I thought about how far we had come from a few years earlier. If this had been back then, I probably would have been so insecure and untrusting that I would have gone with him and then complained the entire time and made both of us miserable. He knew this was not my kind of thing. It was in the middle of a desert; it was going to be hot and dusty. It would take him two days of driving to get there. This was a pilgrimage he needed to take on his own, and he had my full support to do it.

CHAPTER 62

Haley was supposed to leave for college the weekend before Bryan left for Burning Man. Two days before her move day, I looked at her and said, "You haven't packed a single thing. I need you to start packing something. Even if it's not all of it, at least get something done tonight."

She had been feeling particularly lazy as the summer had continued, so she replied, "I don't feel good. I'll get it done later. I'm going to go lay down."

Not interested in fighting with her, I accepted her answer and let it go. About 20 minutes later, she walked out of her room and said, "I'm going to go hang out with my friends. I'll be back later."

Oh, hell no. Not tonight, baby girl. "No, you are not going out with your friends. You're going to go pack. Seriously. You are not leaving. You are packing."

Now, with a regular teenager, this answer wouldn't have gone over well. With my daughter? My insistence that she stay home and finish packing was about to turn my house into a scene from Apocalypse Now.

As tensions started rising, she continued arguing with me in her mouthy teenager way and I stood my ground in a calm, rational, EBD teacher kind of way. After several more minutes of this, Owen finally walked up the stairs and stood up to her. I was pretty proud of him because he's a relatively docile kid most of the time, but he walked up the stairs and yelled, "Leave her alone! You are the worst sister ever!"

As Owen stood in between us, Haley grabbed his shoulders and said, "Owen! This doesn't have anything to do with you."

Now, I know that Haley would never do anything to hurt any of us. She's not a violent person. She's got a temper. She's got a mouth like Al Pacino in Scarface, but she's not violent. She does, however, get herself worked up to the point that she can't think rationally. I realized it was time to remove myself (and Owen) from the situation and give her a chance to calm down. I took Owen and went and sat in his room with him so that Haley could bring her emotions and her frustration back in check.

Unbeknownst to me, Bryan decided to step in and put an end to the arguing. He came up the stairs to try and calm Haley down, but she was so worked up, that the two of them started yelling at each other. I could only imagine what type of dysfunction this looked like to a stranger looking in.

As I sat with Owen, telling him that we just needed to let Haley calm down, I heard a noise and then screaming. I ran out of Owen's room to see Haley and Bryan falling down the steps, with Haley riding his back as he fell.

I would later find out that Bryan had gotten dizzy, since he was dying of cancer and stuff, and lost his balance as he tried to sit down. Haley tried to catch him but was unsuccessful and fell down the steps with him in the process. Bryan was slightly incoherent and now Haley was screaming at the top of her lungs like she was part of the shower scene in Psycho. So, I did the only rational thing that anyone was doing at that moment; I called 911.

Bryan was taken out of the house on a backboard with a neck collar for an ambulance ride to the hospital. The police took the opportunity to question my hysterical daughter. When she was little, I had prayed that she wouldn't end up dancing on a pole someday. I would have gladly taken the pole over watching her being removed from my house in handcuffs because the police decided she pushed Bryan down the steps. No matter how I tried to convince the police that they were wrong, she was being charged with domestic assault. After an already emotional night, I was now watching my daughter get arrested.

In my desperation, I ran next door to grab Andy, thinking he would be able to do something to help us. "Andy! I need you to come quick. Haley is getting arrested!"

Andy ran over, looked at Haley, hysterical and sobbing, and said in his best cop voice, "Haley, I need you to calm down and just do what they say. You're only going to make it worse if you don't."

I could have told her that! Isn't there some sort of secret cop word that would get my daughter out of this? "Blueberry pie. The code word is blueberry pie!" and they would understand that this wasn't a girl they should be arresting. Unfortunately, it didn't work that way and off she went to spend the night in jail.

Around midnight, Bryan called me from the hospital to come pick him up. I loaded Owen up in the Jeep, and when Bryan got in, he asked, "Why is Owen with you? Where's Haley?"

"She's in jail."

"Are you fucking kidding me? Why is she in jail?"

"Because she apparently pushed you down the steps."

"She didn't push me. I got dizzy and fell."

"Well, the cops didn't believe her."

"She didn't push me. I just fell and she actually tried to catch me."

"Well, there's nothing we can do to get her out now. I'll just go up there tomorrow and try to talk to someone. I hate thinking about her being there. I bet she's scared."

The next day, Haley was released after Bryan spoke with the prosecutor and explained what happened. Once Haley was in my car, she told me about how awful her night in jail had been and the nice "roommate" she had.

"Haley, it is not a roommate. It is a cell mate, and I'm sure you'll have a nice reunion with her when you invite her over for cake on your jailaversary. Let's just stay out of jail in the future. How does that sound?"

"She was really nice, Mom. I cried pretty much all night and she was super nice to me and tried to help me feel better. She's trying to get off meth so she can get her kids back."

I was glad she was making new friends. I just would have preferred she did it in the cafeteria in college rather than a cell at the county jail. After she got home and took a nice long nap, she quietly packed her stuff into several tidy little boxes, and we moved her to college the next day.

CHAPTER 63

L uckily, Bryan didn't have any injuries from his tumble down the stairs and the day for him to leave for Burning Man finally came. I couldn't believe how much we had packed into the Jeep. It reminded me of a Jenga tower; if you moved one item, the whole damn thing was going to collapse. I wasn't sure how he was going to fit anything else in there, including himself. He hooked up the camper and got ready to head out. I couldn't imagine doing this drive, particularly with his cancery status at that moment, but when he needed to find the strength, he would.

Just as we figured, it took him two days to get there. He had a small mechanical problem when he was only a few hours away that caused a little bit of stress, but he finally got back on the road and was almost there when word came out that a dust storm had closed the gates and he wouldn't be able to get in. I had been watching the Burning Man app, and it was an 8-hour wait to get in when they closed the gates because the dust storm was preventing people from being able to see.

"I can't believe this. I'm like an hour away. I've been driving for two days. I'm almost there, and they close the gates? Seriously?"

"I'm so sorry, honey. Do you want to wait it out? The dust storm will have to stop eventually."

"I don't know. What am I going to do? Just sit there for at least 8-hours? It could be a few hours before they open the gates and then it's still going to take half a day to actually get in. I don't fucking know."

"Ok. Here's what you're going to do. You've bouncing around in that Jeep for two days. You're going to spend the next four days covered in dust and dirt with no access to running water. I want you to drive to Reno, which is about 45 minutes from where you are, so you can get a hotel for the night. Get a decent meal. Get a good night's sleep. Shower! Then, in the morning, take off and drive back to the gate. Things should have calmed down by then so you can zip right in."

"Yeah, ok." He sounded disappointed but had accepted that this new plan was for the best. "Even if I did go wait in the line right now, it would be two in the morning by the time I got in, so that makes more sense. Can you look for a hotel for me?"

"Yep! I'll get it handled. I'm sorry that it's more difficult than you thought it would be."

"It's fine. You're right. This is the best plan. I'm just pissed that I'm so close and have to wait another day."

The next day he got up fairly early after getting a good night of sleep and taking a shower to start out clean. The dust storm had died down, and there was no wait time at the gate by the time he got there, so it worked out perfectly. He sent me a picture of himself rolling around in the dirt at the entrance, which is something they apparently make all first timers do. I got sporadic calls and texts from him over the next four days, but his reception was spotty so there wasn't much communicating.

He left after four days and called me on his drive home. He told me how amazing it was and how the Burning Wish people had done a cancer walk that was very healing and emotional. He knew this was the only time he'd ever be able to do this, and he took in as much of it as he could during those four days. I didn't ask a lot of questions because I knew that, for him, this was something more than just a festival that had a lot of drugs and an orgy tent. It was fulfilling dreams. It was the ability to look back and say he had done something, just like he had hoped.

When he got home, I asked, "Of everything you did, what was the one thing you'll always remember? Like the coolest part of the entire thing?"

He thought for a moment and finally said, "Big Sky, Montana. I drove through there on my way home. It was absolutely stunning. I didn't want to leave. Seriously. Every turn you make, there's something beautiful to see. You would have loved it. Can we go back there someday? You and me?"

"Absolutely. I would love to do that with you.

"Promise? I want you to see it with me."

"I promise. But you're telling me that of your entire journey, the best thing about it was the drive home?"

"Burning Man was amazing. It's tough to explain what it's like if you've never been there. It was emotional and cathartic and thrilling and amazing. But I'm 47-years-old with cancer. Day time starts at about 10:00 at night when I was just getting ready to go to bed. I didn't have the energy to do some of the things that other people did.

I'm thrilled that I got to go, but the beauty and solitude in Big Sky was my favorite part. It was quiet, and there wasn't music blaring in my ears until 4:00 in the morning with someone on a loudspeaker yelling 'The Cougar Car is leaving in five minutes!'"

"You realize you sound like your grandpa, right?"

"Yeah. I guess I'm old, but at least I did it. I'm happy that I'm home for Owen's first day of school, though."

"I'm happy that you're here, too, and I'm happy you're fulfilling your dreams."

CHAPTER 64

True to his wishes, we spent the rest of the year making memories. We both had always loved a good adventure, and we spent our life together going on vacations and making sure we gave our children happy memories of their childhood. Now, with a specific timeline in front of us, we knew that cancer would kill him sooner than later and we needed to cram 20 more years of vacations and adventures into a few months.

Bryan used the fall to spend a lot of time hanging out with the Jeep boys and soaking up some of their testosterone riddled activities. They went on a few short camping trips and some trail rides and would get together at various houses on the weekend so they could talk more about the dirt and rocks they all loved to drive on. Now that Bryan wasn't working and I was back at work for the school year, he was able to use their activities as an escape from the day to day monotony of sitting around the house, dying of cancer.

I was still dealing with many of the side effects from my cancer and subsequent hysterectomy. The downside to all of it was that I constantly smelled like an old sock because of the crazy amounts of sweating I did. The upside was that I was still alive so Bryan and I agreed that we'd live with the old sock smell and I would just shower more frequently.

The opportunity to check off another item on his list came when we were contacted by the Minnesota Vikings about coming out to a practice and going to a game on them. They had heard our story when Becky was arranging prizes for the benefit and wanted to invite us to meet with the team. It was an amazing experience. I managed to snag an extra ticket for my nephew Landon. Of all my brother's boys, Landon was always the quietest, so I wanted to give him something special to do with us. Christian and Dillon were pretty salty that I didn't get them tickets, as well, but I couldn't get them all tickets, so I had to make Sophie's choice and I chose Landon. We went out to a practice on a Saturday morning and got to watch from the sidelines and meet all of our favorite players. Latavius Murray spent time talking to Owen. Landon got to talk to Kirk Cousins about cars. Haley got to meet Adam Thielen and pretend she wasn't in love with him. She decided not to mention she had recently gotten a cat she named "Thielen" because she didn't want to seem like a psycho stalker chick. We sat and casually chatted with several of the players and were able to get autographs and pictures. It was phenomenal.

The next week we went to a game and were brought out onto the sidelines of the field before kickoff. Watching the Vikings play was part of our Sunday routine, but we had never been to a game together and we'd only been on a tour of the new stadium. It is an incredible facility and the Vikings pulled out a win for us. We tried to convince the nice lady that was leading us through the facility we were good luck for our beloved team and should be invited back to every game, but she didn't quite agree. It was a very special day and Bryan and I appreciated the attention they gave our family.

CHAPTER 65

Christmas that year was made extra special. Bryan picked out a fantastic tree and, although we didn't do many things differently than we normally did, we were both aware that it would probably be his last one. The opening of presents on Christmas morning had a different feeling to it. We had gotten the kids some special presents and he and I sat on the couch Christmas night looking at the lights on the tree. He felt warm and comfortable and safe, and it was hard to think about him not being there the next year. I hit the button to make my fantastically tacky lights dance, and we broke into the giggles as Deck the Halls started playing during our romantic Christmas moment.

Just before Christmas, I heard about an organization called The Jack and Jill Late Stage Cancer Foundation and applied to receive one of their WOW experiences. Basically, they were going to send us on vacation to Tampa for four days in January all expenses paid. We were very thankful to have that time together as a family. The adventure they sent us on was unbelievable.

The hotel room they set us up with had three different balconies and super swank furnishings we weren't used to, but it felt really good to forget about cancer for a few days. We went on a dolphin cruise from The Florida Aquarium, and Haley got to fulfill her dream of holding a penguin. We took the kids to Busch Gardens to see the Giraffes and spent a day at Universal Studios in Orlando. Bryan finally admitted that he couldn't do all the walking associated with being at Universal, so we rented him a scooter which earned him the nickname of Dr. Nefario for the rest of the day.

It was a wonderful trip where we spent time doing things we normally wouldn't do because I would have said it cost too much money. We were grateful to the Jack and Jill foundation for giving us that time together as a family, not worrying about cancer or money or anything negative. We were focused entirely on family memories.

Our last night in Florida, Bryan and I sat on the balcony, looking at the ocean and reflecting on the day's activities. It wasn't lost on either of us that the reason we were getting these amazing opportunities to go to Burning Man and meet with the Vikings and have an all-expenses paid trip to Tampa was because he was dying. He had outlived the six months that Dr. Laudi had suggested he might have and now we were on borrowed time.

CHAPTER 66

We had one final trip we wanted to go on as a family so Bryan could see Owen fulfill one of his dreams. Owen's favorite TV show was a show called Parker Plays on the Disney Channel. It just so happened that my brother Tom's best friend from high school was the executive producer of the show. I had asked him if it would be possible for Owen to meet Parker and Bryan got super teary when I told him about it.

"Owen is going to be so stoked to get to meet Parker. Kevin's going to arrange it all for us?"

"Yep, I was able to get us airfare already and I'm working out the details with him. I just need to find a hotel. We're there for less than 48 hours, so I'm thinking we'll just stay near the airport."

"That's fine with me. I don't care where we stay."

Unfortunately, the trip to Florida had wiped Bryan out. With our trip to California only three days later, Bryan needed some recuperation, so he spent those three days in bed, sleeping most of the time. He was exhausted and run down by the time we got to California and could barely get out of bed the entire time we were there. I took the kids to get some dinner, but Bryan stayed at the hotel and rested. He didn't want to eat, and he didn't have the energy to go out anywhere. He came down for a few minutes while Owen swam in the pool, but he quickly went back up and got into bed.

The next day, when Owen was going to get to meet his idol, Bryan forced himself out of bed and found the energy to come with us, but we had to take it slow for him. We stopped at the beach and let the kids play for a little while. We went and got cupcakes at a little shop Haley had heard about on some reality show, but Bryan waited in the car for us. We drove through Beverly Hills and down Rodeo Drive. Haley wanted to stop at Starbucks on Rodeo Drive but wanted to sound like she was important while ordering. She practiced her order out loud ahead of time, so she didn't sound like she was from a small town in Minnesota.

As we got out of the car, Bryan rolled his eyes and said, "She knows she's not going to get discovered as the next big thing in Hollywood based on how efficiently she orders Starbucks, right?"

We went to Kevin's house, and Owen was nervous as we got closer. He asked a lot of questions about what he should say and if he could bring his iPad to show Parker some of the games he liked. Bryan calmed him down and reassured him that Parker and Kevin and all the people there were just regular people and he shouldn't be afraid.

When we arrived, several people from the Parker show were there taking care of some business. They stayed and talked with us and treated us like we were part of the group. The day was filled with laughter and games while Parker took Owen on in a couple of video games and Owen "won" an X-Box for his victory. Bryan was talkative and friendly to the people we met, but I could tell that he was dragging by the time we left.

We stopped at the beach again on the way back to the hotel and Bryan and I stood and watched the sunset over the ocean while the kids ran around, happy to escape the snow and cold waiting for us at home. He held my hand, and not a single word was spoken. I got tears in my eyes because I instinctively knew that his time was getting shorter and this would be our last adventure together. This would be our last ocean sunset. It would be the last time we walked on a sandy beach. The last time we would wake up at the crack of dawn to go catch a plane together. The last time he would hold my hand on takeoff and tell me that the noises the plane was making were normal. This was the last. Cancer was killing him, both physically and mentally.

By the time we got back to our hotel, Bryan was exhausted and went right back to bed. Our plane was set to leave early the next morning, but Bryan woke me up about 11:00 that night and asked if he had a fever. I felt his forehead and could tell that he did, but I tried to play it off like it was no big deal. I just needed him to get home to Minnesota without getting stuck in California and unable to travel. I gave him some ibuprofen to bring his fever down so he could go back to sleep. After I was sure he was doing better, I went back to trying to shove a shiny new X-Box and all of our clothes into the single carry-on size suitcase we had brought along.

CHAPTER 67

Two days after we got home, I brought Bryan into the hospital and were told he had ascites. They explained it was a buildup of fluid in his belly that needed to be drained out. Because of who he is, Bryan decided to film the procedure of having his belly fluid drained and then sent it to me. It was disgusting. All those years photographing dancers for the Ballet Project had led him to ask the nurse to line up the bottles his fluid was draining into so he could get a more artistic shot of the nastiness of it all. He came home after a few days of resting in the hospital but was back again a few days after that with the same buildup of fluid in his belly.

We both knew what this second visit to the hospital in two weeks meant. On our way back to the hospital for his second stay, I asked the question I didn't want to ask but knew I needed to.

"Honey, I have to know. We've talked about things before, but I need to know where you're at. If something happens to you… something catastrophic…. do you want to be resuscitated?"

"No." There was no hesitation in his voice.

"You're sure?"

"I just can't do it anymore. I don't want to die, but this isn't living anymore. I don't think you know just how miserable this is. I just can't do it."

"I understand. Well, let's hope they have something that will give you a little more time."

"Or let's not."

I didn't respond to his comment because I knew what he was saying, but I didn't want to accept it. There's a line that a caregiver needs to walk between protecting the person they love by being the chicken hawk that attacks every problem head-on and realizing when it's time to respect the wishes of their loved one by knowing when it's no longer time to push.

He was once again admitted, and this time, Dr. Laudi and Lacey came over to visit. As soon as they walked in, Bryan said, "Heyyy! Dr. Laudi is here!" Then, less enthusiastically, "Oh…. Dr. Laudi is here."

They explained to us that the ascites was getting worse. They felt that further treatment wouldn't be beneficial and suggested that we pursue home hospice care for him. It was a devastating gut punch. We had known it was going to happen eventually, but we still weren't ready to hear it. As they walked out, Dr. Laudi grabbed my hand as I choked out the words, "Thank you for trying."

After they'd gone, Bryan and I cried. There wasn't much to say until Bryan looked at me, sitting in a chair at the foot of his bed and said, "What are you doing way over there? Get over here!" I moved to his side, and we held each other and cried some more. We cried for the years that were being taken from us. We cried for the years we had wasted fighting with each other. We cried for all the things on his bucket list he would never get to do. We cried for our children who would grow up and get married without their dad. We cried for the life that was being cut short.

The plan was for Bryan to stay one more night in the hospital so he could have a permanent drain placed the next morning. I was able to drain the fluid from his belly at home and make him more comfortable that way. We met with the hospice and palliative care team and were told what life would look like on hospice care.

I went home that night and slept in my bed alone. I had slept in our bed alone many times over the years; when he had been away on a work trip, when he had been in the hospital, when he was out camping with his Jeep boys. But this night felt a little lonelier. I fell asleep, emotionally drained, prepared to think about the details of what the next few weeks would look like the next day.

. . . . .

I received a call from Bryan early the next morning, and he was confused and crying and didn't understand what the doctors were saying anymore. I had gotten a few strange text messages from him over the past two days I tried to dismiss as an overload of pain meds. He had asked me to bring him mustard, which he doesn't even like, and had made a comment about gnats I still hadn't figured out. Now I was questioning whether it was the pain meds or if something else was going on.

"The doctor came in and said I couldn't sit in my chair because I'm a flight risk. What the fuck is that? What's even going on? I don't understand what's happening anymore."

"Ok, try and calm down. What exactly did the doctor say?"

"I wanted to sit in my chair because I hate these beds and she said I couldn't because I was a flight risk. Am I in some sort of prison? What the fuck is happening? I don't want to be here anymore, Jen. I'm scared."

"Ok. I'm on my way. I'll handle it."

I jumped in the Jeep and made my way to him, all while calling into work and let them know that I couldn't be there that day. Haley was home with Owen to get him on the bus, so I didn't have to worry about that. When I arrived at the hospital, Bryan was much calmer than he had been and explained that they let him sit in his chair now, so he was feeling better. They came to take him for his procedure to get the permanent drain placed, and while he was gone, I decided to investigate what had happened that morning that had gotten him so upset.

The nurse explained to me that the doctor had made a joke that Bryan had misunderstood, and he took it to mean he was actually imprisoned in his hospital bed. I met with the doctor who said the same thing, although she came short of actually apologizing for her ill-timed joke.

"Ok, he'd like to go home."

"We'd like to see his numbers stabilize before he goes."

"What numbers? He's going home to die. They aren't going to stabilize."

"His white count is a little high, and his blood pressure has been low all morning, and he has had difficulty urinating."

"Ok, again, he's going home to die. What exactly do you expect to have happen?"

Just then, the other doctor we had been working with walked up and explained that it was ok to discharge him. He was going to put in the orders, but he confirmed that we had the appointment for hospice set up for the next day. "I agree, though, that he should be able to urinate before he leaves or else I'd like to see him get a Foley catheter before he goes."

"Ok. I'll talk to him." When he got back from his procedure, he was pretty groggy but said again that he wanted to go home. After he woke up a little more, I tried to talk to him about his pee.

"Honey? You awake?"

"Yep! Hi! You came here for me!"

"Of course, I did. You want to go home?"

"Yes, I can't stand being here anymore. I just want to be at home."

"Ok, they don't want to let you go until you pee."

"Ok, I can pee."

"The doctor said that you had a hard time peeing before so they don't want to let you go unless you can pee."

"I can pee. There were four people in the room, and one of them was actually looking over my shoulder at my junk to see if any pee came out and kept saying things like 'Looks like we're not getting anything yet!' I can't pee under those conditions."

"Gotcha. I wouldn't be able to pee in that situation either."

"If they want me to pee, I'll pee."

I handed him the bedside urinal and told him to pee. I walked out and waited in the hallway. A couple of minutes later, Bryan yelled to me he was done.

The nurse came in and told me they wanted to do a few more things before he was discharged. A bladder scan, some blood work, and so on. I looked at Bryan, and the look on his face told me everything I needed to know. It was time for me to protect him in other ways now.

"No, you're not doing any of those things. I'm taking my husband home."

"I'm sorry?"

"He's going home. We're not staying here any longer."

"You understand that if you leave against medical advice, then the insurance company won't pay, right?"

"Excuse me? This isn't against medical advice. The doctor that was here earlier put in discharge paperwork. We've spoken with home hospice. We've spoken with palliative care. We've spoken to his oncologist. He's going home to die. He's signed a DNR. He doesn't want to die here surrounded by the company of strangers in a bed he can't stand. He's going home. Get Dr. Fredrickson on the phone from palliative care. Get the home hospice social worker. Go talk to whomever you'd like, but my husband is going home. By the way, here's his pee." I handed her the warm plastic container he had recently peed into. "Go find someone to discharge him because he's getting dressed and we're leaving."

I looked over at Bryan as she walked away, and he had just the tiniest smile on his face. He closed his eyes and quietly said, "Chicken hawk."

Five minutes later, I had discharge paperwork in my hand and a nice nurse was giving him a ride in a wheelchair to the front door.

. . . . .

That night, I took to Facebook to make the update that Bryan insisted I make, even though I didn't really want to put it into words. He had asked me to do it so that people would understand why he wasn't responding to messages and texts. We had always kept our Facebook people updated throughout his journey but posting this update was harder to write than most. It would be out to the masses, and for some reason, that made it real.

The very first post I made about Bryan's cancer said that there was one word you never want to hear. I thought that word was "cancer." I was wrong. The word you never want to hear is "hospice."

After meeting with oncology and several other doctors, they have all agreed that Bryan put up an amazing fight. He got poison in spite of pain. He had his insides burned with radiation. He forced himself up out of bed when he felt awful so he could play games with his boy and attend his daughter's graduation. He fought like I didn't know he could fight. Unfortunately, cancer was just too strong, and his body isn't able to take anymore.

They doctors have recommended that he takes the time he has left to be with his friends and his family and find the comfort he needs as he faces the final chapter of his life on Earth. The coming weeks and (hopefully) months will be another battle for all of us .... an emotional battle none of us want to fight .... but I know my husband will face it with courage and dignity and do it the way he's lived the rest of his life .... his way and on his terms.

CHAPTER 68

I got Bryan home where he was comfortable, and the kids could spend some time with him. He sat in his favorite chair while Owen played video games and I could hear him with his usual encouragement, although it was quieter than it had been a year ago. "Go get him, buddy! Behind you! Behind you! Yes! You got him! Nice job!" Owen loved the encouragement since Bryan treated it like it was a serious sport that Owen was participating in.

We had planned to go the Shawn and Becky's house on Friday for a little get together at their house, but as we got closer, it became evident that Bryan wouldn't be able to make it over there.

"What if we come to you? We'll bring pizza."

"That could work. I think he's going to have a hard time getting to your place. He's pretty weak and gets confused easily. I think it would be better to keep him home."

"That's fine. We'll be there around 6:00."

It was a lovely evening. They brought pizza. Haley had stopped and picked up cupcakes on her way home from college. Bailey brought some chips and dip, and I had some other snacks and beverages I put out. We threw together a little party in no time at all. Bryan was able to sit up for about an hour and a half while they were there and tell stories and jokes and laugh and have a good time with them.

As the night was starting to wind down, Shawn started talking, which brought everyone to tears.

"You know, I have to tell you, buddy, there are friends of convenience. Those are the people you know and talk to and enjoy their company... the people you talk to at your kid's hockey game. Those are friends of convenience. Then there are real friends. The friends that would give you the shirt off their back. The friends that would drive an hour out of their way to help you change a tire. Those are real friends and that's what you've been to me... to all of us. You're someone who has made my life better by being part of it and I thank you for that. It's been a privilege to be your friend and I'm going to miss you. Love you, Brother."

As soon as he began to speak, Haley threw a blanket over her head and refused to look at him. We all knew what we were doing there. It was nice to pretend for a little while it was just a regular weekend, hanging out and telling funny stories, but the truth was, they were there to say goodbye to their friend. It was beautiful and bittersweet to hear his words.

After they left, Bryan needed to go lay down, so I picked up the remnants of our party and put Owen to bed. As I tucked him in and went through the nighttime routine I had taken over from Bryan, I knew there was something he wanted to say to me.

"What's up, boo?"

"Nothing. Well, maybe something, but I don't want to tell you because I don't want to make you sad."

"It's ok to be sad, buddy. This is a sad thing that's happening to us, but if it makes you feel better, I'll try not to be sad. What do you want to tell me?"

"I'm scared." He hugged me and burst into tears.

"Oh, sweet boy. I'm scared, too. Would it be ok if we were scared together?"

"But then neither of us will feel better!"

"How about this…. We'll both be scared, but I promise I'll be here to protect you and take care of you and help you still feel safe. Does that sound like an ok plan?"

"Yeah. Is Dad going to die soon?"

Owen and Haley both knew that there was no cure for Bryan's cancer, but Owen hadn't yet figured out what the word "hospice" meant. I chose my words carefully because helping him understand what was happening was one of the hardest jobs I had to do through all of it. "I think so, sweet boy. I'm so sorry. His cancer is getting worse, and his body is having a hard time. Some nurses will come to the house tomorrow to check on him and let me know how I can keep him comfortable so he's not having a lot of pain."

His tears kept coming, and I could see him struggling to say something more. "It's ok, bud. What do you want to ask me?"

"I don't want to make you cry, though. That just makes me sadder."

This was an opportunity to help him not make the same mistakes I had made when I lost a parent. "I'll try my very best to be strong for you. I know you don't like it when I cry, but you know it's ok to cry? When sad things happen, people cry, and that's ok. Sometimes the best way we can show someone how much we care is by letting our tears out. I'll be here to hold onto you. And, if it makes me cry, that's ok. This is a sad thing."

"What are we going to do without dad, mom? We're not going to survive!"

I could see the worry on his face. Bryan had always taken care of all the big projects around the house. He fixed things and built things and took care of the cars. Owen was worried about how we would all function without his dad.

"Buddy, listen. I know we're going to miss Dad. It's going to hurt a lot. But, anything Dad did, I can do. I can fix things. I know how to use tools. I can take care of the house and the lawn and both you and Haley. If there's something I don't know how to do, we'll just call grandpa or Shawn so they can help us out. I promise you ... I can do anything that Dad did."

He thought about this for a moment and then, through his tears, said, "Yeah, but you can't fight hand to hand combat!"

I laughed at him, which made him laugh, and I finally said, "When did Dad ever have to fight hand to hand combat?" Owen just laughed at the goofiness of what he had said. I finished it off by saying, "You're right. I don't know how to fight hand to hand combat. But I can learn if it's important to you."

He smiled at me and gave me a big hug. "Will you lay with me for a while and rub my back?"

"For sure! Do you want me to tickle you like Dad does?"

"No." He waited for a few moments and then, "Yeah, maybe a little."

I started tickling him and singing the Mahna Mahna song that Bryan always got him with. He started laughing some more and had a giant smile on his face. We roughhoused a little bit the way he and Bryan would always do before bed until I told him it was time to settle down. I said the prayer that Bryan always did with him and he squeezed my hand extra tight while I was saying it. I rubbed his back for a couple of minutes and kissed him goodnight and went to see Bryan in our room.

"How's my bug doing?"

"He's sad. He's scared, but mostly, he's worried about you."

"I think more than anything else that's the hardest thing for me. I can't imagine him growing up without a dad."

"I know." I thought for a few moments and told him, "You know I'm going to do a good job, right? I promise I'll raise him the way that you would have done it. I promise I'll make sure he knows all about you and how important you were to all of us."

"I know. You'll do great. I just wish I was going to be here to see it."

"You will be. You'll still be with us in some way. You tired?"

"Yeah, I need to sleep. What time does the nurse come tomorrow?"

"2:00. I'm taking the day off to take care of you until they get here. This weekend the Jeep Guys want to come see you if you're feeling up to it. A bunch of people have been messaging me since I put the Facebook post out about you entering hospice. Would you be ok if I just open the house up from 1:00 to 3:00 on Saturday? That way everyone can just stop by and say what they want to say, and I don't have to keep arranging times with people?"

"That sounds excruciating."

"Yes, it does. But so many people want to come see you before they can't anymore. You can literally just lay in bed while people come here to see you."

"Yeah, I suppose. Would you lay with me for a while?"

"Yep. Whatever you want." We laid in bed holding hands as I thought about all the regrets I wouldn't be able to make up for and it crushed me. I thought about all the times I had been short with him, or the words I wished I could take back. All the things we never got to do. All the places we never got to see together. Before I could stop them, the tears rolled down my cheeks as I thought about all the things I wished I could do over. He pulled me a little closer, and he knew what I was thinking without me having to say anything.

"You know, I had a pretty good life, didn't I?"

"Yes, you did. You had an amazing life. It might not have been fancy or filled with glamour or mansions or vacations all over the world, but it was pretty dang good."

"Do you remember that time we met up the highway in Eden Prairie when you broke up with me?"

"Yeah. Are you going to finally admit that you were stalking me? Because more than one person has suggested you were."

"Ha! No, I wasn't stalking you. I was just thinking about how that was the day we got back together and stayed together after that. I was thinking that if I had left the house five minutes later or if I had taken a different way or you had stopped at McDonald's for a cheeseburger, we wouldn't have seen each other, and none of this would have happened. Fate played a part in our story that day. Even when things were tough, we didn't give up, did we? We kept working to stay together. If I had gone a different way that day, we wouldn't have this house or that little bug. You're the reason I made it this long. You're the reason I was able to fight. You're my everything. Just like our first dance. I wanted to be your everything then, and I still want to. I'm sorry I won't be here to be your everything forever."

"I'm sorry, too. I love you."

"I love you, too."

CHAPTER 69

The home hospice nurses came the next day and got him set up on their program. They would be coming by once a day to check on him and see how he was doing. I was shown how to drain his fluid from his belly when it was starting to build up. They explained the medication and the schedule he needed to be on. He couldn't be left alone anymore, so I needed to arrange for my mother-in-law to sit with him when I went to work. They did an excellent job of making me feel comfortable and supported.

That night I assumed my new favorite place to be; lying in bed with my head on his shoulder enjoying the fleeting time we still had left. I knew there were some logistics I needed to take care of, but I was careful to find a balance between handling the details and still allowing myself to feel the sadness.

"I went and met with a funeral home today with Becky. The people were really nice, and they seem like they'll take good care of you."

"That's good. I'm glad you're taking care of some of that ahead of time. It will be harder to do once I'm gone."

"Do you want to have an open casket? I was planning to have the visitation and the memorial and everything there."

"No, I'd rather be cremated. You can put me on the bookshelf and keep me around for a while."

"Ok. I'll get rid of all your World War II books to make room for you. Should I move you to the table each night for dinner?"

"No, that would just be dumb."

"But keeping you on the bookshelf is normal? What about music? Is there a certain song you want me to play at the funeral?"

"Metallica?"

"Seriously?"

"I don't know. I think Sexy Back would be most appropriate, cuz this right here looks good. I got my sexy on all the time."

"How would your mother feel about that?"

"It's my funeral. I can have whatever I want. You should play The Circle of Life then raise my urn up over your head."

"Like Lion King baby style? I'm not sure that's dignified."

"Is Sexy Back dignified?

"At least I'm not recreating a scene from a Disney movie in the middle of your funeral. I'll go with Sexy Back and maybe throw some Keith Urban in there. He seems to have defined every stage of our life together. I mean really, I can't think of a time that Keith Urban wasn't part of our life. So, you want me to have you cremated and leave you on the bookshelf?"

"Yeah, I guess. I mean not forever, but for a while. When you're ready, you can spread my ashes somewhere. Maybe in Germany on that mountain we went to."

"That was beautiful, but then I'd never get to visit you."

"That's true but I'd love the view. You'll find somewhere nice to leave me. Find a Jeep trail somewhere and leave me there."

We sat quietly thinking about the morbid conversation we were having, my head still on his shoulder, just enjoying our time together until I finally asked, "Do you think when you die, you'll know how the Star Wars trilogy ends?"

Without missing a beat, he said, "Oh, I'm sure of it." He knew how much I hated waiting for the final episode of any show or movie. He stayed off Facebook for weeks before the previous Star Wars movie came out because he didn't want to accidentally see any spoilers. I, on the other hand, read every article and watched every trailer trying to guess what was going to happen. I didn't read the spoilers, but I read the theories and crafted my own ideas. Finally, he said, "I know what you're getting at and I'm not going to come back to tell you. Don't expect to have a dream some night where you have a sudden realization who Rey's parents are. I wouldn't ruin it for you like that. But yeah, I'll know what happens long before you do."

"Asshole. I'm your wife. If you have info, I should be told."

"It's not happening. What are you gonna do about it?"

That weekend I opened the house like we had talked about so that people could stop by and visit. We had a total of 72 people come over to see him. The Jeep Guys all came, Bryan's best friend from high school and his wife stopped by, family friends, and a few people he worked with on The Ballet Project. I put chairs up in our bedroom so that Bryan could stay in bed and they took turns going up to have a few laughs and spend some time with him. Most of the eyes that went in were dry but were red and full of tears on the way out. By the end of it, he was exhausted and got some good sleep that night. The drugs they were giving him seemed to do the trick, so he was more comfortable than he had been for a few days.

By Tuesday, things were a different story. Owen woke me up at 6:00 a.m. and told me that Bryan needed me. Bryan had been in the bathroom throwing up for a couple of hours which I couldn't hear because I had a fan on in our room to help with my profuse sweating.

I sat on the edge of the tub while he vomited, and I rubbed his back. "I'm sorry, honey. I didn't hear you calling me."

"I just can't …. ehhhhh…. I can't stop puking. Isn't there something they can give me to make it stop?"

"I can try calling the hospice people and see what they recommend."

"Yeah, do that."

"Ok, I'll be right back. You stay here."

"I'm not planning to go …… ehhhhh…. anywhere."

I walked into the hallway, and Owen was standing there with a look of fear in his eyes. "Is Dad ok?"

"Yeah, buddy. His belly is just pretty sick right now. You want to go lay in my bed for a while?"

"No, can I go downstairs?"

"Sure. That's fine. I need to go call the nurse people that take care of dad." I came back a few minutes later, and Bryan's vomiting had settled down a little bit.

"What did they say?"

"You're not going to like it."

"What?"

"They want you to use the suppository."

"What the fuck is that?"

"It's the medicine you need to put up your butt."

"For fuck's sake… seriously? Not only have I been puking for two hours, but I also need to shove something up my ass?"

"They said it's the quickest way to get your vomiting and nausea under control."

"I'm not shoving something up my ass. Go get me my bat."

"You'd rather be high than shove something up your butt?" I stopped. "I just heard it when I said it out loud, so I think I know the answer to that."

"Wouldn't you?"

"Yeah... Ok." I found his weed and let him smoke a little of it in the bathroom, and it seemed to help. He was able to get back into bed, and I was able to get ready for work. His mother would be there soon to get Owen off to school and sit with Bryan while I worked a half-day. I called the hospice nurse on my way to work and told her about what had happened that morning.

"I feel awful that he was in there for two hours throwing up and I couldn't hear him. Owen had to come tell me that Bryan needed me. I was just exhausted and couldn't hear him."

"Jen, don't feel bad about it. I know how you feel. I think it's time to send him to a hospice facility."

"Already? He's only been on the hospice program for less than a week."

"Yeah, but things are moving quickly, and I want you to feel comfortable, too."

"So, you really think it's time?"

"I do. Just based on what's been happening the past few days, I do think it's time."

I went to work as I had planned. The escape from all things cancer was nice. I was able to help a few students that I knew were close to graduating. I could take my mind off everything happening at home, even if it was just for a short amount of time. The people at my work were supportive of me and I was able to leave on a moment's notice if things went south quickly.

When I got home, I let Louise know that transportation would be coming in another hour or so to take Bryan to JA Wedum Residential Hospice. I felt bad about it, but I asked her to leave. This was the last time they would take my husband out of his home. The last time I would ever be with him in the home we had created. The last time he would see his room or his garage or his things. This was another last, and it was excruciating. I needed just a few moments with him before they came to take him, and I didn't want anyone around to see it. I knew how hard this was on her with Bryan being her only child, but this was my husband, and I needed these few moments with him before he was gone.

"Honey, your mom just left, and your transportation should be here soon."

"Ok, they're coming to take me?" It was a day where he was confused more easily, and I didn't know if he understood what was happening.

"Yes, they're going to come take you to Wedum now. They have a nice room there for you."

"Ok. They're going to give me a ride?"

"Yes."

"And I'm going to stay there?"

"Yes, honey. They can make you more comfortable than I can. They know how to take care of you. I don't know how to give you this kind of care."

"Ok. Will you come with me?"

"Yes, I'm going to follow behind you in the Jeep."

"In my Jeep?"

"Yes."

"Ok. I think I understand."

He looked at me with fear in his eyes. I knew that he really understood what this meant. The end was getting near.

As he was wheeled out our front door for the last time, I told him I would be right behind him. I put on my shoes and grabbed my jacket, and I couldn't fight the tears any longer. I sat down as sobs shook my whole body. It was just too much for one person to handle. He would never be in the home we had built together ever again, and it was devastating. I looked around at the quiet of the new home I was going to live in and felt the enormity of what the coming days would bring. I took that moment to feel sorry for myself, then composed myself, grabbed my keys and went to meet my husband at the place he was going to die.

CHAPTER 70

I followed closely behind his ambulance to Wedum, which was about 25 minutes from our house. The facility was beautiful. It had dark cherry wood throughout the building, a fireplace room with a stone surround, and a grand piano in the lobby. I wanted to get Bryan settled before I brought the kids back to see him.

"So, what do I do? Lay here and die?"

"I mean... no.... But yeah, I .... I mean.... You're just supposed to be more comfortable here. Do you want me to stay? They have a couch I can sleep on."

"No, you need to go home to be with the kids."

"I can find someone to come stay with them or Haley is old enough she could stay home with Owen overnight. I'll stay if you want me to."

"No, I don't want them to be scared. They need you there."

"Ok. They're at Shawn and Becky's right now for dinner. I'll go pick them up and bring them back. Are you going to be ok?"

"Yeah. I'll just lay here and wait for Death."

I knew he was trying to joke, but I couldn't hear the finality of his statement at that moment. I left to pick up the kids and during the ride back to Wedum, I could tell that both of them were nervous. Haley kept asking me how long he was going to be there.

"I mean, is he going to die soon?"

"I don't know, honey. They can just take better care of him than I can."

"Yeah, but what did they say? Did they say it would happen soon?"

"They didn't say, honey. Here's what I do know. He's still alert. He still can communicate with us, but that might change in the next few days. It's important that you both say everything you want to say to him tonight. Don't have any regrets you didn't tell him something or ask him something. Say what's in your heart and what's on your mind. Owen, do you want me to tell you what it looks like, so you're not surprised?"

"Yeah, I guess."

Owen was quieter about his emotions than Haley was. He didn't like to upset people and never made himself the center of attention. He was my helper and thought helping me now meant keeping control of his emotions. As we were driving to see his dad at the hospice facility he would spend his remaining days, I knew that Owen was trying his best to be strong, but it was harder for him than Haley.

We arrived at Wedum, and I showed the kids the fireplace room, and where they could get a snack. I showed Owen where the playroom was and showed him the video games in case he wanted to play. We walked down to Bryan's room. The lights were low, and the room was quiet as he rested comfortably in the bed they had given him.

Watching my children say goodbye to their dad was, and will forever be, the most heartbreaking experience of my life. I didn't interfere and let them say what they needed to say, but I choked back tears as I listened to them cry. I watched them try to find the words to convey what they felt. It was the most gut-wrenching, horrible thing I've ever had to watch. Haley thanked him for being the dad he didn't have to be and apologized for all the times she had treated him poorly. She was trying to make peace with her horrible teenage years and not have any regrets. Owen had a harder time finding the words but eventually told him he was the best dad anyone could ask for. They told him they would miss him, and he promised he would check in on them from time to time from Heaven. They both sat holding his hand, crying for the dad that wouldn't be around to see their accomplishments.

I thought back to the day my mom died and how I never wanted my children to have to feel the pain I had felt that night. When we knew her death was close, I asked everyone to leave the room so I could say what I needed to say without everyone watching me and allowing them into the heartbreak I was feeling. I could see myself sitting next to her hospice bed, begging her not to leave me. I remembered how I told her I didn't know how to be half the mother she had been. I remembered the despair I felt as I watched her slowly fading away in front of me.

And now, I watched my children have to go through that same anguish I felt that night. It's a feeling I never wanted them to know at such a young age. I don't know how I managed to drive after that, but I had them tucked into bed shortly after we got home, and then I went to our bed and cried my eyes out.

CHAPTER 71

Bryan had been at Wedum for a few days, and he had grown increasingly weaker. He had requested that we restrict visitors to just close family and Shawn and Becky. Too many visitors were overwhelming for him. On Thursday, I was getting ready to leave for the night and reminded him that Shawn was coming the next day to sit with him. I had used up so much of my vacation time I was having to take all my days off unpaid, so I was trying to work when I could find other people to come sit with him. Typically, I would find someone to sit with Bryan in the morning so I could work and then stay with Bryan in the afternoon until his mom could get there. When she arrived, I would head home for a little while to feed the kids and regroup and then head back to sit with him in the evening.

"Who's coming tomorrow? Do you remember?" He looked at me, and I could tell he was confused, but I tried to give him a minute to process. He looked at me again, and his eyes told me he didn't know.

"Shawn is coming, remember?"

"I know. I know! I was working it out. I'm not as fast as you."

My heart was in my throat. I could tell he was frustrated, and I didn't know what else to do to try and help. The situation we were in was painful and foreign, but still had the familiarity that I had been there before. My husband had quickly deteriorated in front of my eyes until all that was left was a shell.

By Sunday, he was more confused and had been agitated all morning while I was there. After his mom arrived, I headed home for a break. I fed the kids and waited for my dad to arrive so he could feed them some dinner. I called Louise on my drive back and asked if he was still as restless as he had been that morning. She said that he was. I knew it was going to be a long night, but I brought a book and a snack and headed back to my love.

When I walked in, I kissed him on the forehead and told him I was there. He had been twitchy for the past few days, and the nurses had told me they were going to give him something to help him calm down a little bit, so he wasn't so twitchy and agitated. The nurse came in and gave me an update on how things had been going. He still wasn't showing any of the classic signs that death was getting closer, so she gave him a double dose of his medication that would help him to calm down and then left me to be with him.

As soon as she walked out, Bryan started moaning. I told him about what we had done that day at home and told him that the kids missed him to try and help him calm down. I sat down in the reclining chair in the room and turned on the TV. I thought we could watch something together, even if it was really just me watching.

"I'm going to sit over here and watch some TV. Do you want to watch it with me? The Oscars are on tonight. We always watch that together. Gaga and Bradley Cooper are going to sing, and we don't want to miss that!" He continued moaning with every breath he took, and it was getting louder.

"You're ok, honey! I'm right here." I was hoping that the sound of my voice would help him calm down. "Are you uncomfortable?" I didn't know what he was trying to tell me, but the moaning was getting worse with every breath. "I'll have the nurse come back in and get you more comfortable. Is that why you're moaning so much? Is it because you're uncomfortable? Do you need something?" *I can't fucking stand this! Oh, my gosh…. Just stop moaning. It was supposed to make him more comfortable for him to be here.* "I'll be right back. I'm going to go get a nurse."

I walked down to the nurse's station and could still hear Bryan moaning while I walked down the hall. "Excuse me?"

"Hi. How are things going?"

"Not very well. The nurse that was on the last shift gave my husband some medicine to make him more comfortable, but he won't stop moaning. He's clearly in some sort of pain, and he's still twitchy. They had talked about sedating him. Could someone please go give him something? Bringing him here was supposed to make him more comfortable, and he's clearly not." As I realized I was slightly more aggressive than I needed to be, I could hear Bryan calling me a chicken hawk in my head.

"Yes, the last nurse talked to me about it. We're going to give him something that will help for a while. Are you ok with that? It would essentially put him to sleep."

"Yes, please. I can't stand to watch him like this. If you could just find some way to sedate him, so he's not aware of his pain, that would probably be best."

"Yep. We'll be down there in just a few minutes."

I walked around the facility for a few minutes. Hearing him like that was awful, and I couldn't listen to it anymore. I went and got myself some spaghetti from the kitchen where they kept meals in a crock pot for the families that were visiting their loved ones. I figured I would give the nurses a few minutes to get him settled and let the medicine they were going to give him kick in.

When I walked back to the room, two nurses were in his room with him quietly talking. They had straightened him up on his bed and covered him up with the blanket I had brought him.

"Hi. Were you able to give him that medicine?" He was still moaning so I was hoping it would kick in fairly soon.

"Well, no. Is this what he's been doing?"

"Yes, for like the last hour. He lets out a moan with every breath. It's unbearable to listen to him like this."

"Honey, I don't think he's in pain. I think he's actively dying."

I stared at her and didn't know what to say. *This whole time he wasn't moaning because he was in pain? He had been yelling at me to get my ass out of my reclining chair and come sit with him. I could hear it, "Are you fucking kidding me? You can watch the Oscars when you get home. Get over here! I'm ready now."*

"Oh. Ok. Ummm.... So, should I not leave?"

"No, you need to sit down and be with him now."

"Oh. uhhhh.... Ok. Are you going to give him that medicine still?"

"No, I can't do that because I believe that would hasten his death. He's already in the process of dying, so we can't administer anything to him now."

"Ok. Ummm.... So, I should stay here with him?"

"Yes. That's what you need to do now."

The nurses both walked out and I hesitated for just a moment. I had escaped watching my mom die by volunteering for mundane tasks that my neighbor could have done. I had always been thankful that she chose to die while I was still in the parking lot, but now ... at this moment ... I couldn't escape the promise I made to the man I loved. I pulled the little folding chair closer to his bed and sat down next to him. I took his hand in mine and looked at the man I had loved for the last 18 years. I didn't want him to go, but I wanted his pain to be over and knew that he had been trying to make peace for the last week with his life ending. I sat holding his hand until I finally found the words to tell him it was ok and quietly said, "I'm sorry I didn't understand you sooner. I'm here now. You're safe. When you're ready, you can go. I'll just sit here and hold your hand until you're ready."

As soon as I said those words and held his hand, his moaning stopped, and he became very quiet. His breathing became slower and softer. I continued holding his hand as I watched the transformation from agitated and upset to peaceful and ready to let go. His breathing was becoming choppier, and the time between each breath was getting longer, but there was no fear on his face. There was no looking to me for help. He was ready. He had made peace with what was happening to him.

The nurse walked back in and saw me sitting with him and said, "Oh! He's close!" It had been no more than 10 minutes since they had told me that I needed to sit down and be with him. She ran back out to get another nurse as I sat there, still holding his hand. I watched his face and his breathing and sat there quietly loving him as I watched his final breath leave his body.

That was it. He was gone. I refused to let go as the anguish hit me like a wave. He was gone. I just sat there, not wanting to let go of his hand. His was the hand I had held for the last 18 years. The hand that fit perfectly in mine. I knew every bump and every callous. It was the hand that meant safety and love, the hand that was always there to catch me when I needed it. The hand that would hold mine when we went on a summertime walk even though my palms were sweaty. It was the hand that held mine as I begged for drugs while I was giving birth to his son but never let go once, even when my nails were digging into his palm. He was the man I promised to love for the rest of my life, and once I let go, I would never hold his hand again.

I didn't want to leave him. I didn't want to be done. I wanted to take every decision back and try more chemo or a clinical trial or find a new doctor that was willing to operate. I wanted to go back in time and tell them to do the endoscopic ultrasound earlier so they could have gotten to the tumor before the blood clot formed. I wanted to skip back to the years we were hurtful to each other and change the things I said to him and not waste those years with criticism and foolish pride and anger. I wanted to take it all back so I could have just a few more minutes with him. After what felt like an eternity and only a moment all at once, I finally took his hand, held it to my lips, kissed him one more time and let go.

I stood up and walked over to the couch as a hazy reality floated around me. I was seeing it all happening from a distance as the nurses came in and out of the room. After several more minutes, I started making the calls I dreaded making. First, to Haley. "Hi, baby. Are you home now? Yeah? Is grandpa still there? Ok, honey, Bryan just passed. I know you wanted to be here, but by the time we realized what was going on, it was less than 10 minutes before he was gone. You wouldn't have made it back in time. I know, baby. I'm sorry. I'm going to finish up here and then come home."

Next, I called his mother and let her know that he had finally found the courage and peace to let go and that he was no longer in pain. Listening to her cry on the other end of the phone was one of the worst sounds I had ever heard. Hearing a mother find out that her only child was gone tore at my heart. I told her I would be in touch in the next few days so we could work out the details of his service.

I slowly packed up his things I had brought to hospice with me so he would feel comfortable; A bright orange and red blanket, pictures of Haley and Owen, a drawing of a tiger that Owen had made for Bryan. I made the nurses promise they would treat him with dignity when the funeral home came. I also confirmed that they had contacted the organization that would come and take his corneas so he could donate them. He had always wanted to be an organ donor, but with his cancer, the only thing he could still give was his corneas. He made me promise that something good would come from his death, and this was the only thing I could think of to do.

I walked out to the Jeep and made the drive home with tears streaming down my face. I promised him I would be there until the very end, holding his hand, and I had fulfilled that promise, as much as it hurt me to do it. I had wanted to run and hide and be anywhere but there, but I promised him I would be there with him when he was finally ready to let go. As was Bryan's way, he did it on his time, at his pace and when he was ready. And once he knew it was time, it was over quickly and quietly. That was how he had always operated his life. Once you made a decision to do something, you did it and didn't second guess.

CHAPTER 72

The day after Bryan died, Owen and I spent the day playing hooky from work and school and doing fun things to remember his dad. Haley wanted to be with her friends, and I had no problem with her surrounding herself with the support system she needed. We went to a movie in the middle of the day, and we were the only ones in the theater, which was a special treat for Owen. We went and played laser tag and ran around charging each other with our laser guns and then assuming sniper positions to defeat the other player, "Just like Dad taught me."

We stopped by his school so Owen could see Ms. Ashley, the school social worker who had been doing wonders for him through both Bryan and my illnesses. She was kind and patient and understanding and handled the situation with skill. We also stopped by to see Mrs. N, Owen's 4th-grade teacher who gave us each a hug. Of all the teachers Owen could have gotten that school year, we lucked out when he got Mrs. N. Some teachers believe that math, reading, and science are all that matters at Owen's age, but Mrs. N saw the whole student and how the social aspects are just as important as the academic. She was excellent, and precisely what Owen needed during a confusing time for such a young boy. They had both loved my son enough to make the hard times just a little bit easier, and I was confident they would continue to do that through the rest of the school year.

We planned Bryan's funeral for March 9th. It gave people who were out of town some time to arrange to come to the cities. Bryan had asked that the people he worked with in Nashville be notified, so I sent a message to his old boss, Kirsten, and asked her to let everyone know. As we got closer to the day of his funeral, the news started reporting a giant storm was supposed to hit Minnesota right around the time that Bryan's service was about to begin.

"Are you fucking kidding me? Snowmageddon is going to hit the cities right during the funeral." Bailey had brought Mac to play with Owen for a while. It was a nice distraction for Owen and a good reminder that it's still ok to have fun and laugh and continue on with life.

"Yeah, I saw the storm was coming. Could you change the date?"

"I doubt it. Besides, Bryan would have hated that. Once you decide on something, you're supposed to stick to it. It's already in the obituary, and I can't change the day now."

"Well, maybe it won't snow as much as they say."

"They're predicting the apocalypse. People are stocking up on canned goods and bottled water. I have never been so annoyed by the timing of a storm in my life. Seriously. He'll be the only one there, and that's only because he's already there!"

"People will still come. I'm sure of it. All those Jeep guys with their big tires?"

"That's a valid point. At least I'll have them."

I had planned his funeral to perfection. I knew what readings I wanted, what songs I wanted to play, the poem I would have Becky read, and now the one thing I couldn't plan for was happening: The weather. All I could do was hope that the perfect funeral I had planned still went smoothly.

I knew I wanted to speak at his funeral. I knew him better than anyone, and I wanted to capture both the love we had for each other, as well as the humor that was a staple of our relationship. I had written my eulogy when Bryan was still alert enough to understand it so he could approve it. As I was reading it to him in our bed a few days before he had left for Wedum, he looked at me and said, "I've got five bucks that say you don't make it through the 3rd paragraph before you break down."

"I will not! I'm very talented. I can get through it."

"Jen, you just read it to me and made it through like three sentences before your voice started catching. I've got five that says you crumble."

"I am not going to crumble. I'm doing this for you. I have a heart of stone when I need to."

"That's true. You are tougher than anyone I've ever met. You'll do great. I withdraw my bet."

"Nope. You owe me five dollars if I make it through without crying."

"Good luck collecting on that one!"

"Asshole…. I'll make it through. I'm a stone robot."

"You realize that doesn't even make sense, right? A robot can't be made of stone. You can't be both a robot and be made of stone."

"Seriously? Shut the fuck up." He laughed as I stood up to walk out of the room. I leaned against the doorway and folded my arms. "I can be whatever kind of robot I want to be. Either way, I'll do better on your eulogy than you ever could have done on mine. I'm going to crush that bitch." I smiled at him.

"I'm sure you'll do great. You did a great job of writing it. You're a talented stone robot."

Now, as I sat there with the perfect funeral only a day away, I was pissed off that the one thing I couldn't plan was going to screw it all up.

"People will still come, Jen. Don't worry. He was loved by a lot of people. Besides that, we're Minnesotans; A March storm is nothing. People will make it through."

CHAPTER 73

The worst of the weather managed to hold off long enough for the room to be packed. Every seat was filled, and the outer walls were standing room only. We had an hour of visitation ahead of the funeral, and it was exactly as I had hoped. People walked around, looking at the pictures of him and telling stories and laughing. There was sadness in the room, as well, when people would go up and see the urn I had specially engraved with a line drawing of Bryan's Jeep. Several people asked me if they could take a picture of it, and I was happy to have that happen. Bryan's photos from The Ballet Project lined one side of the room. Images from his pilgrimage to Burning Man filled the other side. I had small, flat rocks and markers for people to leave a message or a phrase I could keep and remember all the ways people loved him.

The funeral was supposed to start at 2:00, and at 1:59, true to form, I saw Dena walk in. I turned and waved at her and resisted the urge to jump out of my seat and go hug her, or at the very least yell,

"Hey! You're one whole minute early! Amazing!". We hadn't seen each other often in the past few years, but she was still there to support me, and I loved her for it. At precisely 2:00 the service started, and Pastor Dave gave a great opening by saying, "If I were to say there's a Jeep in the parking lot with its lights on, I think I could clear the room." We all laughed, realizing just how many Jeeps filled the parking lot.

After Pastor Dave said a prayer for Bryan's life and read Psalm 23, I had one speaker talk about the Ballet Project and the difference he made to the ladies and gentlemen he worked with. The Ballet Project was something he was so proud of, and I hated seeing it come to an end. One of the Jeep Guys talked about their off-roading adventures and how much they all enjoyed having Bryan around and what he meant to the guys in the group. Haley spoke about how grateful she was that Bryan made the choice to be her dad. I was incredibly proud of her for making it through without losing it. Haley is a nervous public speaker so for her to speak in front of all those people was a huge accomplishment. Finally, Becky went up to read the poem I had picked out for her. She took a few moments to compose herself, and I almost stood up to go help her, but she pulled it together and made it through.

Finally, I heard Pastor Dave say, "Jennifer? Do you want to come say a few words?" I stood and walked in slow motion to stand behind the podium and looked at all of the people staring at me. Tom and Angela were sitting with their boys …. Shereen was clutching a box of Kleenex …. Scott had a look on his face that told me he was there to support me … Bailey looked like she'd been crying…. Shawn had a big shit-eating grin on his face, impervious to the emotions that were in the room… Owen had created a kid's section in the back so that he could sit with his friends and Haley was looking at me like she was scared, but every seat was filled. It was difficult to see all those faces that missed Bryan, but a sea of love was staring back at me. All of these people had braved the storm to support me and show their love for my husband. It was amazing to see so many people there.

Ok.... you can do this. You are a stone robot. I got a little smile on my face and knew I would make it through his eulogy with no problem. He was with me.

"Before I met my husband, I had gone on a lot of really bad dates. I was a divorced single mom, and I had waded into the worst imaginable dating pool with tragic results. There was the guy who dressed all in purple. He walked in wearing a purple mock turtleneck, purple pants, purple socks, and purple shoes. I'm not sure what he was going for, but I could instantly tell that it didn't work for him. There was the guy who showed up two hours late with a case of beer and asked if he could sleep on my couch. No… No, you cannot sleep on my couch. There was the guy who kept farting. I ended that date pretty quickly. There was the guy who arrived in a Winnebago to the restaurant I was meeting him at. He asked me if I wanted to come hang out in his Winnebago in the parking lot after dinner. My untimely death flashed before my eyes and I decided to pass.

And then I met this completely average guy who loved to talk about his Jeep and considered watching the movie Beauty and the Beast at home with my kid to be a great first date. He even had the forethought to call me before he came over to see what kind of candy he should bribe her with …. nummy nummy M's became a go-to item any time he came over after that.

So, there I was… vulnerable single mom, coming off a bad divorce and wading into the worst dating pool imaginable, and I'm afraid to pull the trigger and get serious with this guy who seemingly is completely normal and kind. His clothes weren't monochromatic.

He kept his bodily functions to himself and he drove a regular vehicle... and a fun one at that. And still, I'm a little gun shy to let him in.

I actually broke up with him once and told him I just wasn't ready to date. He hung his head and walked away, and we got used to the idea we wouldn't be together anymore. Then, one day I was driving home from Eden Prairie, somewhere I would usually never be in the middle of the day, and on the entrance ramp I see this Jeep pull up beside me. I looked over, and there was Bryan.... like a flashing neon sign from the universe. He gave me the pull over signal, and I thought, 'ah crap.... this really is the guy.' He insisted he wasn't stalking me, no matter how many times I asked him. What are the odds of us both being in an area we wouldn't usually be and meeting up on 494 by chance? If he was a crazy stalker, it worked because my heart melted, and I realized this was the guy I was going to spend my life with, and it was silly to keep fighting it.

You couldn't have picked two different people to form the team we did. He, with his go with the flow attitude, and me with my need to plan everything. He, who would pack for a trip three hours before his plane left, and I, with a checklist and clothes set out a week ahead of time. I had my spreadsheets that indicated what time was allocated for having fun, and he was continuously finding a new adventure in the moment that wasn't on our schedule of activities. He had an artistic eye and a free spirit. I copied my best ideas off Pinterest. There were his serious moments when I had to remind him to smile, and times he had to remind me that not everything is a joke. But that was the great complement we had with each other. It wasn't opposites attract .... it was where can I fill in your gaps and where can you help mine?

He knew me better than anyone and knew when I was trying to work an angle and wasn't afraid to call me out on it. One night, when we knew the end was getting near, we were lying in bed, my head on his shoulder, and I mentioned that it would be pretty cool if, as soon as he died, he would know how the new Star Wars trilogy ends. Let's just say, he made it pretty clear that he wouldn't be coming back to share any insight with me. We made a great team by loving each other and checking each other when our BS started to show.

Bryan and I didn't have the easiest life. We went through some pretty hard times, but we managed to find the humor in most everything we did. Whether it was losing a job, a broken furnace in the middle of winter, or eventually surgeries, chemo, and radiation, we found a way to laugh at what was happening around us. I can remember late nights, no money to go out and do anything and we spent hours at home talking and laughing with each other. Other nights were spent at our favorite neighborhood bonfire listening to music and telling inappropriate jokes and stories until it was obvious that everyone needed to go to bed. There were camping trips in a busted-up pop up camper that he bought for $500 off Craigslist that he spent time fixing up only to have to fix it again, but many camping trips were had in that busted up piece of junk and many late nights just enjoying the quiet of nature. Life was better when it was less complicated.

That's not to say they weren't complicated at times, but we took it all in stride. We shared the responsibility of being the rock the other could lean on when it was needed. After I found out I had breast cancer, I got pretty good at hiding the emotion behind it. I'd say it like I had gone to Walmart for snacks. 'I stopped at the store to get some juice and some chips. Oh, and I have breast cancer.' However, the morning of my surgery, I had gotten the kids off to school when it all of a sudden hit me: I have breast cancer. As I started to break, Bryan was to me in three giant steps letting me break on him rather than on my own. The day we learned that further treatment wasn't going to help his cancer, I was sitting across from him, both of us feeling the weight of what the doctor had told us, and he called me to his side so that we could cry together rather than apart. It was my turn to hold him and promise him I would be there, holding his hand until the very end.

Our kids were everything to Bryan. He took on the role of instant parent when he met me. I didn't always make it easy for him, either. Many battles were fought with me trying to maintain my control and him reminding me that kids need to fall in order to learn. Regardless, his pride when he talked about his daughter was evident … not stepdaughter. He considered her to be his. He taught her about Jeeps when she was little and the fancy windows you had to turn a crank to roll up instead of pushing a boring old button. He taught her that Jeepin naked did not mean you had to take off your clothes, but still used the phrase to freak out her friends from time to time. He played tea party and dance party including a dance moved he nicknamed 'The Sparrow' which looked like a full-body dry heave with his arms flapping at his side. He bragged about how beautiful his daughter is. He sat at basketball tournaments cheering her on when he didn't really understand the rules. He sat through hours of dance competitions to show her he cared.

When we decided we wanted to have a baby together, that was also a struggle. After years of failed attempts and a couple of miscarriages, we finally got the sweetest boy through IVF. When his son was born, the emotion and love were palpable. He sat holding that baby boy just staring at him. He thought he had cracked the baby code when Owen fell asleep in his arms while Bryan was stroking his eyebrow. Yes, he fell asleep, but he's like seven minutes old. He cried for the first six minutes, and now he's exhausted, but you are absolutely the baby whisperer. Watching his son grow up was the highlight of his existence. He relished the tasks of teaching him about cars, wrestling with him, playing video games, teaching him how to be a gentleman, and then in the very next breath teaching him that a sniper needs to have a perch above everyone to get the best shot; all the things a dad needs to teach a young man. In fact, once Bryan got sick, his son was the one thing that was off limits to talk about. Having his son grow up without a dad was the one thing he couldn't think about.

I promised Bryan that in his absence, I will do my very best to raise a young man that is kind and respectful the way that his father was. I promised him that I'll walk our daughter down the aisle. I promised him that his presence will be known and felt, and we'll remember him and honor him through our actions, our words and our intentions.

When my mom passed away from cancer, I would listen to the Garth Brooks song, "The Dance" and wonder if my dad would have changed anything knowing the pain he was going to go through losing my mom. Theirs was the great love story that none of us could measure up to. But, knowing the heartbreak that came with losing her, I often wondered if Garth was on to something or if it would have been easier to not know that kind of loss.

I now know that the dance is what makes it all worthwhile. If I had driven off instead of pulling over that day or if I thought a completely monochromatic purple clothing choice was sexy, I could have missed the heartbreak I feel today. I wouldn't be aching inside missing my best friend and the one person I turned to whenever I needed someone. But I also would have missed all those late-night

Jeep drives holding his hand, getting lost on back roads and then finding our way home. I never would have had all the camping trips with the quiet of the stars surrounding us. I wouldn't have experienced him making me laugh so hard that I'm about to pee my pants, and then him, realizing I'm about to pee, steps up his game and makes me laugh even harder. I would have missed all the good things that come with the pain I feel right now, and I wouldn't trade those good things for anything."

A couple of months after Bryan's funeral, the turn signal on my car burned out. I had spent two years remaining stoic and composed and the rock that everyone could lean on. I was there to scoop up anyone that fell and be the solver of problems, even when it was my own health that was in question. I had maintained my sense of humor and kept everyone laughing so that we could tackle the next problem with optimism and a smile on our faces. That burned out turn signal sent me into a crying spell that took a good hour to recover from.

It's a very surreal thing when someone you love dies after a prolonged illness. When you find out they're sick, you spend all of your energy trying to find ways to save their life. You spend hours and days looking at options and statistics. You look for anything that might be a glimmer of hope and convince yourself the next thing is going to work. However, when they die, you are left in a void where you don't

have anything you're working toward anymore. After a month, the phone calls and the cards and the well wishes from the people around you come to an abrupt end, and everyone continues on while you're still immersed in the void. The direction of my life had changed the day Bryan was diagnosed with pancreatic cancer, and now I was left not remembering what "normal" looked like since the only normal I could remember was fighting cancer.

I laid there, thinking about that $3 lightbulb and everything it represented and realized how easy it would be to become cynical and angry again. Bryan had continued loving me the way he promised he would. I had finally gotten comfortable letting him love me, and then he was gone. My tough exterior had been softened over the years as he systematically took down my wall brick by brick, and now I was exposed. Even after he cheated, I learned to trust again with hard work and our commitment to becoming a better couple. He had been patient and kind while I tested him at the beginning of our relationship, waiting for me to realize that having a man in my life did not diminish my accomplishments or detract from my independence. He had loved me for, and in spite of, my tenacity to tackle every crisis that came our way. And now, it was just me… no wall… no man…. Exposed to the emotions I didn't want to feel.

For the past 20 years, I had been managing other people's bullshit. When something bad would happen, I would go into a certain mode and start controlling the details. People looked to me to be the voice of calm when everyone else was panicking. Over all those years, the crises had slowly started to define who I was and control the story of my life. I didn't know who I was without them.

Now, I was defenseless against the last crisis I needed to manage. And it wasn't just the death of Bryan that I was grieving. I was feeling the weight of two years of cancer treatments. I was grieving the loss of

my boobs. I was crying because I missed his companionship. I was crying because I still didn't have my origami nipples. I was crying for the tree I would have to put up by myself next Christmas and that no one else was around to stop and grab milk when we were out. I was grieving two years' worth of shit that I had gone through.

I had thought that my mother's death taught me how to fight, but as I laid there, I realized it taught me how to grieve. Yes, her death had made me diligent about advocating for my own health and led me to find my BRCA status, which led to me finding my cancer at Stage 1. But, after my mom died, none of us talked about her. We didn't acknowledge the sadness inside. I didn't want to have to teach my kids how to grieve, but losing my mom had made me stronger, wiser and we talked about Bryan every day. We talked about memories that made us laugh and we kept his spirit alive in everything we did.

After I had satisfactorily cried a river over my burned-out light bulb and all that it represented, I got my ass out of my bed and walked downstairs. I sat down at his computer and saw the familiar wallpaper of one of his photos from Tettegouche from the last time we were there. I knew that this time, I needed to face the grief head-on. After some searching and a few clicks, I had a plane ticket to Bozeman, Montana for just after the school year was out. He hadn't stopped talking about Big Sky for months after he returned from Burning Man. *Maybe I can rent a Jeep while I'm there. He would have loved that.* There was a photo he took of a bridge and a small stream I had used for the cover of his funeral program. I wanted to find that spot and fulfill the promise to go to Big Sky, even if I had to do it without him.

It was an absolutely beautiful day and after a long Minnesota winter, hitting the upper 60's for the first time in months felt wonderful. I walked outside looked at the Jeep that Bryan loved so much and thought, "What would Bryan do on a day like today?" I got out his tools and tried to remember how he had taught me to take the doors and the top off the Jeep. I knew that I needed to learn how to do this, so I dug into my memories and thought about all the times he had gone through this routine of getting his Jeep naked.

Ok, first the doors. You have to use that squirty WD40 stuff to loosen them up the first time. Where is that funny shaped tool to remove the bolts for the hard top? I need the ratchet straps to hook up to the hoist. Remember to get it right in the middle so the top doesn't tip. I looked at the results of my work, and I was proud of myself. I had a fully naked Jeep.

I jumped in and started driving and took a moment for myself. I turned the radio up and drove aimlessly as I looked at the small Yoda figurine that was on his dashboard and saw him staring at me. *Yes, Bryan. I won't turn the radio up too loud and blow your speakers. I remember.* I drove through all the quiet back roads he loved, and I felt content, or at least optimistic that every day would get a little easier if I was willing to do the work. I had to allow myself to feel the emotions that accompany losing someone you love. I knew it would make my heart ache, but I also knew it was an important part of recovering from the chaotic life I had lived. I hadn't done it when my mom was sick. I hadn't acknowledged it when she died. Instead, I distracted myself with an abusive relationship which ended up making things worse. But the lesson I learned through the 20-year shit show I lived is that feeling the pain is part of the process. It's how we begin to heal.

When I got home, I sat down in my favorite spot in our living room and looked around at all the memories of him; His urn sitting proudly on the bookshelf with a rock on top of it that I had picked up on the beach the last time we were in California... a picture of him and Haley from Europe.... A little Lego Jeep that he and Owen had built... some fake flowers that he put in a vase because he knew I would kill real ones. He had been the love of my life, through good times and bad. He had taught me to trust. He had taught me that it was ok to be vulnerable and admit when you're scared. He taught me that asking for help didn't minimize what I was capable of. I was a better person for having known him and loved him. I was a better person because he had loved me.

As I sat thinking about all the memories in that room, my phone rang. I looked down and saw "Haley Bell" show up on the caller ID.

"Hey, honey... what's up?"

"Mom! I have a question."

"Ok... ask it."

"Is it ok to put tinfoil in the microwave?"

Are you fucking kidding me? How is she surviving away at college? "No, Haley, it is not ok to put tinfoil in the microwave."

"What about the little pans that you make those frozen cinnamon rolls in?"

"Well, that's also made of tinfoil, so no. Just warm them up on a plate." I looked over as Owen walked in and stared at me.

I heard Haley say, "Well, if I use a plate then I would have to wash a plate."

Owen started whispering at me. "Mom.... Mom.... Mom.... Moooooommmmm!"

I looked at him, "Just a second, buddy…. Haley do not put tinfoil in the microwave. It's a lot less work to clean a plate than it is to clean up your kitchen after your microwave starts on fire."

Owen was still by my side and whispered, "Mom! I need you to sign my permission slip so I can watch the puberty video in class on Friday. Here." He handed me his permission slip and waited for me to sign while I was still on the phone with Haley. I started making the pen motion with my hand like I was writing in the air, but he just held up his hands, shrugged his shoulders, and stood there.

I heard Haley say, "Ok… I'll just eat them cold."

"What? You'll eat what cold?"

"My cinnamon rolls. I don't want to blow up the microwave. Do you think they'd charge me for that?"

"Yes, honey. I'm sure they would. Go find something to eat, and please don't blow anything up. Love you."

I hung up the phone and looked at Owen. "I need a pen, bud. You got one for me?"

He rummaged around in his bag for a pen and handed it to me. "Can we have some dinner?"

"Sure. You want to talk about the puberty video? Do you have questions I can answer?"

"No. If you told me all of it, I wouldn't need to watch the video and then they'd just make me sit in the library. When can you make something to eat, though? I'm kinda hungry." The doorbell rang and the dog started barking at one of Owen's friends standing at the door.

"Sure. Just give me a minute and I'll get it started." He ran off to go play with his friends and I yelled, "You've got math homework to do after dinner!"

Life didn't stop. I was, once again, a single mom putting out fires and taking care of the people who depended on me. But this time

I was doing it unafraid and assured of who I was as a person. This time I was doing it with the knowledge of how to start the healing process. There would always be field trips, and play dates, and puberty videos, and math homework, and life lessons on how to not start your kitchen on fire. The important part was finding a healthy way to continue on so that I didn't end up with my jagged edges and giant emotion blocking walls. Life continued to move forward, and so would we.

CPSIA information can be obtained
at www.ICGtesting.com
Printed in the USA
LVHW041200141019
634125LV00006B/2593/P